Theo-
logy
&
Life

THEOLOGY AND LIFE SERIES

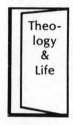

Volume 15

Vatican II
and
Its Documents

An American Reappraisal

Edited by

Timothy E. O'Connell

A Michael Glazier Book
THE LITURGICAL PRESS
Collegeville, Minnesota

About the Editor

Timothy E. O'Connell, Ph.D., is a priest of the Archdoicese of Chicago, ordained in 1969. He holds a doctorate in theology from Fordham University, as well as several other degrees. Father O'Connell is Director of the Institute of Pastoral Studies at Loyola University of Chicago. He is also Associate Professor of Theology at Loyola, Adjunct Professor of Theology at Saint Mary of the Lake Seminary, and Associate Editor of *Chicago Studies.* Father O'Connell is the author of four books, most recently *Principles for a Catholic Morality* (Seabury Press, 1978), and numerous articles.

A Michael Glazier Book

published by

THE LITURGICAL PRESS

All quotations from the documents of Vatican II are from:

Vatican Council II: The Conciliar and Post Conciliar Documents, Austin Flannery, O.P., General Editor. Costello Publishing Co., Northport, N.Y., 1975.

Cover design by Lillian Brulc. Typography by Debbie Farmer.

ISBN 0-8146-5537-8

Contents

Preface

In times of transition there is a tendency to return to sources. It is a way to evaluate where you are today. It is a sound instinct to see what was said at the start, to see what has happened since, and to see where we are now headed. The Second Vatican Council was perhaps the most profound religious event of the twentieth century. A World Church was gathered to consider who it was and where it wanted to go. Much was said and much followed. Today there is still much to be said, and much to be done.

This book collects a series of papers examining the Vatican II documents. From 1982 to 1984 a small group of scholars and pastoral ministers of the Great Lakes Region met in Chicago to use these papers as a basis of discussion. Their particular interest was to talk about the documents in the light of a North American perspective.

The papers deal with specific documents of the Council. Each participant chose to write in an area of his or her particular expertise or interest. These papers present the basic content of a document, what has happened since, and where the present discussions are focused. There is a wide range of thought as well as some concise statements of critical issues.

On the basis of the group discussion, each author has revised his or her paper. Nonetheless, no attempt has been made to achieve group consensus on any essay or on specific items within essays. Rather, the content of the essays represents solely the thought of their individual authors.

Indeed, while the concluding essay, by Timothy O'Connell, attempts to capture some of the insights generated during the discussions and to pull together the threads of thought that connect Vatican II documents, even this chapter does not necessarily represent the mind of the group.

The editor wishes to thank all the authors for their generous cooperation in bringing this project to completion.

Timothy E. O'Connell

The Constitution on the
Sacred Liturgy
Sacrosanctum Concilium, 4 December, 1963

Kevin W. Irwin

Introduction

The shape of the liturgy prior to the Council was fixed, rubrical, and clerically-oriented. While some "options" did exist, such as the "solemn," "high," or "low" Mass, there was little variation within a given model, and congregations were largely passive no matter what the rite going on. Rubrics concerned the performance of ministers, and the correct performance of the rubrics had to be insured for valid/licit celebration. Essentially what the *Constitution on the Sacred Liturgy* did was to move away from this model of liturgy to one which would allow variety, option and flexibility, and which took seriously the participation and involvement of worshiping assemblies.[1] Such a victory was

---

[1]The pre-conciliar advances toward popular participation and the influence of the liturgical movement should be recalled here. The European-inspired liturgical movement had sunk roots in America (see E.B. Koenker, *The Liturgical Renaissance in the Roman Catholic Church* (Chicago: Concordia, 1954). There was

not easily won, as is attested in the debates on the Council floor. In many ways the contribution of the Constitution was to endorse the "liturgical movement" and to insure on-going liturgical renewal by calling for the revision of all the liturgical rites then in use (25).[2] It was a watershed document, yet now a rereading understandably reveals many pre-conciliar presuppositions some of which were modified in later conciliar and post conciliar documents.

This paper is concerned with a review of the Constitution's strengths and weaknesses as seen from our present perspective. It then attempts to sketch the effect of this reform document in the life of the American Church noting contributions, tasks still to be undertaken or completed, and areas requiring further exploration which relate the liturgy with other areas of church life.

Strengths of the Liturgy Constitution

SETTING THE CONTEXT

The Introduction to the Constitution reveals the "aims of the Council." These are appropriately placed and outlined here since this was the first Conciliar document to appear. These statements provide a helpful context within which to consider the liturgy in general. The broad vision of the Council "to impart an ever increasing vigor to the Christian life of the faithful," "to adapt more closely to the needs of our age those institutions which are subject to change," "to

indeed liturgical participation in the "dialogue mass"and in the "four-hymn"mass before the Council. Instructions from the Holy See from the early 1900s on early and frequent communion, the revival of Gregorian chant (Pius X) and the encyclicals *Mystici Corporis* (1943) and *Mediator Dei* (1947) of Pius X in their own way led to the theological and liturgical climate in which the Liturgy Constitution would develop.

[2]The Constitution on the Sacred Liturgy called for the revision of all rituals in use in the church. Each revised rite contains a "General Instruction" sketching the theological and pastoral issues involved in the revision, as well as full explanations of the rite. It is in the revised rites themselves where the notions of flexibility and option are most clearly evident.

foster whatever can promote union among all who believe in Christ," and "to strengthen whatever can help to call all mankind into the Church's fold" (1) is enunciated here and provides a helpful context for what follows concerning liturgy. While this brief paragraph about aims becomes dwarfed when compared with the legal detail to follow, nevertheless it is a significant starting point. The Council's consideration of liturgy involves ritual revision based on a pastoral and theological perspective. Pope Paul VI stated that "the liturgy was the first subject to be examined and the first too, in a sense, in intrinsic worth and in importance for the life of the Church."[3] The context is liturgy for the life of the church; worship in the context of real renewal of the pastoral life of the church.[4]

SOUND TRADITION

The investigation to be made of the existing liturgical rites was to be based on "sound tradition" (23), that is involving theological, historical and pastoral perspectives. This statement validated the kind of investigation that had been undertaken largely in Europe as part of the theological ferment and liturgical movement that preceded the Council. Although the Liturgical Conference here in the United States stirred some interest among a select crowd of clergymen and lay activists, the inspiration, the substance of liturgical theology and criteria were set in Europe. Hillenbrand, Hellreigel, Morrison and Virgil Michel did spark some pastoral application in America but once legitimized the Conference and some of its leaders seemed tired and even left behind. Criteria were thus established for going beyond Tridentine theological formulations and ritual

[3]Paul VI, as quoted in C.J. McNaspy, "Liturgy," an introduction to the Liturgy document in Walter M. Abbott, ed., *The Documents of Vatican II* (New York: America Press, 1966) p. 133.

[4]On the (helpful) distinction between "reform" and "renewal" see, Richard J. Neuhaus. "Has the Liturgical Movement Failed?" *Una Sancta 24* (1967) 49-58.

directives to rediscovering riches that were part of the church's "tradition."[5]

COMPLETE REVISION

The revision of the liturgial books was to be completed "as soon as possible" (25) and it was to be a complete revision. Where formerly revisions had been partial (e.g. the Roman Missal and Breviary at Trent, Holy Week in 1955) now there would be a total reform of the liturgy. Implicit in this statement is the admission that the Roman rite then in use was in need of "correction."[6] The states of revision, however, were more far-reaching than first imagined or even envisioned by the Constitution. Once the books were revised according to the directives of the Constitution and guided by post-conciliar committees, the Church then had a universal starting point for a truly pastoral liturgical reform, not a completed revision.

RESTORATION

The revision aimed at restoring to the church's liturgical life practices which over the course of centuries had been overshadowed or encumbered by other ceremonies or had been eliminated entirely. "In this restoration both texts and rites should be drawn up so as to express more clearly the holy things which they signify. The Christian people ...should be able to understand them with ease and take part in them fully, actively, and as a community" (21).

The question raised here involves the much debated issue over what can or should be changed in liturgy, a debate which has come into its own in more recent years with the

---

[5]See, Pope Paul VI, *Apostolic Constitution* promulgating the Roman Missal, *Sacramentary* (New York: Catholic Book Pub., 1974) 8*-9*.

[6]Pope Paul VI uses this term to describe the reform undertaken after Trent by Pius V. He then goes on to speak of further progress in liturgical study in the past four centuries. See, *Apsotolic Constitution.*p.8*.

encouragement of ongoing cultural adaptation in liturgy.[7] Examples of preferred usages which are presently restored in the liturgy include greater attention to the symbols used in worship,[8] the pluriformity of liturgical roles, and communal sacramental and liturgical celebrations.[9]

PARTICIPATION

One of the most frequently repeated aims of the liturgy constitution was "full, conscious, and active participation in liturgical celebrations...demanded by the very nature of the liturgy" (14). "In the restoration and promotion of the sacred liturgy, the full and active participation by all the people is the aim to be considered before all else..." (14). The 1958 Instruction on participation was something of a partial preparation for the council,[10] but its tone is tentative as compared with the Constitution. From about the twelfth century liturgical rubrics had become so concerned with clerical performance and correctness (especially at "private" Mass) that the Council had to state: "When the liturgical books are being revised, the people's parts must be carefully indicated by the rubrics" (31).

The participation envisioned by the Council involves doing things (singing, proclaiming) and also being attentive to what was occurring liturgically (listening, observing). To this end the council decreed that "the rites should be distinguished by a noble simplicity. They should be short, clear, and free from useless repetitions" (34).

[7]See, among other works, those by Anscar J. Chupungco, *Towards A Filipino Liturgy* (Manila: Benedictine Abbey, 1976) and *Cultural Adaptation of the Liturgy* (NY/Ramsey: Paulist Press, 1982).

[8]For a brief treatment of "symbols" and their function in liturgy see below, section "A Didactic Model for Liturgy?"

[9]CSL, nos. 28-29 (roles) and nos. 26-27 (communal celebrations). On liturgical roles see, *Roles in the Liturgical Assembly* The Twenty-third Liturgical Conference, Saint Serge, (New York: Pueblo Publishing Co., 1981).

[10]"Instruction of the Sacred Congregation of Rites on Sacred Music and the Sacred Liturgy According to the Encyclical Letters *Musicae sacrae disciplina* and *Mediator Dei* of Pope Pius XII" AAS 50 (1958) 630-663.

PROCLAMATION OF THE WORD

Of the reforms undertaken by the Council regarding liturgy pride of place must be given to the restoration of the proclamation of the Word to a position of prominence. The conciliar texts about the importance of the Word, and that a more representative portion of the Scripture be read at the liturgy (35,51) ushered in a new era in the liturgical life of Roman Catholicism. That this emphasis has been carried out in the revision of all rituals is clear since the proclamation of the Word is a major focus in all liturgical celebrations today.[11] This restored element of the liturgy was called "Protestant" by many critics.

VERNACULAR

The statements of the Constitution about permission to use the vernacular are prime examples of the idiom involved in ecclesiastical decree. The Latin language is given due emphasis as the language of the "Latin rite" but then the Council states that the use of the mother tongue "may frequently be of great advantage" (36). In the years since the Council most "territorial ecclesiastical authorities" took partial and then full steps to allow the use of the vernacular in liturgy. Once again, this major shift in Roman Catholic liturgy is a reason why the reformed liturgy has been called "Protestant."

LOCAL CONFERENCES OF BISHOPS

A major change in the way of dealing with the liturgical life of the church is seen in the Constitution where it states that the Apostolic See and the local bishop share "the regulation of the liturgy which belongs also to various kinds of bishops' conferences, legitimately established, with com-

---

[11]This is not to suggest, however, that the Roman Lectionary reform is not without flaws. See, Gerald Sloyan, "The Lectionary as a Context for Interpretation" *Interpretation* 31 (April, 1977) 131-38, and William Skudlarek, *The Word in Worship*. Preaching in a Liturgical Context (Nashville: Abingdon, 1981) pp. 3-39.

petence in given territories" (22). While the relationship between what is to be approved in Rome and what remains for local conferences of bishops at times remains unclear, nevertheless the fact that provision is made for local initiative is significant. Like the statements on the vernacular, these too have a certain restrictive and legal tenor, which is not surprising considering the fact that the Holy See was the only place for liturgical clarification and change at this point in history.

CULTURAL ADAPTATION

Among the more significant statements of the Council on liturgy are those concerning "Norms for Adapting the Litrugy" (37-40). These important statements about adaptation begin with the observation: "Even in the liturgy the Church does not wish to impose a rigid uniformity in matters which do not involve the faith or the good of the whole community" (37). Hence, "legitimate variations and adaptations" are encouraged provided that the "substantial unity of the Roman rite is preserved" (38). Certain adaptations are for the local conference to determine, others that are "even more radical" are to be referred to the Holy See (40).

What makes this statement so important is the fact that the church's liturgy is seen to relate to particular cultures and that variations among and within cultures may well call for changes in the liturgical patterns of the church. In addition, and perhaps even more importantly, this moves the center of focus from rigid uniformity given from Rome to a substantial unity of the Roman rite as celebrated in local churches. Rome and the local church are to play a great part now in the further development of liturgy. What some have called the theological imperative of our times is here endorsed and promoted for the church's liturgical life as well.[12]

One aspect of the variety proposed here is apparent in the

[12]See, Karl Rahner, "Towards a Fundamental Theological Interpretation of Vatican II," *Theological Studies* 39 (December, 1979) 716-727.

revised rituals themselves for they contain many options from which to choose for a given liturgical celebration. Options include scripture readings, prayers and other liturgical texts, the forms of gesture and movement in the liturgy, and the amount and style of music possible. The choice and use of such options have become commonplace as aspects of the postconciliar reform. While they trace their origin to the Constitution, they are more clearly stated and demonstrated in the revised rituals.

Weaknesses of the Liturgy Constitution

THEOLOGY OF LITURGY

In the first chapter of the Constitution the Council fathers present "The Nature of the Sacred Liturgy and its Importance in the Life of the Church." While this section does continue the important context within which the Council considered liturgy,[13] nevertheless, it is to be observed that these paragraphs are sketchy and leave much to be desired. What is evident throughout the Constitution is the particularly Western preoccupation with a certain external approach to worship. Conventional Western treatments of liturgy concerned the "how to," not the "why" or "what" of worship.[14] Unfortunately, this flaw in preconciliar treatments of worship is not completely eliminated in the Constitution. In fact, this flaw is indirectly underscored and endorsed.

Specifically, the importance of the paschal mystery is stated but left largely unexplored and undeveloped (6). While it is clear that liturgy is pastorally oriented and the conciliar document is both theological and pastoral in tone and content, it is the "pastoral" aspect (i.e., practical) which receives the greater attention in the Constitution. The theological implications of the liturgy are not drawn sufficiently,

---

[13]See above, and CSL nos. 1-4.

[14]See, for example, Alexander Schmemann, *Introduction to Liturgical Theology* (New York: St. Vladimir's Seminary Press, 1975).

nor is the traditional principle "lex orandi, lex credendi" given much credence throughout. Since the liturgy document does not have a sustained theological perspective and enunciated vision, it may be counted weak. Establishing some fundamentals about the theology of liturgy and then developing them under each subsection might have been one way of alleviating the still rubrical and extrinsic approach to liturgy that is evident here.

HIERARCHICAL MODEL OF CHURCH

Throughout the liturgy constitution the then prevalent hierarchical notion of church is underscored. This is derived from the prcconciliar assumptions about church and liturgy. While the Constitution makes a contribution in the direction of local adaptation, nonetheless, it does weigh heavily in the direction of "top-down" ecclesiology. When compared with the Dogmatic Constitution on the Church this document pales. Where the Church document begins with "The Mystery of the Church"and "The People of God" and then addresses the "Hierarchical Structure of the Church,"[15] the Liturgy document contains a reverse ordering. The very section on "Norms Drawn from the Hierarchic and Communal Nature of the Liturgy" bespeaks this approach, as does even a comment on the presence of Christ: "To accomplish so great a work Christ is always present in His Church, especially in her liturgical celebrations. He is present in the Sacrifice of the Mass, not only in the person of his minister, 'the same one now offering, through the ministry of priests, who formerly offered himself on the cross,' but especially in the eucharistic species...He is present in his word. Lastly, he is present when the Church prays and sings"(7).

ONE MODEL OF LITURGY

This observation raises a question about what is assumed

---

[15]See, Dogmatic Constitution on the Church, Chapters 1-3.

in the Constitution and what has influenced the revised rites. When describing the revision of each liturgical rite the Constitution gives some general and some particular guidelines.[16] Yet, in the light of the very theological, historical and pastoral investigation called for by the Constitution another aspect of the church's tradition of liturgy becomes clear— varied styles of celebration. With regard to the eucharist this involves, for example, a large scale cathedral liturgy with many ministers, a local church liturgy less expressive in scale, a liturgy held at a place of pilgrimage or shrine, and a domestic model.[17] For the liturgy of the hours there is strong evidence in the tradition for "cathedral" and "monastic" liturgies.[18]

Hence the issue raised here is whether the Constitution assumes that there is one model of liturgy on which to base contemporary adaptation and particular celebration.[19] Even when the Constitution speaks about adaptation, or postconciliar documents speak about further variation as in the Directory of Masses for Children, what appears stable is one model of worship. Providing for alternative models of liturgy would go a long way toward the desired goal of fostering full, active participation in the church's liturgy.[20]

[16]The very structure of the Constitution shows concern for general norms first (in Chapter 1) and then particular norms for each liturgical rite in succeeding chapters.

[17]With regard to the frequency and setting of eucharist see, Robert Taft, "The Frequency of the Eucharist Throughout History" in D. Power and M. Collins, eds., *Can We Always Celebrate the Eucharist?* Concilium 152 (New York: Seabury, 1982) 13-24, and R. Kevin Seasoltz, "Monastery and Eucharist: Some American Observations" in R. Kevin Seasoltz, ed., *Living Bread, Saving Cup.* Readings on the Eucharist (Collegeville: Liturgical Press, 1982) 259-284.

[18]See, among others, William J. Storey, "The Liturgy of the Hours: Cathedral versus Monastery," in John Gallen, ed., *Christians At Prayer* (Notre Dame: University of Notre Dame Press, 1977) 61-82.

[19]In certain sacramental celebrations modifications of the one model do exist; for example, the continuous rite of anoiting and viaticum for those near death, or baptism in cases when an infant (or adult) is in danger of death. Such are regarded as exceptions and even here what exists are modifications of the revised rite.

[20]See, for example CSL no. 11; General Instruction on the Roman Missal, nos. 3,5,313; Appendix to the General Instruction (for the U.S.A.); Music in Catholic Worship nos. 3, 6, 17, 21.

This lack of pluriformity shows itself in two other ways: in language and ecclesial structure. Besides the supposition of one model, the demands of the vernacular are very simple: translate the Latin into English, French, Spanish, etc. The supposition is that the same English is suitable for Pakistan, Ireland, the United States, etc. When looking at the ecclesial structures of territorial conferences of bishops again the supposition seems to be that the culture, language and customs are quite common under each territorial conference. In no way was it seen that single dioceses or even parishes would take seriously the cultural diversity of the community. The ecclesial structures that would guide the reform were not set up to deal with this sensitivity to pluralism.

ECUMENICAL CONTEXT AND IMPLICATIONS

Understandably the *Constitution on the Liturgy* is directed toward the revision of the forms of Roman Catholic liturgy. Yet, when compared with statements from the *Decree on Ecumenism* about the importance of conversations about sacraments and about the liturgical life of churches,[21] the Liturgy Constitution may be termed weak in ecumenical context and implications. Its only explicit statement on the ecumenical nature of the contemporary reform is in the "Appendix" on the revision of the calendar. This is particularly striking to observe from our present perspective since much of the work undertaken in the reform of Roman Catholic worship is shared by other Christian churches.[22] Clearly, the historical studies on which the present forms of common prayer are founded have been ecumenical in the sense that research and findings have been shared across denominational lines.

If, as the Council states, one of its aims is a greater ecumenical awareness and collaboration among the

[21]See, Decree on Ecumenism, no. 22.

[22]See below, "Ecumenical Sacramental Conversations."

churches,[23] a more decidedly ecumenical foundation in liturgy would have been helpful. In fact, the present liturgical reforms of many churches are so similar that this similarity is a force toward greater ecumenical convergence and union.[24] Would not the Council have taken greater steps toward real ecumenical collaboration if it had validated the existing degree of consensus on the roots of worship and called for deliberate collaboration in the preparation and trial use of revised liturgies?

RUBRICAL, LEGAL TONE

A counter-point to the lack of theological depth evidenced in the Constitution (noted above) is its rubrical tone. Understandably the Council Fathers were concerned to get the liturgical revisions underway; hence they speak about the kind of work that needed to be done in terms that are legal and prescriptive in tone. And yet, this kind of language can often give a mixed signal when viewed from the perspective of what has come to be an assumption in contemporary liturgy—flexibility and option. For example the text about the "General Norms" for the revision states:

1. Regulation of the sacred liturgy depends solely on the authority of the Church, that is, on the Apostolic See, and, as laws may determine, on the bishop.

2. In virtue of power conceded by the law, the regulation of the liturgy within certain defined limits belongs also to various kinds of bishops' conferences, legitimately established, with competence in given territories.

3. Therefore, no other person, not even a priest may add,

[23]Decree on Ecumenism, no. 1.

[24]See, Kevin W. Irwin, "The Holy Communion" *Exploring the Faith We Share* edited by Glenn C. Stone and Charles LaFontaine (New York/Ramsey: Paulist Press, 1980) pp. 42-64. As James White has remarked: "I often wonder: Why teach ecumenism when you can teach worship?" in "The Teaching of Worship in Seminaries in Canada and the United States," *Worship* 55 (July, 1981) 317.

remove, or change anything in the liturgy on his own authority. (22)

In another place the Constitution states:

> Pastors of souls must therefore realize that, when the liturgy is celebrated, something more is required than the laws governing valid and licit celebration. It is their duty also to ensure that the faithful take part fully aware of what they are doing, actively engaged in the rite and enriched by it (11).

There does appear to be a mixed signal here.

In sum, it may be said that the *Liturgy Constitution* ushered in a new era in liturgical piety and celebration. The document made great strides in overcoming the Tridentine heritage of conformity and uniformity in liturgy (with emphasis being given to sacraments celebrated validly and licitly). Yet, the Constitution is not without its flaws and apparent contradictions. It stands up well under the scrutiny of the intervening years of evolution and change in the church, and some of its weaknesses have been set in a new context by local initiative and adaptation. Such is the contribution of the local, American church in the intervening years. It is to these initiatives and questions that we now turn.

American Implementation of Liturgy Constitution

PRACTICAL IMPLEMENTATION

Among the things most notable about the American implementation of the liturgy document was the efficiency with which the "changes" were made. This was most clearly evidenced in the implementation of English in the liturgy, the publication of service books, and the first major shifts in decor (altar, lectern, chair).

In addition, the American revision of the liturgy was

accompanied by a spate of literature on "how to" reform and catechetical material to "explain the changes." Some on-going efforts at liturgical education mark the American implementation, along with many homily services and planning guides for those involved in worship.[25] Of the latter, generally speaking, the quality and tenor has improved over the years with more attention given to variety and possibilities rather than "this is what to do."

BISHOPS' COMMITTEE ON LITURGY

The American reform of the liturgy has been aided and directed in no small measure by the bishops' committee on liturgy of the National Conference of Catholic Bishops. After the council the Bishops' Conference faced the task of restructuring itself and adding new offices to serve the implementation of Vatican II. Among the more significant, considering the fact that worship concerns the day-to-day activity of all levels of church life, is the Liturgy Committee.[26]

Among the more enduring publications produced by this Committee are the monthly *Newsletter,* the *Study texts,* and practical commentaries from the American experience of liturgy, such as *Music in Catholic Worship* (1972), *Environment and Art in Catholic Worship* (1978) and *Liturgical Music Today* (1982). These last three documents are significant statements because they come from a process involving many experts in the field, revision and reconsideration of various drafts, and then publication of the "final" document.[27] This is a clear example of local implementation of the reforms envisioned in the Liturgy Constitution. These

[25]See, for example, the kind of publications from the Liturgy Training Publications, Archdiocese of Chicago.

[26]An individual whose contribution to the BCL was formative for the implementation of the Liturgy constitution is Fred McManus.

[27]The process involved here included experts in respective fields, those involved in implementation and the Committee itself. These were for the expressed purpose of aiding in pastoral implementation, and are helpful for the present.

particular texts emphasize the relationship of music and art to the liturgy and deal with the theological, liturgical and pastoral issues involved in this relationship in a substantive way.

ACADEMIC PROGRAMS

The *Liturgy Constitution* directed that liturgy be established among the major courses to be taught in seminaries (16) and that "professors who are appointed to teach liturgy in seminaries, religious houses of studies, and theological faculties, must be properly trained for their work in institutes which specialize in this subject" (15). In addition to the international centers in Paris, Trier and Rome, the American church has had the advantage of on-going academic formation in degree programs offered at the Catholic University of America and at Notre Dame University. Both of these offer Masters degrees and Doctorates in Liturgy. Both rely heavily on theological and historical methodology, and each has contributed significantly in terms of providing needed credentials for those involved in teaching liturgy and in implementing the Constitution's reforms in America.

PASTORAL PROGRAMS

Besides the more strictly academic programs, Notre Dame has a Center for Pastoral Liturgy which sponsors workshops on various topics of liturgical implementation, most often geared for those in leadership positions in pastoral settings.[28] Notre Dame continues to offer a major annual conference on pastoral liturgy, and the papers delivered have most often been published in volumes that reflect the tradition of historical theological research as this back-

[28] While much effort has been expended in aiding the renewal of liturgy in parish settings, more recent efforts from the Notre Dame Center have been aimed at other settings such as liturgy for religious communities.

ground is brought to bear on pastoral implementation.[29] In addition, other institutes have recently opened to help develop on-going implementation on a pastoral level. These include the Georgetown Center for Liturgy and the Arts in Washington, D.C., and the Loyola Pastoral Institute in New York City.[30]

NORTH AMERICAN ACADEMY OF LITURGY

A decade ago an "invitation only" meeting of people involved in liturgy was held at Scottsdale to determine the state of "American liturgy"[31] and to reflect on the criteria used when teaching or reflecting on the liturgy. This group has grown into the North American Academy of Liturgy, an ecumenical, professional organization that meets annually. Much of the time at these meetings is devoted to on-going seminars on a variety of topics[32] with participants expected to do research or other work in between meetings of the Academy. Some of the papers presented at these meetings have been published in *Worship*. Most often this meeting provides academicians and those involved in pastoral implementation with a unique opportunity for exchange and dialogue about matters liturgical especially because of its ecumenical nature.[33]

[29]See, *The Roots of Ritual* (Grand Rapids: Wm. Eerdmans, 1975) *Made, Not Born* (Notre Dame: University of Notre Dame, 1976), *Christians at Prayer* (Notre Dame: University of Notre Dame, 1977), *Liturgy and Social Justice* (Collegeville: Liturgical Press, 1980), *Parish: A Place for Worship* (Collegeville: Liturgical Press, 1981).

[30]Interestingly, each of these is associated directly with a parish: the former with Holy Trinity, Georgetown, the latter with St. Ignatius Loyola, New York City.

[31]See John Gallen, "American Liturgy: A Theological Locus," *Theological Studies* 35 (June, 1974) 302-311.

[32]These include: Eucharistic Prayer; Liturgical Theology; Liturgy of the Hours: Christian Initiation; Social Sciences; Fine Arts; Liturgy and Spirituality; Liturgy and Social Justice; Music; Liturgical Year; American Parish; Liturgical Preaching; Liturgy in Religious Communities.

[33]While this ecumenical orientation adds to the diversity of the group and to discussions, it should be admitted that the majority of members are Roman Catholic and that a certain "Catholic" undergirding is evident. This is partially due to the fact that Roman Catholic worship was in the forefront of liturgical reform in America.

FEDERATION OF DIOCESAN
LITURGICAL COMMISSIONS

With the establishment of liturgical commissions in most dioceses in the United States, the step was taken in 1969 to establish a federation of such commissions and to establish an annual meeting for this group. Early in its history, this group took on the identity of a "grassroots" organization that would raise questions and propose ideas to the Bishops' Committee on the Liturgy. Unlike the NAAL this federation is composed of those who work on day to day implementation of liturgy in pastoral settings.

Most often the committee charged with planning and executing the annual meeting puts together a study booklet in preparation for the convention whose purpose is to acquaint participants with an overview treatment and some depth on the topic to the considered.[34] This booklet is also helpful background material for regional representatives of commissions who meet to discuss "resolutions" which the entire federation then votes on for approval or disapproval at the annual meeting. The approved resolutions are then sent to the Bishops' Committee on the Liturgy for action and possible implementation. Over the last few years this process of discussing and passing resolutions has been refined greatly and kept alive issues when they were deemed potentially explosive such as communion in the hand, music copyrights, communion under both kinds and American adaptations.

NATIONAL ASSOCIATION
OF PASTORAL MUSICIANS

In 1977 the National Association of Pastoral Musicians was established to help implementation of the Council's direction that liturgical music be an "integral part of the

---

[34]See, for example, the booklet prepared for the 1982 meeting in Buffalo, *Symbol: The Language of Liturgy*. Contributors include: Emil Lengeling, Peter Brown, Joseph Gelineau, Adrien Nocent, Peter Fink, Robert Hovda, Walter Burghardt, Don Saliers, James White and Jean-Yves Quellec.

.... liturgy" (112). This group is directly concerned with the American context for developing music and continues to hold annual conventions (whether on a national or regional level). The organization publishes the journal *Pastoral Music* and occasional books for pastoral musicians.[35]

FROM "ROMAN" TO ECUMENICAL LECTIONARY

A most significant contribution toward ecumenical progress in American liturgy was made as the three-year cycle of readings of the Roman lectionary came to be adopted (and adapted) by the Episcopal Church and many other Protestant churches. A further proposal is now being made by which in the U.S. and in Canada the Episcopal Church, the United Church of Christ, the Christian Church (Disciples of Christ), the United Methodist Church, the Lutheran and Presbyterian churches would unify even further their Sunday and Feast Day cycle of readings. This, in turn, has inspired biblical commentaries on the Sunday readings to come from ecumenical sources such as the *Proclamation* series of commentaries.[36] The contribution which such a move can make to ecumenical progress and more honest and thorough study of the scriptures by Roman Catholics is just beginning to be felt.

American Implementation: Not Complete or Not Begun

DEPTH OF PREPARATION

While it has been stated that the American implementation of the *Liturgy Constitution* was practical and fairly

---

[35]See, Virgil Funk, ed., *Music in Catholic Worship* (Washington: National Association of Pastoral Musicians, 1982); V. Funk and Gabe Huck, eds., *Pastoral Music in Practice* (Washington: NPM and Chicago: LTP, 1981); and Ralph A. Keifer, *To Give Thanks and Praise* (Washington: NPM, 1980).

[36]See *Proclamation*, Aids for Interpreting the Lessons of the Church Year (Philadelphia: Fortress Press).

efficient, it must also be admitted that what was lacking in many areas was a real appreciation of what was involved in the "changes." In fact, the issue involved not changing *things*, but rather changing attitudes and developing new ways of looking at the relationship between liturgy and pastoral life, of liturgy as a cult and liturgy as the means by which communities celebrate common identity forged in Christ's Paschal Mystery. Training leaders and congregations about the depth involved in liturgical reform and renewal was most often spotty and incomplete.

QUALITY OF PREACHING

While the Liturgy constitution ushered in a new era of awareness of the importance of the Word in liturgical celebration, and the importance of biblical preaching (24,34), the depth of such appreciation and quality of preaching is cause for self-examination. The causes for disappointment are many. Sometimes biblical homilies came to mean explaining the readings—a didactic exercise. Sometimes the reformed liturgy exposed clerical weakness in the area of theological and biblical competence, sometimes due to the lack of preparation in preconciliar seminary education. What is clear is that the conciliar emphasis on preaching in theory has not been evident in pastoral implementation.[37]

LITURGY AND CATECHETICS

Despite advances made in both liturgy and catechesis, the fact that they once were united in inspiration and pastoral concern has more recently given way to a divorce between them. Centers of religious education do not necessarily have programs that are strong in liturgy, and vice versa. To continue to separate liturgy from catechetics would be to

---

[37]See, Philip J. Murnion, "Parish Renewal: State(ments) of the Question" *America* 149 (April 24, 1982) 314-317. For some insightful commentary on the quality of preaching see Nadine Foley, ed., *Preaching and the Non-Ordained* (Collegeville: Liturgical Press, 1983).

continue a divorce unforeseen in the church's tradition of communal prayer and instruction.[38]

LITURGICAL LANGUAGE

Although the International Commission on English in the Liturgy (ICEL) set out to translate the Latin into a usable English vernacular and hurried to present texts to English speaking conferences of bishops it has suffered criticism for its work. At first the aim was simply translation. But the critics, self-criticism, diverse literary talents and pastoral use have broadened out the concern to one of developing a solid liturgical English. ICEL has already begun a revision of texts project beginning with the Rites of Christian Burial. This project will encompass all the liturgical texts and has a timetable reaching over two decades. Efforts are already being made to provide texts that are free of discriminatory language and are more poetic and rhythmic in style. Proclamatory texts need to be developed both for the scriptures as well as for prayers. The nuance of language and the cultural influences on language are now a part of good liturgical research.

LITURGICAL MUSIC

The state of liturgical music immediately after the Council was often a polyglot of "high church" hymns, Gregorian chant, and English versions of the latter. The "folk mass" soon appeared and enjoyed great popularity. In the intervening years the "folk mass" has given way to a model of music in which the folk idiom is more commonly integrated into a liturgy comprised of varying musical styles. And yet, while this is the ideal, and is sometimes achieved, there often

[38]There are contradictions in sections of the *National Catechetical Directory* dealing with liturgy and sacraments, for example those on initiation. At times the liturgists were those influencing statements, other times they were not. The issue here is not where liturgy should dominate; rather the question is how and where liturgists and catechists can collaborate in theory and in practice.

exists a pull between the "high church" music (and, by extension, model of liturgy), and the more folksy style of music (with a more folksy, "personal" style of worship). While this diversity may be considered helpful nevertheless one wonders what the future will hold if some "high church" communities do not experience more modern music and other "folksy" groups never reach beyond the very contemporary to a greater appreciation of the tradition of church music.

EXPERIMENTAL CENTERS

The implementation of the *Liturgy Constitution* by Roman Catholics took place from the top down. The Episcopal Church in the United States, on the other hand, used "trial services" and grassroots experimentation.[39] The advantage of the Roman approach is that at least some reforms had to take place, where if trial services had been offered some argued that the opposition would have been so great that liturgical reform would never have been undertaken at all.

Yet, at our present stage of reform, in order to further the on-going reform of the liturgy in terms of acculturation, the failure of the established experimental centers and the lack of "trial services" is now being felt. The Notre Dame, Collegeville, Woodstock, Composers' Forum "centers" have all but collapsed. For an informed agenda of where to move with liturgy in the future for Americans the revival of more serious attempts at expermentation in both academic and pastoral settings would seem to be in order.[40]

[39]The single exception to the "top-down" approach I know of is the Rite of Christian Initiation of Adults, which was used in experimental centers before final revision and publication. On this, see Andre Aubry, "Le projet pastoral du Rituel de l'initiation des Adultes," *Ephemerides Liturgicae* 88 (1974) 174-191.

[40]One of the reasons why the officially designated experimental centers died was that their mandate was thought much too restrictive. Rome had given criteria for experimentation, rather than inviting grass-roots experimentation to flourish. It is said that Rome is presently intereseted in establishing criteria according to which to "judge" the validity of liturgical indigenization. A methodological difficulty is apparent in such an approach.

DIFFICULTY WITH RITUAL

A particularly acute problem that many Americans face with liturgy involves the nature of ritual. The repetition and familiarity of the rite (which makes the experience a "ritual") often becomes boring repetition for some. For others in America, the liturgy proves disappointing because commonality of assumption cannot be presumed for people of different backgrounds and cultural heritages. The American liturgical situation still needs to address these issues to determine how best to achieve a balance between a ritual that is familiar yet creative, and, perhaps even more importantly, how to provide a ritual that appeals to a variety of peoples.

LITURGY AND JUSTICE

It has recently been pointed out that the pioneers of the American liturgical movement and those involved in justice issues were originally aligned, and that a close association cannot be granted today.[41] In the American experience such a reunification is all the more important so that liturgy can be seen to be an integrating force in Christian life. Without this understanding and appreciation, liturgy and social justice concerns can go separate ways.

While there has been much emphasis (in the 1960s) on the implications of liturgical prayer, these implications often meant involvement in civil rights concerns, peace issues, etc. What is at stake here is the proper understanding of liturgy and justice. It is in the experience of liturgy that God's justice is revealed and experienced primarily.[42] Hence the task for American Catholicism is one of focusing on the liturgy as the locus for establishing and experiencing God's

---

[41]See, J. Bryan Heir, "Foreword," in *Liturgy and Social Justice*, pp. 9-10.

[42]See, Mark Searle, "Serving the Lord with Justice," in *Liturgy and Social Justice*, pp. 13-35.

justice and for reuniting common prayer with Christian witness.[43]

LITURGY AND SPIRITUALITY

Despite the fact that a major point of emphasis in the *Liturgy Constitution* was the important place which the liturgy should have in a person's spirituality (12,13,17) a great gap still exists between liturgy and spirituality movements in America. While some of these "movements" touch on the liturgy or are affected by it, (liturgies at retreats, "healing" masses, etc.) that liturgy is to be central to them seems to remain an ideal. (Part of the reason for this may well be that the implementation of the liturgy has been such that people derive more benefit from personal devotions or prayer meetings.) While "spirituality" is hot-copy in America today, the notion of "liturgical spirituality" or a liturgical component of spirituality seems to be largely unexplored.[44]

A DIDACTIC MODEL FOR LITURGY?

In the present state of liturgical reform in America a suggestion that keeps coming up is that of making a three-year plan for "preaching" so that American Catholics can become better informed about the teachings of the Catholic faith. This suggestion is often countered by liturgists as not in keeping with the nature of the homily.[45] The purpose of a

[43]That these issues should be more integrated is the thesis of John Egan, "Liturgy and Justice: An Unfinished Agenda" *Origins* 13 (September 22, 1983) 245-253. See also, R. Kevin Seasoltz, "Justice and the Eucharist," *Worship* 58 (November, 1984)507-525 and "Social Justice and Liturgy," *National Bulletin on Liturgy*, Canadian Catholic Conference, Number 96 (November-December, 1984).

[44]See, Kevin W. Irwin, *Liturgy, Prayer and Spirituality* (NY/Ramsey: Paulist, 1984) for an attempt to indicate this interrelationship. Two recent popular attempts to address this same issue are found in *Spiritual Life* 27 (Spring, 1981) and *Spirituality Today* 34 (March, 1982).

[45]This suggestion was addressed and effectively tabled at the Synod in 1977 by Cardinal Knox then Prefect for the Congregation for Divine Worship.

homily is not merely or primarily to impart information. It is to lead to deeper faith and renewed conviction in God's presence and God's ways borne of sharing the Word and Sacrament. Yet, the question can be raised as to whether we have devoted sufficient attention to the non-didactic elements in American liturgical implementation. The fact that symbols are often spoken of as "things" or "elements" to be objectified underscores a lack of appreciating their importance as those things of material creation and human industry which are used in worship. These natural symbols and products of human labor are used by the liturgical community in order to become remade and renewed in and through Christ's paschal victory. The issue raised here for American Catholics concerns the way symbols are used and interpreted and the importance of symbolic interaction in liturgy.

Liturgy and Other Areas of Church Life: Issues and Tensions

MINISTRIES, LITURGICAL AND OTHERWISE

The *Liturgy Constitution* called for the restoration of liturgical roles (28,29) and postconciliar documents have guided this restoration.[46] The same kind of "practical implementation" noted above with regard to the Liturgy Constitution in general can be applied here. Great attention has been given to implementing liturgical roles and to training a variety of liturgical ministers.

However, this advance is not without its own inherent tensions and problems. With regard to liturgical ministers specifically the alternate side of implementation at liturgy requires that they be restored to their appropriate context, that is service in church life outside the liturgical setting. Diaconate programs are generally among the more acute instances where this issue surfaces. How best to reintegrate

---

[46]These include *Ministeria quaedam* and *Ad pascendum.*

liturgical ministries with other kinds of ministry outside of liturgy itself is an issue that remains unresolved and in need of attention. "Sacristy clergy" may well have provided a poor role model for contemporary liturgical ministers.

In addition, there has been a significant shift away from the liturgy as a focal point for ministry in the church in the sense that various episcopal conferences have seen the limited impact derived from restoring liturgical ministries in isolation from developing other kinds of ministry in the church.[47] To surface this part of the question is to raise the value of implementing norms from "on-high" as opposed to developing roles and ministries from "below," or rather from the contemporary ecclesial context in local communities. To raise the issue of liturgical ministers, therefore, is to raise the question of ministry in general, of who calls to ministry, and what are the criteria for the development of ministry in the church today.

In America a significant context is set for the worldwide consideration because of the advances made in greater participation by women in liturgical ministries, save for that of liturgical presidency. While in the implementation of the Liturgy Constitution the American church may be credited with effective practical implementation, the area of liturgical ministry is a point of real tension, both for the liturgy and for the whole of church life in America. It is an issue and a source of tension that cannot be ignored.

THE CONTEXT FOR WORSHIP

The most commonly experienced setting for worship for American Catholics is the parish. Despite efforts of theologians and practitioners to direct attention to special interest groups and to have them form "parishes,"[48] in America the geographical parish is the most common setting for the

---

[47]See, David N. Power, *Gifts That Differ:* Lay Ministries Established and Unestablished. (New York: Pueblo Publishing Co., 1980), pp 36-54, 149-158.

[48]See, for example, Karl Rahner, *Theology of Pastoral Action* (New York: Herder and Herder, 1966).

liturgy. However, this is not to suggest that the liturgical community is the local parish. In fact, the setting for liturgy is less the territorial parish and has become more and more "the voluntary parish."[49] What this evidences is often a judgment against the liturgy offered in one parish and in favor of what is offered in another.

Parishes provide a full experience of life especially when compared with other more homogeneous settings,[50] and yet what is often sought is a parish that provides for the felt needs of Catholics. This suggests that the liturgical question is often the parish question. Good liturgy often is reflected in good community life, and vice versa.[51] How is the American church to face the reality of the voluntary parish, and what adjustments does this require in terms of appropriate liturgical celebration and the continuation of that worship in common life and service? Christian liturgy traditionally reflects belonging; it is not just cultic. How can these important issues be faced in determining the appropriate context for liturgy? Another important question about parish life in America that effects the liturgy and vice versa is the size of our parishes today and in the future.

SACRAMENTAL SERIOUSNESS

In the late 1960s and through the 1970s a popularly conceived and established way of approaching sacramental preparation for children was the parish sacrament programs. These most often involved sessions for parents as well as children prior to the sacramental celebration. Sometimes these included interviews to determine readiness on

---

[49]See, Jay Dolan and Jeffrey Burns, "The Parish in the American Past," in *Parish: A Place for Worship*, pp. 51-62. The authors sketch the historical evolution of the American parish under the headings: "The Congregational Parish," "The Devotional Parish," and "The Voluntary Parish."

[50]Nathan Mitchell, "Teaching Worship in Seminaries: A Response," *Worship* 55 (July, 1981) "the seminary community is a very thin slice of Christian humanity." (324)

[51]See the findings of Philip Murnion on the American Parish.

the part of both parent and child. This approach is now giving way to programs modelled after the Rite for the Christian Initiation of Adults (RCIA). This involves what is essentially a liturgical process with the whole community electing, scrutinizing, and sharing in the sacramental initiation of candidates. As the RCIA is implemented various ministries envisioned in the rite are becoming more apparent: sponsors, catechists, etc. What is most helpful is that this model for making new Christians restores the essentially ecclesial context for initiation.

As this approach has been implemented on other levels of sacramental involvement,[52] it continues to run into some of the same problems faced by the former approach: readiness for sacraments, sense of community participation, liturgical formation prior to and consequent upon sacramental celebration. Is the RCIA the appropriate model to choose when dealing with other sacraments? To what extent is the vision of church life enunciated in this document apparent in parish life?[53]

LITURGY AND SOCIAL SCIENCES

In the twenty years since the Liturgy document came forth as the first result of the deliberations of the Second Vatican Council there has been a significant change in the conventionally accepted method of liturgical study. While the Council clearly enunciated theology, pastoral life, and history as important for the required investigation of the various forms of liturgy, today in America these components often stand alongside an investigation from anthropological, sociological and psychological perspectives.[54]

---

[52]See, as a model of such an approach adopted by the Diocese of Rochester, N.Y., "To speak of Sacraments and Faith Renewal," *Origins* 10 (April 9. 1981) 673-688.

[53]While not directly concerned with this issue, the talk by Philip J. Murnion, "A Sacramental Church in the Modern World," *Origins* 14 (June 21, 1984) 81-90 is most insightful and thought-provoking.

[54]See, for an overview, Raymond Vaillancourt, *Toward a Renewal of Sacramental Theology*, trans., Matthew O'Connell (Collegeville: Liturgical Press,

Clearly, in America there has been much movement in the method of liturgical/sacramental study. However, despite efforts at underscoring the importance of the social sciences, liturgists are divided on the place which these should have in such important investigations, and the weight to be given them as a result.

In addition, the question of how carefully these other sciences are respected is an important issue to address. Making over another discipline into an image and likeness that is needed for liturgy is methodologically harmful, not to say dishonest. Are the advances in method evident in liturgical journals[55] in the past two decades real advances? How can these advances be integrated into an approach to pastoral liturgy today?

CULTURAL ADAPTATION

The last statement above leads directly to this concern. Since the Liturgy Constitution calls for adaptation of the liturgy by local churches, what approaches are being taken, or are to be taken in America toward this end?

One current example of a process that could well move in this direction is the study of the Order of Mass co-sponsored by the Bishops' committee on the Liturgy and the Federation Diocesan Liturgical Commissions. The study is an investigation of the present Order of Mass with the aim of determining what has proven effective in implementation and what has proven ineffective or not needed. The method of implementation of the liturgy of the eucharist is important to recall: conciliar decree, postconciliar commissions, revised rite in Latin, translation into vernacular, implementation. The Order of Mass study now adds an on-going part

1979). From an American perspective see Michael J. Taylor, ed., *The Sacraments.* Readings in Contemporary Sacramental Theology (New York: Alba, 1981). Some of the articles collected here reflected such an approach.

[55]In the past years the issues of *Worship* have contained more and more articles from the perspective of the social sciences. A comparison of the method employed in *Worship* articles from its inception to the present would yield much insight on the question of liturgical method in America.

to this method: review, evaluation and proposals for further revision. Some issues raised by this study concern how helpful this method is in the first place, how should one deal with responses that are based on education and those which rely on impression alone, who is to determine whether and what further revisions are in order, and who is to implement the proposed changes, Rome or the American bishops?

ECUMENICAL SACRAMENTAL CONVERSATIONS

On the theological level the newly agreed upon "Lima" statement on baptism, eucharist and ministry of the Faith and Order Commission of the World Council of Churches[56] will focus attention once again on mutual recognition of ministries, intercommunion, and the present recognition of baptism among the churches. The multilateral and bilateral conversations held since the Council are clear testimony of the important place which liturgy and sacraments have in the life of member churches.

Yet, it is often the case that such ecumenical conversations are held at a level that ignores the grass-roots or they are engaged in by theologians who have not taken the liturgy seriously as a starting point for their endeavor.[57] This is paradoxical for at the very same time many churches are engaged in liturgical actions which are remarkably similar. With this new climate ecumenical understanding and "common" liturgical forms, what are the steps that need to be taken for full communion among churches? Who is to determine them? How can the apparent agreement in liturgical form and disunity at sharing sacraments be explained today? Do local and more universal notions of church order come into play here? How does one approach these issues?

[56]What is conveniently called the "Lima" Statement is actually *Baptism, Eucharist and Ministry*. Faith and Order Paper No. 111 (Geneva; World Council of Churches, 1982).

[57]See, Eugene L. Brand, "Response to the Berakah Award: Ecumenism and the Liturgy," *Worship* 58 (July, 1984) 305-515. See also, Kevin W. Irwin, *American Lutherans and Roman Catholics in Dialogue on the Eucharist:* A Methodological Critique and Proposal (Rome: Editrice Anesemiana, 1979).

Conclusion

In a sense, these last points about issues and tensions in church life as a result of liturgical reform should not be surprising when one considers that the Liturgy Constitution was a theological and pastoral document. The renewal of pastoral life was a chief aim of the council, and the fact that liturgy and theology are intrinsically connected could not but present new questions once the liturgy was reformed and implemented. A new context for understanding liturgy, theology and pastoral renewal is provided by a review of the *Liturgy Constitution* at this time. The fact that issues and tensions remain may well be the greatest testament left by the *Liturgy Constitution*. On-going reform and renewal stand clearly as necessary agenda items for the Church in any age. An advantage for our own age is that documents such as the Liturgy Constitution continue to point us in that direction.

Dogmatic Constitution on the Church
Lumen Gentium, 21 November, 1964
and
Decree on the Pastoral Office of Bishops in the Church
Christus Dominus, 28 October, 1965

John Linnan, C.S.V.

Historical Background

Prior to the Protestant Reformation, there were no treatises which provided a synthetic theological vision of the Church. The Church was in large measure un-selfconscious about her own nature from a theological point of view. The Church took her existence, nature, and role in the mystery of salvation for granted. It was a given. The Church's self-understanding was embedded in theological reflections on faith, the sacraments, and the Incarnation, and in the various canonical collections which vindicated the rights and powers of the Church over against the civil authority of emperors and kings.

It was the Reformation that challenged the Church to define her own nature, to clarify her role, and to vindicate her exercise of authority in purely religious matters. Out of this challenge emerged a Roman Catholic theology of the

Church, which given the circumstances was highly polemic. In response to Protestantism, this theology of Church tended to focus on hierarchical and institutional dimensions. These were the elements most frequently called into question by what Rome could only consider a "revolt." Because polemic always distorts one's vision, many other elements in the Church's self-understanding were neglected or even overlooked. This Roman Catholic theology of Church emphasized structure, authority, the sacred power of the Pope, bishops and clergy, and adherence to propositions defining Catholic faith as criteria for Church membership. It constructed a monolithic Church. The pluralism in thought, practice, worship, and organizational structures which characterized the patristic and medieval churches was cast aside. A fortress mentality could not afford the luxury of diversity.

For four hundred years this theology dominated Roman Catholic thinking on the Church, in spite of vigorous challenges from concilarism, gallicanism, and erastianism (the Church, as nothing more than the department of religious affairs subject to an all powerful secular authority). This theology knew its moment of triumph in the definition of Vatican Council I (1870) of the primacy and infallibility of the Pope. Yet, the definitions of the first Vatican Council themselves gave evidence that already there were forces at work in the Church that within a century would radically alter the way the Church had come to understand herself.

From an historical perspective the various reform movements in the Church which began in the 14th century and eventuated in the Protestant and Catholic Reforms of the 16th century were not a satisfactory response to the challenge which the Renaissance mounted to faith and to Church. The Renaissance shifted the focus of western civilization from God to the human person, and in the last analysis, the ecclesial reforms, both Protestant and Catholic, were unable to vindicate the place of faith in a universe whose thought, life, and culture had undergone a Copernican revolution. And if confirmation of this failure is needed, the Enlightenment produced it by forcing the issue of faith and religion from the center of the arena of public concern to the periphery of the private judgment of the individual. Modernity had arrived.

It was only in the 19th century that the Church seemed to begin to grapple seriously with the real challenge posed by the modern world. Officially, of course, the position of the Roman Catholic Church was for most of that century one of outright rejection of a worldview which, however, had already been assimilated by most of the faithful. Pius IX in his *Syllabus of Errors* (1864) clearly stated this rejection. One purpose for calling the First Council of the Vatican was to ratify this rejection and to reaffirm in the strongest terms the authority of Pope and Church over against the individualism, rationalism, materialism, liberalism, scientism and statism of the modern world. But in the 19th century there were movements in the Church which before the end of the century would recover forgotten or neglected elements in the Christian tradition and would lay the foundations for a more positive vision of the role of the Church in the modern world. These movements included the renewal of biblical studies, the systematic recovery of the patristic tradition, the liturgical movement, the shift from abstract metaphysical modes of understanding to more experiential and existentialist ways of thinking, and, finally, the growing consciousness of a world of diverse cultures, a consciousness which tended to relativize the Western European culture.

These movements each in its own way opened to serious theological reflection elements in the life of the Church which had long been overshadowed by the prevailing juridical and institutional conceptions of Church. The results of biblical research not only challenged certain historical assumptions about the origins of ecclesial institutions, but drew attention to the role of Jesus and the Spirit in the life of the Church and relativized the historical Church in the the light of the Kingdom of God as an eschatological reality. The recovery of the Patristic tradition likewise called attention to the richness of ecclesial forms and traditions and to the historical character of the Church as a developing and changing institution. The liturgical movement restored the sense of the Church as the primordial sacrament of Christ and shifted the focus from universal institution to the particular worshipping community. The ecumenical movement began among Protestant Churches in an effort to remove the scandal of ecclesiastical division and conflict from the 19th century missionary effort. This same movement also forced the Roman Catholic Church, with some reluctance, to respond to the scandal of division and to reconsider its own polemical interpretation of other Christian Churches and other religions. The philosophical shift from classical metaphysics to the post-Kantian critical philosophies led to a greater emphasis on the actuality of existence and experience. This shift changed both the method and language of theological reflection and gave rise to a body of theological thought which was a major resource for Vatican II. Finally, two world wars, the revolution in worldwide communication, the end of the colonialism, and emergence of non-European Catholic Churches, created a situation in the Church analogous to the major shifts in perspective required when the Church moved from the semitic world into the Hellenistic, and from the Hellenistic world into the Latin West. Account now had to be taken of cultures and civilizations that were non-European.

The ecclesiology of Vatican II, expressed in the Dogmatic Constitution on the Church and in the Decree on the Pastoral Office of Bishops in the Church, is the product of a confrontation between an understanding of the Church inplicitly required by these movements and the classical Roman theology of the Church centered on Pope, hierarchy and institution. What emerges is a theology that is rooted in the teaching of Sacred Scripture and takes into account an historical tradition more ancient and inclusive than that of the post-reformation period, or even that of the medieval West. Its emphases are shaped by the *lex orandi* and by the real experience of a believing community. It is set in a context which strives to embrace the whole world, its history, cultural diversity, and religious pluralism. While it preserves the fundamental elements of the classical Roman theology of Pope, hierarchy and institution, it radically alters and relativizes these by stressing the mystery of the Church, the relationship of Church to the Kingdom of God, the people of God, the particular Church, the episcopal college, and finally, by clearly recognizing that the Church of Christ cannot be simply indentified with the Roman Catholic Church.

The Constitution on the Church

This *Dogmatic Constitution on the Church* was discussed in the first three sessions of the Council. In the first session (1962) the initial draft was so sharply criticized that the text was sent back to the theological commission for a thorough re-writing. What in fact occurred was the substitution of another draft which had been composed earlier by Msgr. Gerard Philips, the professor of dogmatic theology at the University of Louvain, a Council consultant, and later to become secretary to the theological commission. This alternate draft represented the views of bishops and theologians from northern Europe. This second draft was re-worked by the Commission and submitted for discussion at the second session. More than 4000 amendments were suggested. The document was thoroughly revised, and early in the third session was discussed and voted upon chapter by chapter, and in the case of the third chapter (on the hierarchy) was voted upon article by article. Later in the third session, after further revision, the document was once again submitted for a chapter by chapter vote. On November 21, 1964 it was finally approved at a solemn session of the Council presided by the Pope. The vote was 2151 positive, 5 negative.

The *Dogmatic Constitution on the Church* is a seminal work which will affect the development of ecclesiology for decades to come. It is perhaps the greatest achievement of the Council. It is filled with ideas and statements which have yet to be developed. In one sense it represents a revolution in the Church's self-understanding. So rich is it, that it is difficult to know how to adequately state the contribution it has made to the theology of the Church. The structure of the document is itself a major contribution to a renewed theology of Church.

The Constitution begins with a consideration of the inner nature of the Church, its participation in the life of the Trinity, the mystery revealed in Christ. It then treats the whole people of God prior to considering hierarchy, laity and religious in order to emphasize that regardless of diversity of ministry and role in the Church all its members are equally God's People. Only then does it treat of the hierarchy to insure that there is no false understanding of Pope, bishops and clergy as somehow being above and apart from the Church. The laity, their dignity and mission are next to be discussed, followed by the vocation of all Christians, clergy and laity alike, to holiness. Only afterwards is the vocation to religious life treated, and then, as a particular way to that holiness of life to which all Christians are called. The document then speaks of the Church as a pilgrim in history moving inexorably to the Kingdom that God will establish. Finally, it was at the express decision of the Council that the treatment of the role of Mary in the mystery of salvation should be discussed in the context of mystery of Christ and the Church.

The structure of the document clearly reestablishes a more traditional order in the understanding of the Church, and in the process, undercuts the tendency to absolutize both institution and heirarchy.

The Decree on the Pastoral Office of Bishops in the Church

In the preparatory phase of the Council, two schemas were foreseen: "On Bishops and Diocesan Government" and "On the Care of Souls." Initial drafts of each were prepared in 1962, and distributed to the Council Fathers on April 22, 1963.

The proposed decree "On Bishops and Diocesan Government" was discussed in general sessions of the Council between November 5-15, 1963. The draft encountered considerable criticism and was returned to the Commission on Bishops for revision. The Coordinating Commission also asked the Commission on Bishops to combine the proposed decree "On the Care of Souls" with the Decree on Bishops. The reason for this request was the lack of time in the Council to deal with these matters separately. On April 27, 1964 a new draft, entitled, *Decree on the Pastoral Office of Bishops in the Church*, was presented to the members of the Council. It was discussed on September 18, 21, 22, 1964. It was submitted for vote on October 30, 1964 after being revised in accord with amendments submitted during the discussion in the previous month. Neither the first nor the second chapter received the required two-thirds affirmative vote. Only the third chapter was approved by the Council at this time. Instead, the decree was again carefully revised and re-submitted for vote. Individual questions relating to major changes made in Chapters I and II were approved in voting between September 9 and October 1, 1965. Neither chapter was ever voted as a whole. The decree as a whole was approved October 28, 1965.

In the final text the office of bishop is considered from three prespectives: the bishops in relation to the universal church; the bishops in relation to their own churches or dioceses; and the cooperation of bishops in councils, synods, and episcopal conferences.

Despite this seemingly simple outline, the Decree on Bishops is a complex document. It suffers from the rapidity with which it was assembled and from the lack of clarity which resulted from combining the two preceding schemas. It breaks no new ground from a theological perspective. Thus, to rightly understand the Decree, it must be read in the context of the Constitution, as well as that of the Decree on the Ministry and Life of priests and the Decree on the Church's Missionary Activity. Perhaps, too, in this decree more than in any other, the skills of a canonist are needed to elicit the significance of nuances and shifts of emphasis, and to clarify the meaning of a new terminology and the new ecclesial structures created here.

Major Contributions of the Documents

When first published, the *Constitution on the Church* and the *Decree on the Pastoral Office of Bishops* seemed to be filled with "new" insights. On reflection, it became apparent that the Church, like the scribe learned in the reign of God and the head of a household, can bring out both the old and the new. What had occurred was that the Council drew attention to rich elements in the Church's tradition which had been neglected or obscured by emphases generated by the polemics of the past. Looking back on these documents now, it is clear that their contributions to the development of the theology of the Church were many. It might be useful to recall several of these.

CHRIST

The theology of the Church emerging from the Constitution on the Church is clearly Christocentric. Christ is the head of the Church. The Church is the primordial sacrament of Christ.

> The head of this body (the Church) is Christ.... He is the beginning, the firstborn from the dead, that in all things he might hold the primacy (cf.Col. 1:15-18) (7).

In the very first paragraph of the document, the Council declares that "the Church, in Christ, is in the nature of sacrament—a sign and instrument, that is, of communion with God and the unity of all men" (1). Later, the Constitution expands on this assertion in these terms:

> The one mediator, Christ, established and ever sustains here on earth his holy Church, the community of faith, hope and charity, as a visible organization through which he communicates truth and grace to all men. But, the society structured with hierarchical organs and the mysti-

cal body of Christ, the visible society and the spiritual community, the earthly Church and the Church endowed with heavenly riches, are not to be thought of as two realities. On the contrary, they form one complex reality which comes together from a human and divine element. For this reason the Church is compared, not without significance, to the mystery of the incarnate Word (8).

THE SPIRIT

While emphasizing the Christo-centric character of the Church, the Constitution on the Church gives a new impulse to a theology of the Holy Spirit, by focusing on the role of the Holy Spirit as the life of the Church, its guide, the source of its gifts, the principle of its internal unity and of its unity with God.

> When the work which the Father gave the Son to do on earth (cf.Jn.17:4) was accomplished, the Holy Spirit was sent on the day of Pentecost in order that he might continually sanctify the Church . . . . The Spirit dwells in the Church and in the hearts of the faithful, as in a temple (cf. 1 Cor.3:16; 6:19). . . . Hence the universal Church is seen to be "a people brought into unity from the unity of the Father, the Son and the Holy Spirit (4).

SALVATION

The document radically alters the notion that "outside the Church there is no salvation," when it states:

> This Church, constituted and organized as a society in the present world, subsists in the Catholic Church, which is governed by the successor of Peter and by the bishops in a communion with him. Nevertheless, many elements of sanctification and of truth are found outside its visible confines (8).

Thus the Constitution clearly affirms that the Catholic Church is not to be identified absolutely with the Church of Christ.

> For there are many who hold sacred scripture in honor as a rule of faith and of life, who have a sincere religious zeal, who lovingly believe in God the Father Almighty and in Christ, the Son of God and the Saviour, who are sealed in baptism which unites them to Christ, and who indeed recognize and receive other sacraments in their own Churches or ecclesiastical communities (15).

Further the Council affirms that people in other religions or without explicit knowledge of God have access to salvation.

> Those who, through no fault of their own do not know the Gospel of Christ or his Church, but who nevertheless seek God with a sincere heart, and moved by grace, try in their actions to do his will as they know it through the dictates of their conscience—those too may achieve eternal salvation. Nor shall divine providence deny the assistance necessary for salvation to those who, without any fault of theirs, have not yet arrived at an explicit knowledge of God, and who, not without grace, strive to lead a good life (16).

PLURALISM

The *Constitution on the Church* also recognizes the legitimacy of cultural diversity and pluralism and affirms the principle of enculturation.

> ....each part contributes its own gifts to the other parts and to the whole Church, so that the whole and each of the parts are strengthened by the common sharing of all things and by the common effort to attain to fullness in unity....
>
> Holding a rightful place in the communion of the Church

there are also particular Churches that retain their own traditions, without prejudice to the Chair of Peter (13).

The Council implicitly abandons, at least in principle, the Western form of ecclesial life as the sole norm for all Churches and recognizes the legitimate differences and traditions which may characterize a particular Church.

KINGDOM

The Constitution also helps to clarify the distinction between the Church and the Kingdom. In so doing, it undercuts those triumphalist tendencies to identify the Church as the Kingdom of God on earth.

> Henceforth the Church.... receives the mission of proclaiming and establishing among all peoples the kingdom of Christ and of God, and she is, on earth, the seed and the beginning of that kingdom (5).

PEOPLE OF GOD

One of the most helpful teachings of the Constitution on the Church is its description of the Church as People of God, a community called to be a sign and agent of human unity.

> For those who believe in Christ..... are finally established as a "chosen race, a royal priesthood, a holy nation...who in times past were not a people, but now are the People of God. (1 Pet. 2:9-10) (9).

This community, no matter how small, is "a most sure seed of unity, hope and salvation for the whole human race (9)." It is "an instrument for the salvation of all." (9). God has gathered all those who in faith look to Jesus and established them as Church, "that it may be for each and everyone the visible sacrament of this saving unity (9)."

PRIESTHOOD OF THE FAITHFUL

In developing its understanding of the People of God, the Constitution for the first time explicitly affirms the common priesthood of all believers. While it notes that the ministerial priesthood differs not only in degree, but in essence, from the priesthood of all believers, the Council does not determine the exact nature of the common priesthood of believers. It does, however, affirm that "each (priesthood) in its own proper way shares in the priesthood of Christ (10)." The priesthood of the faithful is also more than a spiritual reality. It is communitary and public.

> The faithful indeed, by virtue of their royal priesthood, participate in the offering of the Eucharist. They exercise that priesthood, too, by the reception of the sacraments, prayer and thanksgiving, the witness of a holy life, abnegation and active charity (10).

In the Council's reflection on the ways by which all the faithful participate in the royal, priestly, and prophetic character of Christ, the foundation is laid for a new consideration of the fundamental equality of all Christians in the sight of God, and the abolition of all ecclesiastical distinctions which are not rooted in the divine call to serve the people of God (10-13).

COLLEGIALITY

In the third chapter of the Constitution, the Council considers the hierarchical nature of the Church. Here, too, significant new ground is broken. While reaffirming the traditional teaching of the Church concerning the office and role of the Pope and the bishops, and the primacy and infallibility of the Pope as defined in the First Vatican Council, the Council teaches that the Pope and bishops constitute a college, and that this college in communion with the Pope as its head has supreme authority in the universal church.

Just as, in accordance with the Lord's decree, St. Peter and the rest of the apostles constitute a unique apostolic college, so in like fashion the Roman Pontiff, Peter's successor, and the bishops, the successors of the apostles, are related with and united to one another.

. . . .

The order of bishops is the successor to the college of the apostles in their role as teachers and pastors, and in it the apostolic college is perpetuated. Together with their head, the Supreme Pontiff, and never apart from him, they have supreme and full authority over the universal Church; but this power cannot be exercised without the agreement of the Roman Pontiff (22).

It is this principle of collegiality, as carefully defined in the Explanatory Note added to the Constitution by the doctrinal commission of the Council, which offers a new context in which to develop further the understanding of the primacy and infallibility of the Pope. In this sense, the Council's teaching on collegiality complements the definitions of the First Vatican Council. It also proposes a mode of participation and sharing in the government of the Church applicable at other levels in the Church's life.

The Decree on Bishops (4,6) also reaffirms the theological status of episcopal collegiality. Significantly, it begins its discussion of the episcopal office with the responsibility which the episcopal college has, in union with the Pope and under his authority, for the governance of the universal Church. In fact, the Council seems to teach that the first effect of episcopal consecration is membership in the episcopal college. Throughout, the decree reminds the bishops that whatever their role within particular Churches, they have in union with the Pope a major responsibility for the universal communion of Churches. This seems to be a necessary element in an ecclesiology which emphasizes both universal communion and particular Church.

SYNOD OF BISHOPS

The synod of Bishops was not established by the Council, but by Pope Paul VI, on his own initiative, in response to the request of the Council (Decree on Bishops, 5) for some kind of episcopal council which would in a regular way assist the Pope in the government of the universal church. Such a council would give visible expression to the principle of collegiality, representing the college, but not substituting itself for the college. It is representative of the whole Catholic episcopate, and while possessing no authority of its own, being a consultative "auxiliary service" to the Pope, it is a witness to the participation of the episcopal college in the care for the universal Church. The jury is still out on its significance. It does, however, effectively function as a symbol.

BISHOPS

The *Constitution on the Church* teaches that the office of bishop is of divine institution and is conferred by episcopal consecration, and that intrinsically connected with the office is not only the power to sanctify, but also the power to teach and to govern (21). In this way, the Council transcends many of the controversies concerning the power of orders and the power of jurisdiction. While the three-fold power to sanctify, teach and govern is conferred in the sacrament and comes directly from Christ, these powers cannot be exercised except in communion with the Pope and the whole body of bishops and within the limits established by the canonical mission which derives ultimately from the Pope (27). In no sense, therefore, is the bishop seen as a delegate or vicar of the Pope in the particular Church.

> The pastoral charge, that is, the permanent and daily care of their sheep, is entrusted to them (the bishops) fully; nor are they to be regarded as vicars of the Roman Pontiff, for they exercise the power which they possess in their own right...(27).

PARTICULAR CHURCH

It is in describing the sanctifying role of the bishop that the Constitution on the Church focuses on yet another dimension of the Church too often neglected in the past, the particular Church as truly the Church of Christ—and not simply a subdivision of the Universal Church.

> The bishop, invested with the fullness of the sacrament of Orders, is "the steward of the grace of the supreme priesthood," above all in the Eucharist, which he himself offers, or ensures that it is offered, from which the Church ever derives its life and on which it thrives. This Church of Christ is really present in all legitimately organized local groups of the faithful, which, insofar as they are united to their pastors, are also quite appropriately called Churches in the New Testament. For these are in fact, in their own localities, the new people called by God, in the power of the Holy Spirit and as the result of full conviction (cf. 1 Thess. 1:5) (26).

In the *Decree on the Pastoral Office of Bishops,* the Council makes an effort to specify what is meant by a particular church in more concrete terms by defining a diocese.

> A diocese is a section of the People of God entrusted to a bishop to be guided by him with the assistance of his clergy so that, loyal to its pastor and formed by him into one community in the Holy Spirit through the Gospel and the Eucharist, it constitutes one particular church in which the one, holy, catholic and apostolic Church of Christ is truly present and active (11).

This definition ought not to suggest that the term "particular church" is to be identified simply with "diocese." The *Decree on the Church's Missionary Activity* describes "the particular church" in still another fashion.

> This work of implanting the Church in a particular
> human community reaches a definite point when the
> assembly of the faithful, already rooted in the social life
> of the people and to some extent conformed to its culture,
> enjoys a certain stability and permanence; when its has its
> own priests, although insufficient, its own religious and
> laity, and possesses those ministries and institutions
> which are required for leading and spreading the life of
> the people of God under the leadership of their own
> bishop (19).

In this highlighting of the particular Church as the Church
of Christ, there is laid the foundation for the development of
a fuller understanding of the Universal Church as a communion of Churches. Likewise, this teaching establishes a
point connection between the traditional ecclesiology of the
Roman Catholic Church and the Eucharistic ecclesiology of
the Orthodox Church.

EPISCOPAL CONFERENCES

The *Decree on the Pastoral Office of Bishops* also authorized the formation of episcopal conferences—to be
endowed with hierarchical authority. Episcopal conferences
had existed since the mid-nineteenth century. What is new is
that they are now a recognized and authoritative part of the
ecclesiastical hierarchy. Perhaps most important they are
designed in terms of purpose, that is, they are functional
entities (38). While not depriving the bishop of a particular
Church of the freedom and authority necessary to fulfill his
pastoral ministry, these conferences do limit the authority
of the bishops in the name of cooperation and greater good.
It is difficult to determine whether the authority of episcopal
conferences derives primarily from the collegial character of
the episcopal office or from the role of bishop as pastor of a
particular church, though the latter seems more likely, since
auxiliary bishops do not automatically possess voting
rights.

DIOCESES

The *Decree on the Pastoral Office of Bishops* also called for a thorough revision of the geographical boundaries of dioceses and provinces for the good of souls (39). This is one request of the Council that does not seem to have been acted upon.

PERMANENT DIACONATE

In the *Constitution on the Church* the Council also restored the permanent diaconate and opened it to married men (29). This was a significant change in the practice and discipline of the Western Church, where in fact the diaconate had practically disappeared as anything more than a transitional step to the priesthood. Since the Council, the number of deacons has increased in the Church, but their impact on the life of the Christian community has yet to be determined. The restoration of the diaconate has raised many questions about ministry, ordination, celibacy, and the role of women. To date there are still more questions than answers.

LAITY

In the treatment of the laity, the *Constitution on the Church* made a serious effort to make clear the dignity and mission of lay people in the Church and also tried to specify their role both in the world and in the Church. The Council recalls that everything said in Chapter Two concerning the People of God is addressed equally to laity, religious and clergy. The Constitution affirms the fundamental dignity and equality of all members of the Church.

> There is, therefore, one chosen People of God: one Lord, one faith, one baptism" (Eph. 4:5); there is a common dignity of members deriving from their rebirth in Christ, ... a common vocation to perfection, one salvation, one hope and undivided charity. In Christ and in the Church

there is, then, no inequality arising from race or national-
ity, social condition or sex, for "there is neither Jew nor
Greek; there is neither slave nor freeman; there is neither
male or female. For you are all 'one "in Christ Jesus."
(Gal. 3:28 Greek; cf. Col. 3:11)

Their special vocation in the world is to reshape the world in
which they live in accordance with God's will.

But by reason of their special vocation it belongs to the
laity to seek the kingdom of God by engaging in temporal
affairs and directing them according to God's will. They
live in the world, that is, they are engaged in each and
every work and business of the earth and in the ordinary
circumstances of social and family life which, as it were,
constitute their very existence. There they are called by
God that, being led by the Spirit to the Gospel, they may
contribute to the sanctification of the world, as from
within like leaven, by fulfilling their own particular duties
(31).

And in the Church, the laity also have a specific vocation:

The laity, however, are given this special vocation: to
make the Church present and fruitful in those places and
circumstances where it is only through them that she can
become the salt of the earth (33).

The laity can also share in the specific apostolic work of the
hierarchy through deputation.

Besides this apostolate which belongs to absolutely every
Christian, the laity can be called in different ways to more
immediate cooperation in the apostolate of the hierarchy,
like those men and women who helped the apostle Paul in
the Gospel, laboring much in the Lord (cf. Phil. 4-3;
Rome. 16:3ff.). They have, moreover, the capacity of
being appointed by the hierarchy to some ecclesiastical
offices with a view to a spiritual end (33).

HOLINESS

In considering the vocation of the Church to holiness, the Council in the Constitution on the Church emphasizes that all Christians, clergy, laity, and religious, are called to the same holiness of life, even though the ways to that holiness may differ from person to person.

> It is therefore quite clear that all Christians in any state or walk of life are called to the fullness of Christian life and to the perfection of love, and by this holiness a more human manner of life is fostered also in earthly society" (39).

RELIGIOUS LIFE

While the Constitution's teaching on religious life is in large measure traditional, it refrains from using the traditional language of "states of perfection," and in accord with its teaching on the vocation of all Christians to holiness, affirms that the religious life is one of the modes of realizing Christian holiness, and as a stable form of life constitutes a gift of God to the Church for the sake of her mission.

> This form of life has its own place in relation to the divine and hierarchical structure of the Church. Not, however, as though it were a kind of middle way between the clerical and lay conditions of life. Rather it should be seen as a form of life to which some Christians, both clerical and lay, are called by God so that they may enjoy a special gift of grace in the life of the Church and may contribute, each in his own way, to the saving mission of the Church (43).

ESCHATOLOGY

The Constitution also sees the Church as a pilgrim people living out its existence in the eschatological tension of the "already, but not yet."

Already the final age of the world is with us (cf. 1 Cor.
10:11) and the renewal of the world is irrevocably under
way; it is even now anticipated in a certain real way, for
the church on earth is endowed already with a sanctity
that is real though imperfect (48).

MARY

Finally, in its theological consideration of Mary, the
Mother of God, and her role in the mystery of salvation and
in the life of the Church, the Council is thoroughly Christo-
centric.

No creature could ever be counted along with the Incarnate Word and Redeemer; but just as the priesthood of
Christ is shared in various ways both by his ministers and
the faithful, and as the one goodness of God is radiated in
different ways among his creatures, so also the unique
mediation of the redeemer does not exclude but rather
gives rise to a manifold cooperation which is but a sharing in this one source (62).

These "new" elements in the teaching of the Council on
the Church are "new" only in the sense that they had been
neglected in the more recent history of the Church. They
represent elements in the tradition which needed to be
clearly affirmed to restore a more balanced and integral
understanding of the Church.

TASKS FOR A FUTURE COUNCIL

Experience has shown the value of the *Constitution on
the Church* to the development of the Church. It is a seminal
work. There is much in it that has yet to be assimilated into
the life, thought and practice of the Church. It has laid
foundations for structures yet to be built, and the full value
of structures that have been created is still to be achieved.
The *Decree on the Pastoral Office of Bishops* is a derivative
work, heavily dependent on the theology of the Church

Constitution. Its effect on the life of the Church has been less significant. It has, nevertheless, raised some important questions which still need to be answered.

Given the achievements registered in these two conciliar documents, what are some of the issues, questions, and problems that a new council would need to address? For the sake of brevity, a brief discussion of several issues will have to suffice.

The mission of the church, its reason for existence, needs to be given a fuller theological statement. Such a statement would need to give consideration to the Christian life as a specific vocation in the world, different from, but in relation to other vocations generated by other religions and systems of belief. Is it, indeed, the ultimate intention of God that all people should become members of the Church? Might other religions have a providential role in the mystery of salvation? Attending to these issues requires that the mission of the Church be considered in the light of the fact that there is salvation outside the Church.

Papal primacy and infallibility need to be reconsidered in the light of the Council's teaching on collegiality and its practice of subsidiarity. The theological limitations on papal authority need to be given institutional form to establish norms of conduct that will make clearer in theory and in practice that papal authority is a participation in the authority of the Church. The relationship of the infallibility of the whole people of God to the infallibility of the Pope and of the episcopal college needs further clarification. It might also be useful to affirm clearly that those who officially teach what the Church believes, must listen to what the Church believes.

Collegiality of bishops needs to be given a clearer institutional form at all levels in the Church: universal, patriarchal, national and regional, provincial and diocesan. While the development of the concept of collegiality is very important, there is a danger that, in making membership in the episcopal college the first and perhaps primary effect of episcopal consecration, we drive a wedge between universal communion and particular Church. Might it not be in virtue of the bishop's role as pastor of a particular Church that he is a member of the episcopal college?

The concept of "by divine institution" needs to be rigorously defined in the light of biblical and historical research.

The ordained pastoral ministry is in serious disarray. The confusion which exists clearly calls for a thorough reconsideration of the Sacrament of Orders as it relates to the pastoral office in the Church. Is the division of ordained ministries into the triad: bishop, priest, and deacon of divine institution, or is it simply the ordained ministry itself which is of divine institution? In what sense are bishops successors of the apostles (who seem to have been itinerant missionaries, not residential pastors of Churches)? In what sense can we even say that the apostles constituted a "college"? Are we not dealing here with a stage in doctrinal development, rather than with the theological principles at the origin of the pastoral office? The nature of the pastoral office in the Church needs a clearer explanation, and perhaps it should be given more than three forms. The concept of permanent office holders needs to be re-examined as one means of limiting clericalism and making ministry in an ecclesial office a service and not a position in the hierarchy. Limitations placed on access to ministerial offices in the Church by reason of sex or state in life need to be re-examined. Finally, what is the relationship between episcopal dignity and the pastoral office? What is an auxiliary bishop? What is a bishop without a particular church (or diocese)? What is the pastor of a particular church who is not a bishop?

The concept of the particular church is a valuable one and calls for further reflection. How can it be more practically defined? What is the relationship between this concept and the notion that the Church is a "congregated people of God?" What is the significance of geographical proximity to a theology of the particular church?

The laity (the People of God) should be given priority in the next Council's reflection on the nature of the Church. The distinction between work in the world and pastoral ministry should be re-thought and the practice of defining a particular group of persons by the work they do be reconsidered.

Religious life remains a quasi-hierarchical element over-emphasized in the *Constitution on the Church.* Careful thought should be given to "de-canonicalizing" religious life in the Church. It should be regulated no more or no less than any other charismatic gift in the Church.

The Petrine Office is still too narrowly defined in terms of jurisdiction and teaching authority. Consideration should be given to the other services and functions which make this office necessary for the Church. Perhaps, too, more careful distinctions need to be made between the multiple functions of the Pope. He is the bishop of a particular Church, the Primate of Italy, the Patriarch of the Western Church, and the Successor of Peter. How are these multiple offices related in the one person of the Pope and in his service to the Church?

Finally, *the role of the Church in celebrating the sacra-ments* needs clearer definition. How the celebration of sacraments constitutes the Church and makes it the Sacrament of Christ should be given greater theological development.

CONCLUSION

The Council's teaching on the nature of the Church in the *Constitution on the Church* and the *Decree on the Pastoral Office of Bishops* and elsewhere remains a fundamental stage in the contemporary effort to renew the Church. Since renewal is, however, an inherent and perduring need of the Church, it is apparent that because of all that has occurred since the Second Vatican Council, new issues and questions have arisen which call for new responses. It is therefore, possible to celebrate the work of the Council and still look forward to that time when it will need to be completed and perhaps replaced.

Decree on Ecumenism
Unitatis Redintegratio, 21 November, 1964

Agnes Cunningham, S.S.C.M.

In October, 1982, Martin E. Marty was one of four speakers in a symposium sponsored by the Christian Life Center in Indianapolis to mark the twentieth anniversary of the Second Vatican Council. In his presentation, Dr. Marty addressed the audience as members of "the second ecumenical generation." He disclaimed any intention to suggest, arrogantly, that nothing of note had occurred, ecumenically, prior to Vatican II. However, Marty insisted that, for Christians in North America—and, specifically, in the United States—any real experience of ecumenism had to be acknowledged as a post-conciliar development.

The reasons cited by Marty for this state of affairs were neither profound nor theological. In the first place, given the average age of the "typical" American today, only a minority of the population knows the pre-Vatican II Church. Secondly, the phenomenon of "reaching across" religious "boundaries" in North America, as Marty expressed it, is an event that must be measured by the life span of at least one generation. Marty asked his audience to remember with him "what it had been like before," in order to recognize the task and the responsibility that are confided to all Christians in a post-conciliar age. I propose his request as the basic structure of this paper: 1) a review of *the Decree on Ecumenism*; 2) an overview of selected post-conciliar ecumenical efforts and their results; 3) an assessment of the present ecumenical climate.

The Document

The Decree on Ecumenism was promulgated by Paul VI on 21 November 1964, the day of its nearly unanimous acceptance by the Council Fathers. From its modest beginnings, the decree had grown through multiple debates, emandations and several major revisions to what Congar could call "this great and beautiful text" (*Documents conciliaires*, 1965). Like other decrees of the Second Vatican Council, it consists mainly of practical instructions derived from the doctrinal teaching of the Council and was meant to foster an ecumenical attitude among Catholics. Perhaps one of the most important points to note regarding the Decree on Ecumenism is that it is to be interpreted in the light of the doctrine of the Dogmatic Constitution on the Church, even as that Constitution is to be understood according to the doctrine of the decree, itself.

The structure of the *Decree on Ecumenism* is simple. The document begins with a preface which includes a statement of the purposes of ecumenism and of the decree itself.

> The restoration of unity among all Christians is one of the principal concerns of the Second Vatican Council. Christ the Lord founded one Church and one Church only.... In recent times he has begun to bestow more generously upon divided Christians remorse over their divisions and longing for unity.

Everywhere large numbers have felt the impulse of this grace, and among our separated brethren also there increases from day to day a movement, fostered by the grace of the Holy Spirit, for the restoration of unity among all Christians. Taking part in this movement, which is called ecumenical, are those who invoke the Triune God and confess Jesus as Lord and Saviour. . . . Almost everyone, though in different ways, longs for the one visible Church of God, a Church truly universal and sent forth to the whole world that the world may be converted to the Gospel and so be saved, to the glory to God.

The sacred Council gladly notes all this. It has already declared its teaching on the Church, and now, moved by a desire for the restoration of unity among all the followers of Christ, it wishes to set forth before all Catholics guidelines, helps and methods, by which they too can respond to the grace of this divine call (1).

Then follow three major sections in which principles of ecumenism, the practice of ecumenism and separated communions, both in the East and in the West, are discussed. The decree ends with a look, in hope, to the future and a "holy objective":—"the reconciliation of all Christians in the unity of the one and only Church of Christ" (24).

The theological teachings of the decree can be considered, briefly, under three headings: ecumenism, ecclesiology, conversion.

ECUMENISM

According to the decree, "concern for restoring unity involves the whole Church, faithful and clergy alike" (5). It is to be integrated into the daily life and activity of every member of the Church. In describing the Catholic contribution of Christian unity, the terms, "ecumenical movement" and "ecumenical work," are used. These phrases refer to the actions and undertakings that are initiated in order to promote unity among Christians. Such activity presupposes a fundamental orientation which seeks to witness to the "one faith" which already exists among Christians, while fostering the continued growth and increase of the unity Christ wills for his Church.

> Moreover, some, even very many, of the most significant elements and endowments which together go to build up and give life to the Church itself, can exist outside the visible boundaries of the Catholic Church: the written Word of God; the life of grace; faith, hope and charity, with the other interior gifts of the Holy Spirit, as well as visible elements. All of these, which come from Christ and lead back to him, belong by right to the one Church of Christ (3).

ECCLESIOLOGY

The decree is based on an understanding of the *unity* and the *unicity* of the Church. We can speak of the *unity* of the Church, because the Church is a *communion*, that is,

> an organic whole composed of spiritual bonds (faith, hope and charity), and of visible structural forms (the profession of faith, the sacramental economy, the pastoral ministry), and which culminates in the eucharistic mystery, the source and expression of the unity of the Church, or rather of the one Church. This ecclesiology obviously makes use of the essence of the constitutive elements of the Church—the Holy Spirit, theological activity, its ministerial structure, the papacy—but each of these "elements" is considered in so far as it promotes, conditions, realizes or brings about the "communion."

The *unicity* of the Church is best expressed in the biblical image of the one fold and the one shepherd. There is but one Church,—"a standard lifted on high for the nations to see," (2) a pilgrim and servant, brought into history by Christ through the Holy Spirit. The one Church of Christ exists; because of that one Church, all the churches are constantly called to greater unity.

In the light of the unity and the unicity of the Church, the document considers the relationship of other Christian "Churches and ecclesial communities" to the Roman Catholic Church, the constitutive institutional elements which are the "means of salvation" and effective incorporation into the body of Christ, even when visible membership in the Church is incomplete (3). The decree recognizes that membership in the body of Christ is both inward (spiritual) and outward (visible). It can grow or diminish according to an individual's fidelity to the Spirit of Christ and to perseverance in love. Ecumenism is, at one level, a call to renewal and reform.

CONVERSION

This is a key concept in ecumenism. The first of all the activities in the ecumenical movement is renewal of the Church. (6)

To the extent that the Church is renewed in fidelity to her call, to that extent is the union of the churches fostered. As a pilgrim, the Church must constantly seek to be renewed: in Church order and legislation, in ecclesiastical structures and constitutions, in doctrinal formulation, in biblical and liturgical studies.

Conversion is addressed not only to the Church at large, but also to the individual; "There can be no ecumenism worthy of the name without interior conversion" (7). Laity and clergy alike are called to a life of humility, love and service, to acknowledgment of personal guilt and to repentance.

Following its promulgation, the *Decree on Ecumenism* was hailed in both Catholic and non-Catholic circles as "a new beginning full of hopes and promises." It was seen as the "beginning of a new era in the relation of the Churches to one another." Christians received it as a sign that the "demand for unity in essentials" does not exclude legitimate diversity and true freedom in non-essentials and that charity is above and in all things (3). To what extent were these expectations met, in the years after Vatican II?

Post-Conciliar Ecumenism

For at least fifty years before Pope John XXIII convoked the Second Council of the Vatican, an ecumenical movement had been developing outside the Catholic Church. That movement, however, was marked, and most of its participants would affirm was handicapped, by the absence of Catholic participation. With the promulgation of *the Decree on Ecumenism* and the encouragement and leadership of the Secretariate for Christian Unity, the ecumenical scene was to change dramatically. This change was due to the establishment of national dialogue groups, of international conversation commissions and to the publication of a number of post-conciliar documents (cf. Flannery, pp. 471-559). Some of these documents marked historic events, such as the Common Declaration of Pope Paul VI and Patriarch Athenagoras (7 December 1965).

An evaluation of the Bilateral Consultations between the Roman Catholic Church in the United States and other Christian communions was carried out and published by a study committee of the Catholic Theological Society of America (CTSA) in 1972 and again in 1979. In both instances, the assistance of the Bishop's Committee for Ecumenical and Interreligious Affairs (BCEIA) facilitated the work of the CTSA committee.

The first CTSA Report (1972) included the BCEIA-sponsored conversations with eight Christian denominations or communions: American Baptist Convention, the Christian Church (Disciples of Christ), Episcopal Church, Southern Baptist, Orthodox, Lutheran Churches, Methodist Church, Presbyterian-Reformed. In all, twenty significant reports and consensus statements were studied by the CTSA committee. Questions considered by one or another of the groups included: the doctrine of ordained ministry, the status of women, the doctrine of the Eucharist, inter-communion, mixed marriages and method for doctrinal agreement. Three of the consultations also addressed the question of the goals envisioned for the consultations. At the time of the 1972 evaluation, the most elaborate theological consensus papers were those from the Lutheran-Roman Catholic consultations 1) on Eucharist and 2) on Eucharist and Ministry. The most productive conversations, at that point, were those of Roman Catholics with Lutherans, Presbyterians and Anglicans.

The second review of bilateral reports and consensus statements undertaken by the CTSA (1979) included six consultations: Anglican/Roman Catholic, Diciples of Christ/Roman Catholic, Lutheran/Roman Catholic, United Methodist/Roman Catholic, Orthodox/Roman Catholic and Presbyterian-Reformed/Roman Catholic. Nineteen documents, covering a wide variety of questions, were examined. Among the new topics introduced for dialogue were responses to some of the international documents (e.g., The Canterbury Statement, the Venice Statement), authority in the Church, papal primacy and infallibility.

In 1972, the CTSA committee acknowledged the value of the bilateral conversations.

> They have helped to overcome prejudices, to establish friendship and trust, to suggest realistic ecumenical goals, and to prompt a healthy reexamination of the doctrinal positions that have become habitual in the various confessional traditions (CTSA PROCEEDINGS, Volume 27, 1972; p. 228).

The "important convergences" reached on the doctrines of ministry and of the Eucharist were particularly noted.

In the 1979 review, the CTSA committee members pointed to a number of weaknesses that marked the consultation. There were evidences of a lack of investment of scholarly energy. Little interfacing or crossreferencing had taken place among the various groups. The groups seemed, largely, untouched by ecumenical efforts in other quarters. Disagreements were not sufficiently accounted for. Underlying ecclesiologies were too implicit. Ethical questions were rarely addressed.

Strong recommendations were made by the CTSA committee to the consultation groups, to the sponsoring agencies and to the Roman Catholic bishops. The final statement of the 1979 report was more tempered than the earlier review:

> We readily acknowledge with the Second Vatican Council, however, that the realization of this unity "transcends human energies and abilities." We, too, place our "hope entirely in the prayer of Christ for the Church, in the love of the Father for us, and in the power of the Holy Spirit. 'And hope does not disappoint, because the charity of God is poured forth in our hearts by the Holy Spirit who has been given to us'"(CTSA PROCEEDINGS, Volume 34, p. 285)

The national bilateral conversations were to continue after 1979. It was presumed that subsequent evaluation of the reports and consensus statements would be able to discern the influence, at the national level, of achievements and convergences realized in the international ecumenical commissions and in the wider sphere of efforts toward Christian unity everywhere. That study will have to be treated elsewhere than in this paper.

The most dramatic achievement of efforts toward Christian unity in the realm of international ecumenical consultations was highlighted in September, 1981, when the Twelfth-Year Report of Anglican Roman Catholic International Consultation (ARCIC) was submitted to Rome and to Canterbury. In the minds of that commission's members, Anglicans and Roman Catholics had reached a point where conversation had to give way to action. *"Extraordinary* convergences" had been realized. Major obstacles in doctrinal differences had been overcome. The members of the commission presumed that their work had come to an end.

With the reconstitution of a new ARCIC commission and a document, from the Roman side, asking for further clarification of certain statements in the Twelfth-Year Report, it became clear that more dialogue was indicated, even for this commission. Other international groups were still in the process of research, study and discussion, or were awaiting reorganization of membership in order to begin a new phase of the dialogue. That process continues to move forward, if not by "giant steps," at least by one-step-at-a-time.

There are moments when one senses a certain weariness on the part of members in one or another of the international commissions. It seems as if some degree of the initial impetus and fervor of early years has been lost. Questions have been asked about the authenticity of Pope John Paul II's commitment to the ecumenical task. Hindrances and delays in the implementation of ecumenical projects have seemed more frequent. In the October, 1983, issue of *Ecumenical Trends,* Karl Rahner is represented as looking to Church leaders "to take the next steps toward Christian unity. He is looking for bold, courageous action to solidify the gains already achieved and to regain the momentum of the ecumenical movement" (p. 131).

It would be unfair to surrender, at this point, to this mood of discouragement. Pope John Paul II has reiterated, on numerous occasions, his fidelity to the "irreversible commitment" of Vatican II to the ecumenical effort. Persons close to the inner-workings of Centers, Offices, commissions and consultations tend to explain the slower pace of recent years as the result of facing the more difficult questions that lie beneath the surface of real separation.

Evidences of continuity in the ecumenical movement can be found, at one level, in the documents that have continued to be promulgated since the close of the Second Vatican Council. In the volume of *Conciliar and Post Conciliar Documents* edited by Austin Flannery, O.P. (1975), there are twelve official statements listed, along with another related to the Declaration on the Relation of the Church to Non-Christian Religions ("Guidelines on Religious Relations with the Jews," December, 1964). Other documents have followed those in the Flannery volume, notably the ecumenical addresses of Pope John Paul II. The summer, 1983, issue of the *Journal of Ecumenical Studies* (20, 3) carried an article by Archbishop Jean Jadot, on the progress in dialogue between the Roman Catholic Church and non-Christian religions, in years following Vatican II.

Furthermore, from another perspective, documents from the National Council of Churches of Christ and from the World Council of Churches are now being accepted and addressed in the bilateral consultations. The events which transpired at Vancouver and the publication of the Lima Document on baptism, ministry and eucharist are two notable examples of this interrelatedness. Collaboration across confessional lines in work for justice and human rights also carries an ecumenical dimension, at times implicit, but increasingly intentional. Despite such assurances, however, the general impression of a loss of enthusiasm in the ecumenical world cannot be completely dismissed. We feel impelled to insist on the signs of progress, in order to assure energy for continued growth.

It is not enough, however, to test the present ecumenical climate on the basis of bilateral conversations and documents, alone. We hope for tangible signs of progress in the search for Christian Unity. How can we measure the distance still to be traveled, if we cannot truly know how far we have come? How can we identify the questions that manifest separation, unless we can point to treasures that we are sure of sharing, even now? I would like to suggest three "irreversible" gains that have been won since the close the Vatican II. Acknowledgment of these agreements will enable us to isolate at least three critical areas of separation among the churhces. From that point of perception, it will be possible to suggest collaborative efforts that will contribute to our continued pursuit of the vision captured in *the Decree on Ecumenism* (2): "One Lord, one faith, one baptism" (Ephesians 4:5).

Things That Unite Us

One of the most remarkable ecumenical achievements realized since the close of Vatican II is the awareness and understanding of the reality of "spiritual ecumenism." The term occurs in *the Decree on Ecumenism* (8) and was taken from the teachings of the great French ecumenist, Abbé Paul Couturier. It was a concept overlooked and only gradually rediscovered, as bilateral groups probed the nature of the unity they sought together and reflected on the meaning of their goal of "visible, organic unity."

"Spiritual ecumenism" is a gift already given by the Holy Spirit to the one Church of Christ and to all those who are baptized into Christ. "Spiritual ecumenism," is a call from God which allows partners in ecumenical conversation to experience freedom in dialogue and in relationships. "Spiritual ecumenism" sustains and fosters the will for unity shared by the churches. "Spiritual ecumenism" grows out of the conviction that Christian unity is, before all and above all, a spiritual matter. Far from being naive, "spiritual ecumenism" is rooted in the consciousness of the gravity of a situation in which Christians are separated from one another and the Church is torn by divisions. "Spiritual ecumenism" enables individuals and communities to be freed from selfishness so as to share life in a reconciled community. "Spiritual ecumenism" leads to a unity of fellowship in faith, hope, love, peace, joy and patience.

A second irreversible achievement of post-conciliar ecumenism is an understanding of the reality that can be called "evangelical space." "Evangelical space" is a term that implies that *visible* division does not necessarily violate or destroy the given unity of grace. Indeed, it is only within "evangelical space" that authentic unity is possible among separated Christians. "Evangelical space" flows from the life of grace, present and dynamic wherever Christians live the gospel and answer the call to gospel holiness. "Evangelical space" is that *locus* within which the holiness and grace present in each Christian church or communion is affirmed and celebrated. "Evangelical space" enables us to say,

"There will be visible unity only to the extent that unity of grace, already present (at least in some measure) bears fruit" (*Mid-Stream* XVIII, 4; p. 393). When ecumenical efforts of any kind—dialogues, consultations, works of faith or charity—are marked by success, it is because Christians have been able to come together, across confessional boundaries, to meet in an "evangelical space."

A final irreversible achievement of the past two decades of work for Christian Unity is at least initial recognition of the validity of what Jean Tillard, O.P., calls "the First *Yes*." According to Father Tillard, every Christian is invited to say "Yes" twice, in regard to his or her membership in the body of Christ. The "First Yes" is a baptismal "yes": it is the fundamental, essential "yes" of faith. It is acceptance of God's revelation in Jesus Christ and of God's plan of salvation to be accomplished through Jesus Christ. The "First Yes" is the expression of our conversion to the Gospel. In the Words of Tillard, it "expresses a readiness to become in this world, for the glory of the Father," the-one-whom-God-wills, the "one for whom Christ Jesus is the model" (*Mid-Stream* XX 3; p. 289).

The "Second Yes" of the Christian, for Tillard, is the acceptance of the gospel and of the Christian revelation, as they are mediated through a particular Church or ecclesial community. Thus, with the "First Yes," I am a Christian ; with the "Second Yes," I am a Roman Catholic, an Anglican, a Lutheran.... Through the "First Yes," I enter the One Church of God; through the "Second Yes," I adhere to one of the many Christian Churches—all of which are called to a unity willed and prayed for by Christ.

"Spiritual ecumenism," "evangelical space," and the "First Yes" are three realities that have been discovered, affirmed and appropriated by many Christians engaged in efforts to respond to the call to unity in the One Church of Christ. Because they are rooted in and effected by baptism, we ought not be surprised to find that they serve to highlight a number of questions that remain unanswered, even in the light of the unity they signify. Three such questions are particularly difficult to address.

Things That Divide Us

As fellowship and communion deepen among Christians committed to the ecumenical effort, it becomes increasingly difficult to explain why mutual recognition of baptism and agreement regarding the effects of baptism have not led to the solution of problems that derive from baptismal consecration, sacramentality and commitment. The questions most frequently asked are direct and disturbing. If we can recognize the validity of one another's baptism, why cannot we admit mutual recognition of one another's eucharist? Why does not mutual recognition of baptism admit mutual recognition of ministries? This second question is usually phrased in terms of the "validity of orders," for those ecclesial communities or churches professing an ordained clergy. It remained as one of the stumbling blocks in the ARCIC Twelfth-Year Report. However it is asked, the question of mutual recognition of ministries that have been authentically and faithfully validated by specific ecclesial communions is one that remains unresolved, despite significant agreed statements on ministry from several bilateral consultations.

Closely related to this question is that of women in ministry. It is true that concern for the role of women in the Church need not be restricted to that of ministry. However, the first brief statement on women (Presbyterian-Reformed/Roman Catholic), focused on this aspect as an area to be addressed. By the time the second CTSA Report was completed, there had been no major agreed statements on this question, although one senses that it is never far below the surface whenever baptism, eucharist, ministry or ordination is discussed. This question assumes greater significance, ecumenically, when we recall the acceptance of ordained women in many churches of the Reform, in contrast to the position on the ordination of women held by the Orthodox Churches.

Many ecumenists insist that neither mutual recognition of ministries nor women in ministry constitutes the most critical ecumenical question, however. The major stumbling block on the road to Christian Unity is identified, increasingly, as the Petrine office. Once again, the ARCIC Twelfth-Year Report and the agreed Lutheran/Roman Catholic statement, among others, can be invoked in testimony. Two recent publications point to the crucial nature of this problem of the papacy, authority in the Church, infallibility and primacy. The first book, *A Pope for All Christians?*, edited by Peter J.McCord, presents a collection of writings by seven leading theologians from as many Christian Churches on the possibility of an ecumenical papacy. The second volume, *The Bishop of Rome*, by J.M.R. Tillard, O.P., is the result of the author's intense and extensive ecumenical experience. His stated purpose is "to lay the foundations of that ecclesiology of communion which the present situation between the Churches calls for" (Preface).

Validity of orders or mutual recognition of ministries, women in ministry and the Petrine office stand as challenges to be addressed and explored, in faith, in Christian love and in hope. The dimension and scope of these questions seem to place them beyond our capacity to address, as we strain our vision towards the horizons which promise the unity Christ wills for his Church. We look, for our part, to lesser tasks and lesser challenges. Fortunately, these more immediate goals are readily accessible to us.

Things We Can Do Together

The One Church of Christ is always in the process of coming to recognize more fully that there is "One Lord, one faith, one baptism" (Ephesians 4:5). That process is assured and promoted in many ways, at many levels. What are some of the more modest ways in which all Christians can seek to contribute to the effort toward Church unity? I suggest five, simple and possible for us all.

The first contribution toward Christian unity is one suggested by Martin E. Marty in the lecture to which I referred at the beginning of this paper. Marty urges us to develop an ecumenical *spirit*, especially when it seems to us that the ecumenical *movement* is losing dynamism. Marty explains that "movements" belong to groups, commissions, organizations; "spirit" belongs to people. Each of us can find the truth wherever it is and claim it for our own life. Each of us can bring together in mind and heart the insights and intuitions of truth found beyond the divergences and differences of Luther and Newman, of Calvin and Paul VI. The ecumenical *movement* may be more or less healthy, depending on the life (or death) of the group engaged in that movement. The ecumenical spirit can be alive, vital and dynamic within us, if we seek to keep it so.

The second contribution we can all make to the project of Christian Unity is an effort to learn all we can about the spiritual traditions and forms of prayer from Christian communions other than our own. We can learn to deepen our own life of prayer, our life in the Spirit, by learning to appropriate the ways and words by which "other" Christians have worshipped, celebrated, thanked, petitioned and praised God. The heritage of Christian holiness belongs to the whole Church. "The walls of separation do not reach to heaven!" This second suggestion is not unlike Leonard Swidler's "Tenth Commandment" for "Interreligious Dialogue": "Each participant eventually must attempt to experience the partner's religion 'from within'. . ." (*Lumen vitae* XXXVIII, 1983, No. 3; p. 350).

Both spirit and shared prayer or spirituality are important for the third effort: ministry to *ecumenical couples*. The shift of emphasis from concern about "mixed marriages" to pastoral care of "ecumenical couples" is long overdue. It is true that a French periodical like *FOYERS MIXTES* reflects an ecumenical maturity and sensitivity that have developed over the years, primarily, in Europe. However, the 1970 *Motu Proprio* of Paul VI on this very topic has had little consequence, at the practical level. Indeed, in North America, theologians, themselves, have devoted little time or energy to the question. Preparation of two Christians for a marriage in which what they share in faith enables each of them to support the separation of what they cannot share is necessary. Nurturing of their faith relationship, so that their family unity is, in itself, a contribution to the desire and task for Christian unity is also necessary. The 1983 Code of Canon Law (c. 1128) entrusts to bishops and pastors the continued care of couples that can be and grow to be ever more "ecumenical." A few small steps in this direction could prove to be giant leaps for the entire Chruch.

If ecumenism is going to flourish at the parish or diocesan level, there must be ecumenical education. For several years, national and regional ecumenical officers have expressed concern about the lack of ecumenical awareness, interest and enthusiasm among priests and seminarians. An entire program is indicated, here. The challenge consists in trying to provide experiences that can be pedagogically effective, spiritually inspiring, and minimally demanding in time and energy. There are hopeful signs in theological education, but the surface of this challenge has only begun to be scratched, in most instances. The ecumenical movement and the ecumenical spirit cannot thrive without leaders at the "grass roots" level. What has transpired and been achieved, nationally or internationally, has to be "brought home" in palatable and stimulating ways to all the people of God. Ecumenism needs to be promoted among priests and seminarians.

My final suggestion is the most simple and the most practical: *until we can do the best possible thing, we ought to do the most possible thing.* To the extent that a person is convinced that the priestly prayer of Christ (John 17) is, essentially, Christ's prayer for the unity he wills for his Church, to that extent will that person find ways to pray, work and sacrifice that all may be one... "when God wills and in the way God wills." To that extent, will the distance still to be travelled be less, because of the distance we have already come. Inspiration and motivation for this "most possible" effort come to us, still today, from the Second Vatican Council:

> This sacred Council firmly hopes that the initiatives of the sons of the Catholic Church, joined with those of the separated brethren, will go forward, without obstructing

the ways of divine Providence, and without prejudging the future inspirations of the Holy Spirit. Further, this Council declares that it realizes that this holy objective— the reconciliation of all Christians in the unity of the one and only Church of Christ—transcends human powers and gifts. It therefore places its hope entirely in the prayer of Christ for the Church, in the love of the Father for us, and in the power of the Holy Spirit. "And hope does not disappoint, because God's love has been poured forth in our hearts through the Holy Spirit who has been given to us" (Rom. 5:5) (24).

Decree on the Up-To-Date Renewal of Religious Life
Perfectae Caritatis, 28 October, 1965

Carolyn Osiek, R.S.C.J.

The *Decree on the Renewal of Religious Life* was promulgated at the Second Vatican Council on October 28, 1965 after a long evolution. The Dogmatic Constitution on the Church, promulgated almost a year earlier, had already devoted its sixth chapter to religious life. This chapter had been prepared by a joint group from the Doctrinal Commission and the Commission on Religious. The latter was also responsible for producing the *Decree on the Renewal of Religious Life*, which was thus intended not as another treatise on religious life but as a statement on "the life and discipline of those institutes whose members make profession of chastity, poverty and obedience, and to make provision for their needs, as our times recommend" (1).

By April, 1962, after one and one-half years of work, the Preparatory Commission on Religious had produced a first draft consisting of 200 articles revealingly titled "Questions concerning Religious." It was loose, lacking in unity, and represented the traditional Roman position up to the time of Pope Pius XII. It was more juridical than theological and contained many condemnations which were dropped in the second draft "according to the spirit of the Council." The second and shorter draft, completed in March of 1963, was still criticized for its lack of theological foundation, its antiquated view of religious life as a "state of perfection," and its lack of treatment of the role of secular institutes and the involvement of religious in the modern world.

By order of the central conciliar Coordinating Commission the document had to be cut drastically and limited to essential principles of renewal. During 1964 the text underwent third and fourth drafts, during which it was further reduced from 51 to 19 articles. It was presented for discussion and vote in the Council on November 10-16, 1964. There was considerable feeling among a significant number of bishops from two opposite points of view: some felt that the document did not adequately reinforce traditional viewpoints and that the Council was thus in danger of undermining the essentials of religious life; others felt that it did not address the real problems of adaptation to the modern world.

Compromise was obviously necessary at this point. The document went back to the Commission where it was remodeled into the present 25 articles. All were voted on individually and passed by overwhelming majorities on October 6-8, 1965, in the seventh session of the Council. The decree was proclaimed by Paul VI on October 28.

The document expressly deals "only with the general principles of the up-to-date renewal of the life and discipline of religious orders and, while leaving their special characters intact, of societies of common life without vows, and of secular institutes. Particular norms for their exposition and application will be determined after the council by the competent authority" (1). This was done under the title *Ecclesiae Sanctae II* on August 6, 1966 by Pope Paul VI.

The *Decree on the Renewal of Religious Life* set down as its basic principles that renewal can only be achieved by two means. The first is "a constant return to the sources of the whole of the Christian life and to the primitive inspiration of the institutes" (2). Thus Scripture, especially the Gospels, and the unique charism and inspiration of the founder or foundress constitute the basic historical sources for renewal. This principle allowed and encouraged the elimination of much "excess baggage" that had accumulated in many congregations over the centuries and stimulated research into the historical roots, original documents, and unpublished writings of founders and foundresses, which has enabled more direct contact with origins and first inspirations.

The second means for authentic renewal according to the decree is "adaptation to the changed conditions of our time." Adequate understanding of the modern world, good physical and psychological living and working conditions, solid education, and sound good sense are encouraged. Religious are to be instructed "concerning the behavior-patterns, the emotional attitudes, and the thought-processes of modern society" in such a way that it will help to integrate their religious life. To this end, religious not in studies for ordination are to have a period of study immediately after the novitiate before beginning full apostolic work. This "spiritual, doctrinal, and technical culture" does not stop there, but should be a lifetime pursuit (18).

Apostolic, monastic, and secular institutes are all recognized as having their distinct character and therefore the necessity to adapt differently and assume different forms (8-11). The vows are treated within the context of sound psychology and effective witness. Thus chastity "is preserved more securely when the members live a common life in true brotherly love" (12); poverty means not only to be accountable to superiors as regards the use of property, but also to be "bound by the common law of labor" (13); obedience involves not only the subjection of the member to legitimate authority, but also the responsibility of superiors "to listen to their subjects willingly and . . . to promote cooperation between them for the good of the institute and of the Church" while retaining their own authority (14).

Common life is a priority. Class distinctions that had been allowed to develop over the centuries within congregations are frowned upon. Clerical institutes are told that "lay brothers...should be associated more closely with the life and work of the community" and that women's institutes should aim at "but one category of sisters" (15). The religious habit of both men and women is to be simple and modest, healthy and suitable to the needs of the situation (17). Conferences of major superiors are welcomed for better coordination of apostolic efforts and cooperation with episcopal conferences (23).

Simplicity and adaptability are the watchwords. A statement revelatory of the spirit behind the document is the following: "All should remember, however, that hope for renewal lies more in greater diligence in the observance of the rule and constitutions than in the multiplication of laws" (4).

Positive Tone

The overwhelming impression to the reader who remembers the general atmosphere of religious life at the time is of a refreshingly positive tone. The condemnations of the world and its evils so common to such documents formerly are notably absent, very much in keeping with the spirit of the previously promulgated Constitution on the Church and especially with that of the Pastoral Constitution on the Church in the Modern World, which was to be proclaimed less than two months later. The surprising thinness of theological basis in The *Decree on the Renewal of Religious Life* is partly explained by pressure from the Council Coordinating Commission to keep the document brief, partly by the fact that the Commission on Religious had already worked out the material on religious life and its place in the Church in chapter VI of the Constitution on the Church. Indeed, the whole of that declaration must be understood as background for the *Decree on Religious Life.*

The document on the renewal of religious life opened up enormous new possibilities. As with most of Vatican II, it would probably be more accurate to say that the trends at work in the Church which *produced* the document were responsible for the renewed perspectives. The Council documents simply confirmed them and made them official. But for the first time in many centuries the official teaching voice of the Church was actually urging religious to turn their faces *toward* the world instead of away from it.

The Council forces urging reaffirmation of traditional perspectives without the new positive outlook were equally as strong as those pushing for honest confrontation with the real problems in religious life. Like all the Council documents, this one was a compromise between those two forces. It enabled the fearful to know that the essentials remained the same, and it enabled the restless to strike out in new directions.

The decree legitimated some important movements that were already being discussed and beginning to materialize among more visionary groups. The return to simplicity and elimination of layers of unnecessary accretions in customs and lifestyle freed new apostolic energy on the part of religious. The stress on common life as the basis for living the vows brought about new ways of forming and living out the community of brothers and sisters equal under God.

The principle that has probably had the most long-range effect is that of adaptation to situations and particular needs. It is expressed frequently in different ways in the document and communicates a fresh sense of flexibility that can hardly be said to have characterized religious life up to that point. It has opened the way to cultural adaptation not only in frontier situations but everywhere that religious strive to insert themselves into concrete contexts for the sake of the Gospel. It reinforces the conviction that religious life exists for the sake of the world and God's designs for that world, not for itself.

Several Problems

If the decree was indeed a breath of fresh air blowing through cloister corridors, it did not leave us without problems. Its tone is one of calm and harmonious development, without directly addressing the areas of greatest tension. A major problem area is the relationship of religious life to the whole Church, and of the counsels to the commandments. The traditional view that all are obliged to obey the commandments as a minimum, but that religious are those called to go beyond the minimum by embracing the counsels of chastity, poverty, and obedience was seen to be totally inadequate. Originally the section on religious in the Constitution on the Church was to be part of the chapter on the call to holiness. It was wisely seen that this arrangement would have inplicitly expressed the traditional idea. Rather, the call to holiness was seen as the call issued to *all* believers, with religious life standing as witness to that universal call. Thus in the final form of the Constitution on the Church the call to holiness became the sole subject of its own chapter V, with that on religious following it.

This is in fact the theology underlying the *Decree on Religious Life* as well, but it is not very clearly worked out there. Moreover, the document retains the traditional way of describing religious life according to the three-fold structure of the counsels, though it does so in a minimal way. Nevertheless, the experience of religious is not so neatly divided, and few religious conceive of their life in terms of this structure.

A more serious difficulty concerns the way of speaking of the integration of prayer and work in apostolic institutes. The model in both chapter VI of the Constitution on the Church and in the *Decree on the Renewal of Religious Life* is that from union with Christ in prayer religious draw strength and inspiration to give themselves to others in the apostolate. But since union with God is seen as the greatest good, and since that union is equated with contemplation, then contemplation is, even for the "active" religious, implicitly higher than action. This is so in theory even if it may be not only permissible but praiseworthy for a person to leave the enjoyment of contemplation for the sake of needed service.

The Ignatian insight of contemplation in the midst of

action and in the midst of the world, so often drawn upon by apostolic institutes of the past four hundred years, does not seem to have penetrated the thinking behind the Council documents, nor any subsequent Roman document on the subject for that matter. The best attempt was "The Contemplative Dimension of Religious Life" issued by the Congregation for Religious and Secular Institutes in January, 1981 (Flannery, vol. 2, pp. 244-259). Here "the contemplative dimension is expressed... by the constant desire and search for God and for his Will in events and people; by the conscious participation in his salvific mission; by self-giving to others for the coming of the Kingdom," as well as by listening to Scripture and participating in the sacraments and prayer (1). Yet when it comes to speaking of "means which favour the contemplative dimension," we are back to the traditional list of Scripture, Eucharist, Sacrament of Reconciliation, spiritual direction, Liturgy of the Hours, devotion to Mary, and asceticism (7-14). The perennial challenge of apostolic religious life, integration of contemplation and action, has yet to be integrated into Roman thinking.

A third problem resulting from the renewal movement characterized by the document is the question of "how far to go." A classicist interpretation of the documents would suggest that they establish a new norm, allowing for a period of experimentation, followed by evaluation and return to a settled, if changed, way of living religious life. A dynamic interpretation would suggest that the documents attempt to seize a moment in a flowing stream, and that the Council intended to bless an inevitable movement which cannot be artificially stopped or even slowed, a movement that is as irreversible as history itself.

Undoubtedly many developments in religious life have moved beyond what most of the Council participants would have envisioned in 1965. What then needs to be said about religious life today? Here one can adopt either of the two positions articulated above.

Recent Developments

The classicist position regarding apostolic religious life has best been expressed by a recent document published by the Congregation for Religious Life entitled "Essential Elements in the Church's Teaching on Religious Life as Applied to Institutes Dedicated to Works of the Apostolate" (hereafter *EE*), dated May 31, 1983. The document is intended to be "a clarification and restatement" of the Church's teaching on religious life at the time of the promulgation of the Revised Code of Canon Law, the revision of the constitutions of many institutes, and the end of the special period of experimentation mandated at the conclusion of the Council (2).

True to its stated intention, *EE* is a traditional restatement of church teaching on religious life, most of which could have been said even before the Council. According to this document, "consecration is the basis of religious life" (5). This is the key image which is used consistently to explain nearly every other aspect: public witness, vows, mission. *EE* is a strong reaffirmation of the traditional values of religious life.

When the question is asked, however, whether *EE* in any way advances the theology of religious life, the answer must be negative. Rather than advance, it could be argued that this document is regressive, in that it grapples with the problems of interaction with the modern world considerably less even than the Council texts. Whereas the decree stressed openness and adaptation, *EE* portrays religious life as almost self-contained. The focus here is on religious life itself, not its existence for the sake of mission. True, public witness is "of the very nature of religious vocation" and religious life (10), but the treatment of this public function portrays religious life as God's gift to the world, with little need to learn anything from that world.

One other aspect of *EE* is not so much disappointing as disturbing: its view of the relationship of religious life to the hierarchical structure of the Church. The text quotes the *Constitution on the Church* (43) to the effect that religious life is not "an intermediate way between the clerical and lay conditions of life, but comes from both as a special gift of the entire church"(*EE*38). Yet it goes on to say that "In their origins, religious institutes depend in a unique way on the hierarchy. . . . for the authentic discernment of (their) founding charism" (41). While the Council documents referred to here use words like "regulate," "order," and "approve" for the task of bishops in regard to spiritual gifts in the Church, this paragraph suggests that it is only the hierarchy who can correctly interpret to a congregation its founder's charism. Moreover, *EE* 49 states that the governmental structures of religious institutes "reflect the Christian hierarchy of which the head is Christ himself." Even if the word "hierarchy" is to be understood fuguratively rather than juridically here, which is possible but not evident, the implication is that the charismatic role of religious life in the Church is being subsumed into the hierarchical framework far more extensively than that with which many of the best theologians of religious life would be comfortable.

Two Issues

The *Decree on Religious Life* was the closest to a progressive or dynamic model of religious life that has so far emerged from official church documents. Where would its spirit carry us today? I suggest two major directions in which the forces behind Vatican II are still moving, and which have profound implications for religious life.

The first major direction concerns the location of the *sacred.* From a highly sacralized view of reality we have evolved—or, some would say, have been catapulted—into a fairly secularized world in which symbols and metaphors of transcendence in our religious faith and practice (e.g. habit, cloister, elaborate ritual, spatial distance as sign of reverence) no longer hold the power over the believing imagination that they once did. A demythologization has been happening which has its positive and negative effects. Positively, we are rediscovering the simple beauty of simplicity and abandoning symbols when they have outlived their usefulness. Negatively, there is little to take their place that can arise from a contemporary Western Christian culture. This poverty leads many to a fascination with the religious symbols of other cultures, which can be enriching as long as they are not adopted uncritically, with little or no regard for the differences of worldview that may underlie them.

This loss of innocence about traditional religious symbolization of the sacred has had its effect on religious life. When symbols of withdrawal and isolation no longer convey meaning, this indicates that their users' perception of where one encounters the sacred has changed. The former attitude tended to be that all union with God is to be found in solitude, withdrawal, and concentrated prayer, the fruits of which are to be brought with apostolic zeal into the service of the apostolate. That sense of the place of encounter with God has now shifted to the marketplace as well, and to the encounter with Christ manifested in the members of the human community. The world as legitimate place of God's presence becomes a focus not only for mission, but for prayer as well. The integration between prayer and apostolic labor, skirted in the decree and groped for in the Congregation for Religious' "The Contemplative Dimension of the Religious Life," can no longer be avoided, but must be thoroughly explored and articulated.

The second major direction that has continued to develop in religious life in postconciliar years is a result of the first: it is a relocation of the sources and presence of *authority*. The forces at work in the world at large have brought on not only a crisis of traditional authority structures but a correlate loss of innocence in their regard. No longer can it be taken for granted that God-given authority is conferred directly, from outside, hierarchically. No longer will modern persons remain for long uncritical of any form of leadership or exercise of authority.

Once Catholics began to take seriously that the Church is the people of God, all else in ecclesiology flowed from that basic insight overlayed upon the new societal attitude toward authority described above: episcopal collegiality, decentralization, obedience as dialogue, etc. While staunchly maintaining that it is not a democracy, the Church structure has by way of concession taken definite steps toward raising expectations in that direction.

Religious seem to have taken this insight more seriously than anyone else. *Because* mandated to do so by the conciliar Church, they have taken seriously their ecclesial citizenship. Out of obedience, they have probed and questioned, renewed and updated. Somewhat paradoxically, in that process obedience to authority has led them to reassess obedience and authority.

The crisis of authority in religious life has brought about a revolutionary change in the manner of exercising authority and decision-making in many congregations. It has brought on a lively sense of the importance of communal discernment and consequently of the location of authority not only in a superior but also in a community—and even in oneself. This confrontation with the relocation of authority is intimately related to a concomitant relocation of responsibility necessitated by the very concept of the Church as community. This relocation of responsibility has not always been as joyfully welcomed, and given the precarious nature of human freedom, remains fragile. The demythologizing of authority also causes a demythologizing of responsibility. But one cannot be had without the other.

It is under these two major themes, the relocation of the sacred and the relocation of authority, that I suggest a new theology of apostolic religious life needs to be worked out. It is significant that along with the failure of past church documents to adequately address the integration of prayer and apostolate there is complete silence in them about the horizontal dimension of obedience and authority. An adequate dynamic model of contemporary apostolic religious life must grapple with these live issues.

Conclusion

The *Decree on the Up-to-date Renewal of Religious Life* was the product of conflicting forces at the Council. It was meant not to provide an articulated theology of religious life, but only to lay down essential norms for the experimentation and renewal which were to take place within the next decades. In its final form the document represents a compromise between those who were fearful of departing too far from the traditional view of religious life and those who were dissatisfied because the Council was not going far enough to address the changing needs and circumstances of the modern world. In the context of the religious life as lived at that time, much of it was quite progressive.

The modern world, however, has not stood still since then in order to allow religious to catch up. Religious life continues to be caught between the same conflicting forces, those of traditional conservation and those of forward movement. Neither is in itself the Reign of God. But official teaching has yet to take seriously the fundamental transformation in human social and religious consciousness that is happening as a result of the technological and psychological revolutions. The dynamic rather than the classicist modes will ultimately be the only adequate way of envisioning religious life in a world of constant change.[1]

[1]Much of the information on the background of the decree in this paper was drawn from Friedrich Wulf, "Decree on the Appropriate Renewal of Religious Life," *Commentary on the Documents of Vatican II*, edited by Herbert Vorgrimler (New York: Herder and Herder; London: Burns and Oates, 1968) vol. 2, pp. 301-332.

Decree on the Training of Priests
Optatum Totius, 28 October, 1965

Robert F. Harvanek, S.J.

One of the areas of greatest change in Catholic life on the American scene since Vatican II has been in priestly formation. Not all of the change is attributable to the decrees of the Council. Much of it is the result of the same forces that both brought about and were unleashed by the calling of the Council. And of course priestly formation does not stand alone in isolation from the concatenation of actions by the Council. Bishop Carter in his introduction to the Decree on Priestly Formation in the Abbott edition[1] states that it is of a piece with the two central ecclesial decrees, the *Constitution on the Church* and the *Pastoral Constitution the Church in the Modern World*. This is probably true. The Decree on the training of priests was passed by the Council before the Constitution on the Church in the Modern

[1]Walter Abbot, Joseph Gallegher, editors. The Documents of Vatican II. New York, 1966, p. 434.

World, but in the same final (fourth) session. It was one of a group of five decrees passed at the same time. The others were: On the Pastoral Office of Bishops, On the Renewal of Religious Life, On Non-Christian Religions, and On Christian Education.

The Decree is not very long, seven chapters, twenty-two paragraphs, with a brief preface and conclusion, 17 pages in Flannery's edition.[2] Let me first outline the topics of the Decree, then point out some of the things it says, highlighting the items which were changes from previous legislation, and then reflect on it from the viewpoint of the American Experience.

Outline of the Document

Apart from the Preface and Conclusion, the Decree can be divided into three parts, though in its own editing it simply divides into seven chapters. The first part deals with preliminaries. Chapter I sets out the scope and limits of the decree: general principles behind laws which are to be determined regionally or in the different rites according to circumstances of time and place and pastoral needs. Chapter II outlines the responsibilities for fostering vocations and says something about minor seminaries. Chapter III discusses the necessity of major seminaries, their output, their directors and faculty, their students.

Part Two, the core of the Decree, takes up in turn the three major aspects of the formation of priests: their spiritual formation, ecclesiastical studies, and training for ministry.

Part Three is a short paragraph on continuing formation and the induction of young priests into the order of the priesthood.

[2]Austin Flannery, O.P., General Editor, *Vatican Council II*, The Conciliar and Post Conciliar Documents. Costello Publishing Company. Northport. New York.

What the Decree Says

Rather than go through the paragraphs of the Decree one by one and recount what it says, I would like to stand back and look at the Decree as a whole and point out what seems significant and new to me. In proper hermeneutical fashion, let me recall for you, as best I can, my own personal and social perspective. I have been, for the last eight years, an active member of the Philosophy Department of Loyola University of Chicago. I read the Decree from the perspective of a Jesuit who taught philosophy in a house of studies of the Chicago Province which included both parts of ecclesiastical studies, that is, both philosophy and theology. As prefect of Studies of the Chicago Province and later as Provincial I was involved in some of the work and developments of St. Mary of the Lake Seminary of the Archdiocese of Chicago, as well as in the shifts and changes of the philosophical and theological studies of Jesuits in the ten American provinces. I am also acquainted with the Jesuit-conducted institutes of higher studies in Rome and with some of the situations in India and Peru. In recent years I have been acquainted with seminarians studying at Loyola University of Chicago, from different religious groups as well as from the collegiate program of the Chicago Archdiocese at Niles, including one semester in instruction at Niles. Undoubtedly my perspective will need to be corrected and filled out by the memory and projections of others.

A significant affirmation of the decree, perhaps an expressed presupposition, is the unity of the priestly order. The decree acknowledges the diversity of the clergy (diocesan and religious, clergy of different rituals), but it sees them as all forming one priesthood. However, its perspective is not that of a meta-priesthood, or a generic priesthood, which is then diversified in the different forms. Rather, its perspective is that of the diocesan presbyterate. It directs the other presbyterates to make appropriate adaptation of its principles. This perspective has had a great impact on religious priests, tending to move their formation along the lines of diocesan priests. It also has tended to leave out any discussion of special works, such as education, health ministry, or social service. It does introduce missionary activity in non-Christian lands in an effort to redistribute the clergy more equitably. Though it is true that diocesan priests have migrated with their peoples, e.g. to the Americas, they have generally been missionaries only when they have formed missionary societies (Home Missioners, Maryknoll). In the past the explicit missionary work to unbelievers has been the focus of religious orders. Taking the Decree by itself, apart from its reception and implementation, the two presbyterates have been moved closer together, more like one priesthood.

A principle which has affected the sacerdotal world in a most significant way is the principle of regionalism, that each region (or rite) needs to adopt the principles to its own circumstances. This has broken one of the most characteristic structures of the pre-Vatican II Church (Tridentine), the Roman control of seminary education all over the world. Seminary faculty were required to be educated in ecclesiastical studies in the Roman "universities." And the Roman faculties were controlled by the Commission on Seminaries and Universities.

Linked with this principle of regionalism is the breaking of the Latin requirement for teaching and textbooks (Latin is still mandated, but for the purpose of developing the capacity to read the theological sources, hardly a sufficient motive for so difficult a task), and the introduction of training in pastoral ministry during the course of academic studies. More will be said about this, but it must be clear that this has put a strain on the Roman institutes (Gregorian, Lateran, Angelicum, and others). The teaching medium in these institutions has become Italian, with some English, French, Spanish... The core of the academic program in theology was collapsed into three years, and the fourth year is now given over either to pastoral training, back in the home context, or to a two-year academic licentiate. The conflict between the European educational structures, and those of other regions, notably the United States, continues unresolved.

The Decree encourages the use of contemporary psychology, sociology and educational theory, not as objects of study, but as providing directions for formation. This constrasts with the earlier rationalist and scholastic norms of education which placed emphasis on ideas, reasoning and will, and underplayed feelings and emotions. This move coincided with the rise of existentialism and phenomenology in continental philosophy, and resulted in the dominance of the behavioral sciences in seminary education. Howard Gray, S.J. sees religious formation, and I believe he would extend this to priestly formation generally, as moving from what he characterizes as a sociological stage (pre-Vatican II) to a psychological stage (post-Vatican II) to a collaborative stage (present era).[3] It probably should be said that the Decree did not so much initiate this development as itself respond to what was happening in Euro-American culture.

There is not much that is new in what the Decree has to say about promoting vocations. It undoubtedly was aware of the depressed vocation situation in Europe, but probably had no expectation of the change that would take place in the large scale resignation of priests and the turn around of vocations in the United States, Holland and Ireland. What is amazing is the Decree's great faith in Divine Providence and the Holy Spirit's provisions of a sufficient number of priests from the young men of the Church. Though there is evidence of awareness of the challenge to priestly celibacy, there is no indication in the decree of the identification of the priesthood with maleness.

Actually the Decree moves away from the former effort to develop priestly vocations through the minor seminary process and to preserve those so gathered from the distractions and enticements of secular society. There is no advertence to the fact that the great, perhaps greatest source of priestly vocations, at least in the United States, was the presence of religious orders of women in the parochial school system.

---

[3]Howard Gray, S.J. "Religious Formation: Evolution to Revolution" in the New Catholic World. Vol. 226, no. 1349. September-October 1982, pp 235-237.

Teachers are mentioned as having a responsibility for fostering vocations. That assumed that the teachers themselves would not be undergoing vocation problems.

The Decree follows the constant pattern of the Council of viewing the public personality of bishops, priests and laity, in summary, the Church, according to the three-fold personalities of prophet, priest, and king. It adjusts the terminology to the modern world somewhat by using the terms, "teacher, priest, and shepherd." The pastoral intent of the Council conforms to the "shepherd" image, though at other times the image of guide or counsellor is used. However, this triadic description of the hoped-for product of the seminary process is not followed through in the remainder of the Decree, though it harmonizes well with the three-fold division of spiritual formation, studies, and ministerial formation. It is this latter triad that structures the main body of the Decree.

Certainly one of the most significant features of the *Decree on the Training of Priests,* in contrast with the era of seminary training which immediately preceded it, is the principle of integration and concurrence which it prescribes for the three aspects of formation. Spiritual Formation should permeate the whole of the process, and support as well as be supported by studies. Pastoral training is to accompany the process from the beginning to the end.

Perhaps this feature is most clear in contrast with the traditional program of formation in the Society of Jesus. In the Society the sequential principle of studies had been followed, derived from the University of Paris at the end of the Middle Ages. In this pattern the first two years of incorporation into the Society were given over almost entirely to spiritual and religous formation. There was some experience in pastoral and social ministry (teaching catechism, service in a hospital) but it was minimal. The next five years were given over entirely to humanistic and philosophical studies. There followed a period, generally about three years, of total immersion in the teaching ministry in one of the Society's high schools or colleges. Then there was a return to studies, again total imersion in theology for three years. Ordination to all three orders, usually on the three consecutive days, normally concluded the first three years. There was a fourth year which was also mostly academic but containing a little experience in parochial ministry (masses, preaching, confessions on weekends in neighboring parishes that needed assistance). Finally, there was another full year (nine months) of spiritual concentration, but joined with increasing ministerial experience in Jesuit type ministries (retreats).

Though the Decree does not prescribe a separate period of spiritual formation, it does make spiritual formation its first concern. Furthermore, it enjoins that doctrinal studies relate to spiritual formation and not be cut off by itself. This is something of a shift from the scholastic-Aristotelian tendency not only to distinguish but also to separate in time and instruction the practical from the speculative, and spiritual and moral theology from dogmatic theology. The purely speculative mentality of the neoscholastics was not supported by the Decree.

But perhaps what has most modified the process of the recent past is the principle that ministerial training and experience should be present in all aspects and parts of the formation program. This meant that the total concentration on studies which had obtained in the recent past was no longer approved. Time and direction with supervision had to be provided, according to the Decree, concurrently with academic studies.

In the same spirit of integration and concurrence the studies of philosophy and theology are supposed to be closely related with one another. Both (an extraordinary statement for a community committed to the Thomistic distinction of philosophy and theology) are to be centered on and related to the mystery of Christ and the history of Salvation. Clearly, the separate study of philosophy in a period and program distinct from the theology was not recommended by the Decree.

Within the sphere of ecclesiastical studies, perhaps the most significant development of the Decree is the loosening up and broadening of the perspective inaugurated by

Aeterni Patris in 1879, the encyclical letter of Pope Leo XIII which initiated the neothomistic revival. In both philosophy and theology respect is shown for the history and development of systems, and for contemporary developments in science as well as for the current of ideas in one's own particular country or region. Understandably philosophizing is to be done within the tradition of the perennially valid heritage. And theologians are to learn the use of reason in theology from St. Thomas. But the restrictive and determinative formulas of legislation during the Neoscholastic era are missing. This absence is probably more significant than the affirmations which are made; for it opens the door to pluralism, a development which most certainly was not in the intent of the document or its framers.

Both disciplines are to be related to life and to the mysteries of salvation and the Church, as was indicated above.

Scripture is called the soul of the theology and given a primacy which certainly contrast with the centrality of reason in the neoscholastic era. Liturgy is also given a role in theology as well as in spirituality that it did not have before. And even though teachers are enjoined to point out errors in other systems and religions, the tone is much more positive and affirmative than it had been before. Truth and goodness are acknowledged to be in other systems in the spirit of the patristic "spoliation of the Egyptians".

The American Experience

What happened in the United States in sacerdotal and religious life on the occasion of Vatican II was not replicated all over the world. In the winter of 1969-70 I visited Japan and Northern India. The question everywhere was: what is happening in the United States? Stories were coming out of amazing changes and upheaval. In response I attempted to outline the revolution(s) of the sixties: the civil rights revolution against social structures, the youth revolution against the same structures and the authority that was forcing young men into an unwanted and dubious war, the sexual revolution linked with the psychological revolution manifested in the various forms of group dynamics, and the women's revolution, part both of the civil rights movement and the sexual revolution.

Within the Catholic community the revolt against past patterns, structures and authority was perhaps most significant within the ranks of women religious. It was manifested in two ways, in the change from religious habits to secular dress and in the self-determination of ministries and communities. To a lesser degree this revolt was imitated by the younger priests and seminarians. But the major revolt, and most shocking, was the departure of many from religious life and from the priestly profession. Accompanying the exodus was the complementary phenomenon of sudden non-response to religious vocation in the traditional sense, the discovery that all Christians have a vocation to sanctity and to ministry.

The impact of all this of course was that there were suddenly no seminarians to experience the changes mandated by the *Decree on the Training of Priests*. Or, with what seminarians there were, more radical changes seemed required both to retain and to attract young persons to religious life and to priesthood. Suddenly these vocations were no longer in the outlook of Catholic high school or elementary school children. And the departures of formed priests and religious led admission officers to be hesitant to promote and accept candidates out of high school on the ground that greater maturity and experience was necessary to insure a more stable vocation. But the value of a stable vocation was losing ground in all areas of culture. Social scientists were talking about a "temporary society," and philosophers and theologians were doubting the possibility of a "commitment for life." This was being demonstrated not only in religious vocation but also in the world of marriage, and of religious commitment generally. Not only were seminaries becoming empty, but so also were the churches.

Another development on the American scene that did not directly derive from the Decree was the re-location and the re-structuring of major seminaries. This had a three-fold aspect to it.

Perhaps the difference between religious order and diocesan seminaries should be noted, because this set of changes was more evident in religious order seminaries. Religious order seminaries moved more quickly into new patterns and new structures than did diocesan seminaries. Bishops were more resistant to the pressures for change than were religious superiors. The reasons behind that difference can be a subject for reflection in its own right. Perhaps fundamental is the basic difference between the religious vocation and the diocesan as expressed by Johannes Metz: the religious vocation is charismatic, the diocesan is structural.[4] Perhaps, too, the background and training of the bishops in contrast with religious superiors is relevant: almost all American bishops had been brought up through the canon law and chancery route, and almost none of the religious superiors had. Also, episcopacy is a permanent office; religious superiorship is temporary, and commonly elective. Possibly equally important is the fact that the diocesan priesthood dealt directly with the laity in parish situations, whereas religious dealt mostly in special works. No matter. Religious orders moved quickly to locate their centers for ecclesiastical studies out of the country and into the city. And it wasn't only in the city, but in the neighborhood of a university, and generally not a Catholic university. And generally not simply in the neighborhood of a university, but in a cluster of divinity schools, Protestant as well as Catholic.

This move had both an educational and an ecumenical aspect to it. The general theory was that it is not possible to provide a faculty, or it is not financially feasible to do so, which would be able to serve all the varieties of studies that should be available to divinity students, one number I remember is that a complete seminary would require specialists in 92 different subjects. Location in a cluster would allow a particular school to select what it wanted to provide

4Johannes B. Metz. *Followers of Christ.* Translated by Thomas Linton. Burns & Oates/Paulist Press. 1978. Cf. ch. 1: What is the religious life?

from its own resources and make use of what was available in the other schools.

There was, simultaneous with this move from isolation into a cluster, a new respect for Protestant divinity schools, and for the Association of American Theological Schools as an accrediting association. American seminaries began to switch their perspectives from that of the Commission on Universities and Seminaries in Rome to the American Association. Some diocesan seminary faculties and administration wanted to make this change also, but were prevented by their governors.

In some instances religious orders began to join together to form common schools of theology. The Catholic Theological Union in Chicago is perhaps the most obvious and most successful example of that development. Again, diocesan seminaries remained outside of that process.

The hopes and expectations of these moves have only partially been fulfilled in the ten or twelve years since they were made. Catholics did not benefit as fully from the ecumenical association as they had expected. Most churches tended to keep their students home for the greater part of their education. Catholic students did not readily attend courses in Protestant schools. The proportion of Protestant students attending Catholic courses generally tended to be greater than the number of Catholics attending Protestant schools. This perhaps argued for a great Catholic impact on Protestant clergy, but sometimes Catholic faculties thought they were being used. Nevertheless, there was almost a 100% turnaround from the atmosphere of hostility which had obtained between the churches. The worry about doctrinal dilution, however, has not entirely gone away.

Common to both diocesan and religious order schools was the separation of philosophy and theology. This was the reverse of what had been enjoined by the Decree. I know of only one institution in the United States, Bellarmine School of Theology in North Aurora, the Chicago province Jesuit scholasticate, where a serious effort was made to implement the document in this regard. It only lasted two or three years, until the philosophy faculty was removed and philosophical studies were moved to the University of Detroit to be joined with collegian studies.

Instead of the theology connection recommended by the Decree, philosophy in the United States was joined to the college of arts and sciences, an American institution. Philosophy was taken as part of the bachelor of arts degree and in conjunction with the arts and sciences. Seminarians frequently majored in some other subject than philosophy while taking the requisite number of philosophy courses. Philosophy in Catholic colleges had earlier broken the Neoscholastic control and faculties were no longer dominated by priests, and included even some non-Catholics, and occasionally a non-believer or two. Certainly the interest of the college faculties was minimally with theology and maximally with the arts and sciences.[5]

Philosophy in the United States among seminarians and seminary faculties had been held in place by the authority of Rome. In the days of revolution philosophy felt the impact of almost as much hostility as Latin, which dropped out altogether. The utility of philosophy was seriously questioned. This in my judgment was an expression of the empiricist and pragmatic mentality of American culture, and of the biblical and liturgical developments in theological studies. Systematic theology (metaphysics) receded in interest, and with it interest in scholastic philosophy. History, literature, and the social and behavioral sciences rose in importance, along with communication arts. Today there is a perceptible swing back from the first revolt, but consensus has not been achieved as yet.

With the movement toward divinity schools and into clusters, in a university situation, seminaries became schools of ministry rather than exclusively schools for priesthood. This was again primarily true of religious order

[5]Since this paper was prepared, the new Code of Canon Law has been published and made some adjustments in response to the experience of the intervening years since the Council. Canon 250, for instance, allows for linking theology and philosophy together, as the Council advised, or doing them separately, as has been the common practice. It also clearly prescribes four years of theology as the norm.

schools. Laity, if they qualified (and qualifications were generally changed so they could qualify), were admitted into the divinity schools and allowed to register for the degree of a master of divinity. By far the larger number of non-clerics who entered these programs were women, and most of these were women Religious. Up to this time there was no opportunity for women to study theology in a Catholic context beyond the college level. It was reported that half of the women in Harvard's Divinity School in 1965 were Catholic.

Simultaneously there was a development taking place in Catholic universities. Theology was becoming a program of interest. There was a time within memory when Catholic colleges offered only core courses in theology, taught by priests, somewhat like higher level catechism courses. Suddenly it was possible to major in theology, and several universities began doctoral programs in theology. Lay men and women were graduated with such doctorates. The monopoly by priests of graduate theology, and of doctoral degrees in the theological sciences was broken.

The broadening of the notion of ministry to the Catholic community as a whole and beyond the priesthood[6] could be said to be within the purview of Vatican II. What was not expected, and what surfaced vigorously and strongly on the American scene, was the demand of some women for ordination to the priesthood. When some American seminaries, those mainly in the cluster and university situation, opened their doors to anyone qualified and interested, they did not know that they were abetting the movement of women to demand ordination, though as the movement developed many of the priests on the faculties supported the development.

Faculties of seminaries, both on the collegiate level and on the theological level, broadened their membership to include professors from different groups and usually there were women among them. The inclusion of women had a

---

[6]Brian E. Daley, S.J. "Ordination: The Sacrament of Ministry," *America* Vol. 147, No. 19, December 11, 1982, pp. 365-369.

double intention. One was to provide a diversified faculty with different perspectives and backgrounds. The other was to recognize the value of women in the personal development of future priests. This last implied a judgment, perhaps unexpressed, that the total isolation of future priests within an all male community was unhealthy and retarding in effect. There are signs that this view is not in favor of Rome, and there is a process in progress to insist on the education of priests by priests alone.

A development which is less visible to the general Catholic community but very evident within the seminary and theology communities is the movement to pluralism in philosophy and theology. The American (US and Canada) university and seminary communities had been more whole-heartedly receptive to the neoscholastic and neothomistic revivals than continental Europe. During the high time of neothomism, Gilson and Maritain were the heroes of Catholic America. They were almost the exclusive heroes. Teihard de Chardin had some impact but his work was controversial and limited in its acceptance. Blondelianism hardly was heard of. His work, except for a couple of short pieces, was not translated. There were few studies of his philosophy, whereas in continental Catholic Europe he was a major figure. The neoscholastic movement in Europe (Germany) was always in competition with a vigorous Kantian, but especially Hegelian, effort to understand the faith from a contemporary viewpoint.

What has happened since Vatican II is the separation of philosophy from theology, as has been noted, and different directions of the two areas of study. Seminary students study the same philosophers that university student are exposed to. Sartre, Marx, Nietzsche, not to mention Kant and Hegel, are at least as much in evidence as Aristotle and Aquinas. A semester course in either Medieval Philosophy or Aquinas is required, but that is all. Topical courses are no longer taught from textbooks resembling the scholastic manuals using the thesis method, but from selections of readings from modern philosophers with Plato and Aristotle sometimes included. Facilities are put together with an eye to diversity of methods and ideologies: phenomenologists, analysts, dialectical philosophers, Christian philosophers.

Perhaps most notable is a swing from the heavy rationalism of the neoscholastics to something like the fideism of the Protestant tradition. This shift occurs long before the students come to college or seminary. As one student, the product of a "minor seminary," put it, "I can't imagine anyone trying to prove the existence of God." Privatism is the common mind of the young. No one is to be judged. Everyone is to be respected for his/her opinion. The only sin is to interfere with another or to be interfered with. Since there is no consensus, there is no objective truth. "Who's to say who's right?"

Whitehead and process philosophy on the one hand, and Heidegger on the other, are perhaps the principal philosophers studied by Catholics, with Wittgenstein and the Analytic philosophers gaining ground.

On the theological level a similar phenomenon obtains. Biblical and historical theology seems to predominate. This means that hermeneutics and social science replaced metaphysics. Where metaphysics is used, Transcendental Thomism and Process Theology seem to be the recognizable trends. Transcendental Thomism is a combination of Marechal (Kant and Thomas) and Heidegger, Process Theology of Whitehead, Hartshorne, Weiss, and St. Thomas. The Chicago School is introducing a new interest in literary theology (story as the mode of religious knowledge, imagination as the religious faculty). We have come a long way from the neoscholastic revival and there is no clear unity on the American scene except the unity of diversity.

The two features of integration prescribed by the *Decree on the Training of Priests,* spiritual formation and ministerial formation carried on jointly and in relationship to academic formation, have been generally well received and implemented in American seminaries. Though spiritual formation was present in the past, it seems to me that it has received marked attention, principally in the assignment of personnel with both the training and time to make the program serious. Religious Orders have always had the benefit of the time of spiritual formation in the novitiate, and a tradition of personal prayer, usually in some spiritual tradition. There seems to be a desire on the part of diocesan seminarians to develop or discover a comparable tradition.

The concurrence of ministerial formation with academic studies has had a mixed reception. Academic faculty have perceived it as encouraging the anti-intellectualism already prevalent in many American seminarians. When seminarians have mixed with lay students or non-priestly oriented religious students, they have commonly been outshone in their commitment to study. And where the commitment is present, a conflict of time and energy is frequently generated. It is thought by some that academic study demands wholehearted concentration and that it cannot be effectively pursued along with apostolic service. That certainly seems to be true of some people. On the other hand, American college and university students frequently are forced by economic factors to study and work simultaneously. Perhaps the difficulty of joining study and ministry should not readily be given up.

Conclusion

How should this document be written if it were written today? I suppose one answer could be that it should not be written, and the reason would be that there is too much confusion. The lines are not clear. On the other hand, perhaps that is the time when some guidelines are needed. Here are some thoughts.

The distinction between foundational principles for the whole church and regionalism should be kept. This is a difficult distinction to maintain in practice. However, it would seem impossible to return to the monolithic Latin model of the Tridentine era. Room and responsibility needs to be granted for regions to develop their own models.

The formation of priests needs to be set within the broader context of the formation of ministers of the Gospel.

A document is needed for the development of the ministerial Catholic community. Within that context, the role and formation of the priest needs to be developed (Cf.Brian Daley, op.cit., as a first step in that direction.).

The diversity of the priesthood needs to be recognized. The pastoral model needs to be recognized as only one model. The missionary (special works) models need to be developed.

The role of women in ministry needs to be acknowledged and developed. This is needed no matter how the question of the ordination of women is finally settled for our times.

The whole enterprise needs to be put within the perspective of a developing church, in a developing world. History needs to be linked to origins.

Declaration on the Relation of the Church to Non-Christian Religions
Nostra Aetate, 28 October, 1965

J. Patout Burns

The *Declaration on the Church's relation to non-Christian Religions* was promulgated 28 October 1965. It had been the subject of intense interest and no little debate—both theological and ecclesial—beginning in the second session of the Council. The controversy centered on the Church's stance toward Judaism and the complication arising from its quasi-identification with the State of Israel. Other chapters were added to broaden the scope of the document and soften the focus on Judaism by addressing Hinduism, Buddhism and Islam directly and other religious traditions indirectly. The fourth chapter, on Judaism, contrasts with the prior two by its emphasis on the spiritual patrimony common to Judaism and Christianity and the explicit denial of any foundation in Christianity for persecution of the Jews.

Only in the most general terms does the document address the religious traditions other than Judaism and Islam with which the Church shares no historical origin, scriptures and symbols. A concern with the status and significance of these other religions can be discerned elsewhere in the work of the Council, especially in the Decree on the Church's Missionary Activity and the Declaration on Religious Freedom.

Our reflections will not be limited by the objectives and methods of the documents we are treating. We shall raise questions of the relations between Christianity and the other religions of humanity as systems of salvation. We shall also question the relations of Christianity to structures of secular society.

Content of the Document

First let us survey in detail the content of the document itself. It asserts a single origin and common destiny of all human beings. It explains that religions address the mysteries of human existence: the purpose of life, the discernment of good and evil, the origin and meaning of suffering, sorrow and death, the way to happiness, the God who is the beginning and end (1). The church recognizes what is true and holy in the doctrines, cults, and ways of life through which other religions address these mysteries. The Council Fathers recognized the contributions of various religions to the promotion of spiritual, moral and cultural goods as well as to the realization of peace, freedom and social justice (2,3). Finally, the document infers that the cult of God demands a respect and love for every human person since all are created in the image of God. No one may persecute a fellow human being in the name or for the glory of God (5).

The assertions of the document are quite limited but are nonetheless significant. Religions tend to be exclusive and absolute. They address mysteries of human life which escape reasoned determination and do not admit a certitude based upon disputable evidence or a common perception of the truth. Yet human living requires and involves a determination of good and evil, a stance toward the beginning and the end, a view of the meaning of individual and communal life. The reflective person may recognize ambiguity and withold assent but the very process of living demands and betrays a decision. The commitment involved in living may be shifting or stable, strong or shallow. Each person votes with his or her life on the mysteries addressed by religions. Few ballots are entirely write-ins and many are the straight-tickets of a particular culture. Each, however, involves that certitude which is requisite for action.

Religions strive to symbolize this lived perspective in stories, to realize it in rituals, to make it clear and coherent in creeds and doctrines, to promote appropriate practices in the lives of their adherents. As social institutions, religions both inculcate a community's perspective in an individual and provide a communitarian expression through the individual's experience. In this sense, religions are languages for the ultimates of human existence.

Some religions are nonhistorical in the sense that they do not claim a constitutive divine influence in their own origins. Instead, they claim an appropriate or even unique expression or realization of what is always and everywhere the case about human existence and the other relevant parts of the world. If founders are identified, they are characterized as persons who have pioneered in perceiving the truth and in discovering the proper way to respond to it. Divine intervention is at most an enlightenment or revelation given to the founders. Such religions may enter into dialogue with competing traditions, may incorporate complementary insights, and may admit multiple ways of life.

The Council itself took just such a stance toward the nonhistorical religions.

> Throughout history even to the present day, there is found among different peoples a certain awareness of hidden power, which lies behind the course of nature and the events of human life. At times there is present even a recognition of a supreme being or still more of a Father. This awareness and recognition result in a way of life that is imbued with a deep religious sense (2).

The recognition is immediately tempered by an assertion that the fullness of religious life is to be found only in the historical Christ. Christianity, therefore, provides a standard for judging the truth and adequacy of the nonhistorical religions.

Historical religions, by contrast, claim an origin in a creative divine intervention which changes the human world, which constitutes existence in a particular way. Working from its own experience of deliverance, Israel came to recognize the Lord as the ruler of the whole world who had brought order and beauty from chaos. In the Jewish view, God chose and saved a people, gave it a land, and preferred this one people to all others. He so identified with this one people that his blessings on all the others he creates and governs are conditioned by their relationship to this one. For Christians, God himself entered the world in Jesus Christ. In his human life, death and glorification, God constituted and established Christ as the sole way in which humans could attain salvation. Christians quickly identified the Christ, whom they knew as risen and glorified, not only as the judge of all but as the divine agent in creation and governance, the source of all truth in the world, and even the guide in the history of Israel. Islam makes similar claims for the role of the Prophet and the revelation in *Koran*; it has acted upon these claims.

Thus historical religions claim their origin in particular divine actions which structure the human world in a creative way and establish the religion's perspective as normative for all interpretations of existence. The adherents of an historical religion never approach another religious group simply to share their own insight and to learn from the other. They always bring news of a particular event which the other tradition ignores or does not appreciate, and which is thought to make all the difference even for that other.

This perspective is evident in the stance which the Council urges Catholics to take toward the adherents of nonhistorical religions.

The Church, therefore, urges her sons to enter with prudence and charity, into discussion and collaboration with members of other religions. Let Christians, while witnessing to their own faith and way of life, acknowledge, preserve and encourage the spiritual and moral truths found among non-Christians, also their social life and culture. (2)

The Catholic can discern and foster the true and the good in these religious traditions without being challenged by their assertion of a different and definitive divine intervention in history.

In dealing with Islam, the document attempts the same technique which was used with the nonhistorical religions. Agreement on the origin and destiny of humanity, as well as a firm commitment to worship of God and care for the neighbor serve as the foundation for mutual respect. A limited sharing of the heritage of Abraham is also noted. In dealing with the conflicting claims for the founders of the two religions, the Declaration is much more circumspect. Though Muslims reject the Christian assertion for the divinity of Jesus, which serves as the foundation for the absolute claims of Christianity, they do acknowledge and honor him.

Although not acknowledging him as God, they worship Jesus as a prophet, his virgin Mother they also honor, and even at times devoutly invoke (3).

No reference is made to Muslim assertions about the role of Mohammed or the authority of *Koran* as definitive divine revelation. Neglecting the foundation of the conflict between the two religious traditions, the Council asks that past quarrels and dissensions be forgotten, that all strive for mutual understanding and cooperation in promoting human welfare.

The conflict between Christianity and Judaism could not be so easily avoided. The Church finds herself prefigured in the history of Israel's salvation and considers herself heir to God's promises which are fulfilled in Christ. Israel did not accept Christ.

> As holy Scripture testifies, Jerusalem did not recognize
> God's moment when it came [cf. Lk. 19:42]. Jews for the
> most part did not accept the Gospel; on the contrary,
> many opposed the spreading of it [cf. Rom. 11:28]. (4)

The Church's claim to God's favor in Christ does not imply,
the Council asserted, the rejection of Israel. Rather God
has, in Christ, reconciled Jew and Gentile. God has not
withdrawn his promise; he will bring Israel along with all
other peoples to unity in Christ.

> Even so, the apostle Paul maintains that the Jews remain
> very dear to God, for the sake of the patriarchs, since God
> does not take back the gifts he bestowed or the choice he
> made. Together with the prophets and that same apostle,
> the Church awaits the day, known to God alone, when all
> people will call on God with one voice and "serve him
> shoulder to shoulder" [Soph. 3:9; cf. Is. 66:23; Ps. 65:4;
> Rom. 11:11-32]. (4)

Thus the Church looks forward to the day when the division
between Christianity and Judaism will be overcome in the
kingdom of Christ. In the meantime, Christians may not
hold the Jewish people responsible for the death of Christ or
consider Israel rejected by God.

> It is true that the Church is the new people of God, yet the
> Jews should not be spoken of as rejected or accursed as if
> this followed from holy Scripture (4).

The cross of Christ is a sign of God's infinite love and
intention to bring all to salvation. Christ's sufferings can
never be a reason for persecution. Such religious motives,
rather than any political expediency, are the ground of the
Council's rejection of antisemitism.

By these considerations, the Council sought to temper the
implications for the Church's dealings with other religious
traditions of Christian claims for the definitive role of Christ
in humanity's relation to God. The revelation and action of

God in Christ calls for love and service of all humans. On these grounds, the Church rejects all discrimination based upon race, color, condition in life or religion. Christians are called upon to be at peace with all humanity, including those who ignore, disregard, or reject Christ (5).

> Ever aware of her duty to foster unity and charity among individuals, and even among nations, she [the Church] reflects at the outset on what men have in common and what tends to promote fellowship among them (1).
>
> Over the centuries many quarrels and dissentions have arisen between Christians and Muslims. The sacred Council now pleads with all to forget the past, and urges that a sincere effort be made to achieve mutual understanding; for the benefit of all men, let them together preserve and promote peace, liberty, social justice and moral values (3).

Thus the Declaration sometimes seems to accept human values as standards for judging the responsibilites of the Christian and the religious value of other non-Christian religions.

Theological Questions

We must however, face the properly theological question of the *relationship between Christianity and non-Christian religions*. Reflecting on this from a particularly American perspective involves a number of considerations.

First, Christianity must sustain its own sense of epistemological primacy. The Christian foundation for making assertions about God's intention to save humans and the way in which he does this is the experience of Christ within the Christian community. The believer can indeed reflect critically on her or his own religious commitment and can recognize that its assertions go beyond evidence which another person could be expected to accept as probative.

Still, the believer must acknowledge that in this critical stance, distanced from the experience of faith in Christ, he or she can make only the most general assertions about the workings of God in Christianity or any other religion. That is, or course, contrary to the American program of public truth, accessible to all inquirers. Because religious judgments fail this standard, they are regarded as matters of private taste which cannot affect another person.

Second, the Christian cannot separate Christ from his community. Christ need not be so identified with the Christian church, however, that salvation becomes accessible only through membership in it. In fact, the early community's own experience of Christ and his Spirit drew it out beyond the limits of Israel and the established ways of salvation through the religious practices of Judaism. Still, the Christian does encounter Christ through the mediation of the community and responds to his invitation within its worship and way of life. Christ's activity beyond the community can be recognized only on the basis of experience within it. Thus, for example, the apostolic communities had to know Jesus as exercising full authority within the Christian community in order to assert that he would judge the non-believing nations as well. Justin Martyr recognized Jesus as moral guide within the Christian community; then he asserted that this same Word had inspired Socrates and given the Law to Moses. [*1 Apology* 5,46; *Dialogue with Trypho*, 56-60, 63]. Similarly, Irenaeus used the manifest presence of Christ in the Christian martyrs as a foundation for arguing against the gnostics that Jesus had himself suffered and died in obedience and peace. [*Against Heresies,* 3,18]. Because the experience of Jesus and faith in his saving work is mediated by the Christian community, it does not give the believer a foundation for devaluing the Church and asserting that Christ and his Spirit operate indiscriminately through all religious traditions.

The experience of Jesus within the Christian tradition and community has led to the recognition that God intends salvation for all human beings. The Gospel of Matthew may offer one explanation for the way in which Christ will offer non-Christians [ch. 25]. Paul interpreted the of Jesus as an element in the divine plan to to the nations [Rom. 11]. The Acts of the __..._ recounts the way in which the Holy Spirit moved out beyond the Christian community [Acts 5, 10]. Even Augustine recognized the Holy Spirit as the source of the Catholic desire to reconcile schismatics and to spread the gospel to non-believers. The realization that God's love does not suffer the limits of the success of Christian missionaries grows out of this same judgment that the desire for the neighbor's salvation arises in God himself [1 Tim. 2:1-7].

The Process of Salvation

Directed by these and other considerations, Christian theologians have attempted to describe the process of salvation within the Christian community and to discover instances of similar processes outside the Church. Various means of salvation in Christ have been identified. Sincere moral action according to one's lights has been a factor long recognized: the Catholic tradition requires this of Christians and Catholics have thought that it might prove salvific for non-Christians as well. A sincere seeking for God, a concern for the welfare of the neighbor, self-sacrificing love, and a commitment to the future of humanity are other elements which have been recognized. The Declaration on Non-Christian Religions cites the recognition of instability and anguish in the present human condition coupled with a trusting flight toward God as signs of the presence of grace (2). Karl Rahner discovered within the commitment of one human being to another the reality of that trust in the goodness of God which has been recognized as salvific in the life and death of Jesus and his saints. These and many other signs of the operation of the saving grace of Christ in non-Christian religions are leading Christian theologians to an understanding of their relationship to Christianity.

Some of these considerations and explanations neglect

what would seem to be an essential aspect of Christian salvation: its communitarian nature. A bit of traditional Catholic apologetics asserts that if a good pagan had no opportunity to believe in Christ, then God would send an angel to preach the gospel to that person. The solution appears contrary to the nature of Christianity itself. In the Gospels one finds a gathering, training, and sending of disciples who are to preach the good news. In the Acts of the Apostles, the angels sent Philip to preach to the minister of Candace and instructed Cornelius to send for Peter [Acts 8:26-40; 10:1-22]. The Lord converted Paul himself but gave him sight and the Holy Spirit through the ministry of Ananias [Acts 9:1-19]. The origin and transmission of the gospel is by human means, by interaction with the community. So the response, the acceptance of the call and the living of the Christian life, is mediated by the community. Paul's letters clearly indicate that a response to Christ requires certain forms of community life and excludes others [e.g., 1 Cor. 10-11]. Baptism and eucharist, precisely as forms of initiation and participation in a community, were soon recognized as integral to Christian life. Finally, the eschatological fulfilment of Christian salvation is generally presented through social analogues such as a wedding feast or a city [Rev. 21].

The social aspect of Christ's salvation has not been universally and uniformly recognized, affirmed, and practiced throughout the history of the Church. Some forms of mysticism have strained against it, as they have strained at the humanity of Christ. Christianity has, however, recognized the community as the locus of both hearing the call and responding to it. This is not to deny an inner working of the divine grace which accompanies the preaching of the gospel to make it effective nor does it rule out the individual call which moves a person to offer service. It only asserts that all such graces carry some orientation to the community.

A Proposal

If grace and the process of salvation in Christ are essentially communitarian or social, then one might postulate that adherents of non-Christian religions are being brought to God through their religious institutions and not independently of them. Precisely as social structures these religions might be mediators of God's offer of grace and of the person's acceptance. Since the Christian church claims both that Christ is the origin and the goal of all saving grace and that this grace is most fully realized in the Christian community, it must engage these other religious traditions just as it has engaged that Judaism whose salvific function was affirmed against the Christian gnostics. This experience of grace in other contexts may lead to a new and fuller understanding and appropriation of the mystery of Christ. Indeed, the fruits of such engagement are already evident in the reversal of an earlier perspective. Using Augustine's premise that all goodness and holiness come through the operation of Christ's Spirit, Christians are realizing that this Spirit has been poured out upon all humanity.

Through its own history, the Christian Church has also come to recognize that particular community structures may hinder the believer's response to the gospel. The validity of many of the Reformers' charges against late medieval and renaissance Catholicism was recognized even in the sixteenth century. The post-Vatican dialogues with the Orthodox and Protestant communities are moving Catholics to question the way in which they have conceived and pursued the universal ministry of the Roman Bishop. In return, the Roman Church has not ceased to call other Christian communities to a unity which transcends national and ethnic boundaries, to a fuller sacramental practice, and to a concern for social structures. The Christian Church may call other religious traditions not only to the promotion of justice, peace, freedom, and other social and cultural values (2-3) but to a more adequate recognition of the divine being who is both revealed and hidden by any religious tradition. Such a ministry to other religions would appear an integral part of preaching the gospel and the reign of Christ.

Secular Society

Finally, I would like to extend the considerations in which we have been engaged beyond the sphere normally recognized as religious. Through a series of questions, the Declaration indicated the mystery of human life to which religions respond.

> Men look to their different religions for an answer to the unsolved riddles of human existence. The problems that weigh heavily on the hearts of men are the same today as in ages past. What is man? What is the meaning and purpose of life? What is upright behavior, and what is sinful? Where does suffering originate,and what end does it serve? How can genuine happiness be found? What happens at death? What is judgment? What reward follows death? And finally, what is the ultimate mystery, beyond human explanation, which embraces our entire existence, from which we take our origin and towards which we tend? (1)

In many areas of the world, and particularly in North America, the secular culture has a greater influence than any religious tradition in shaping the way in which these questions arise, are considered, and are answered by major segments of the population. Might the twin premises enunciated above, that Christ's grace is everywhere operative and that both call and response are socially mediated, lead to the inference that the institutions and structure of secular society serve an auxiliary or even the primary religious function for most persons? The saving grace of Christ might be operative through the secular culture, addressing individuals and groups through political and economic structures and calling them to respond, to work out their salvation, by action in these spheres.

If secular institutions of government and culture can serve as mediators of Christ's salvation, might the Church have a mission of engaging these agencies as well as other religious traditions? Would this charge not be a properly religious one, an integral part of the preaching of the gospel and ministering the sacraments to all humanity? Could such a mission be regarded as secular, as the responsibility of the laity, a task inappropriate for those ordained or publicly consecrated to sacred ministry?

An example may clarify this point. Just such an insight into the way in which law and custom structure an individual's response to God may be at the heart of the concern of the American Catholic bishops with the issue of abortion on demand during the first two trimesters. The law and the consequent economics of medical practice actually discourage an appropriate weighing of the values of the other parties affected by a pregnant woman's action. A similar religious imperative seems to have moved a generation of Christian opponents to nuclear arms and finds expression in the pastoral letter, "The Challenge of Peace: God's Promise and our Response."

Under certain conditions, the engagement of the clergy in political and economic issues might be inappropriate. Where the Christian church defines the dominant culture, the clergy's influence might be adequately exerted through traditionally religious means. Where the political and economic system is formally opposed to the Christian faith, an identifiable portion of the Church, such as the clergy and religious, might be called to an opposing, prophetic stance rather than to cooperation or collaboration with a government or a society's economic agencies. In a pluralistic, open society, however, might the entire Christian church be called to active engagement?

The role of the Church in addressing the political and economic structures of society has been recognized for some time, at least since the days of Leo XIII. What seems to be in question at this time is the religious nature of this task, its relation to the preaching of the gospel and the ministry of the sacraments. The preceding observations would recognize that political, economic and cultural institutions might serve the properly religious function for a large number of persons.

These considerations have grown out of an attempt to identify a properly religious and Christian motive and call for engagement in the secular. One approach which has been regularly employed elaborates a theology of divine creation which is not specifically Christian. The present essay attempts another, through a theology of salvation in Christ. The argument has proceeded from the structures of the process of salvation in Christ as these are evident in the Church, through the same processes as they may be identified in non-Christian religions, and thence to the operation of Christ's grace in and through nonreligious societal structures. If one assumes the universal operation of God's saving will in Christ and further accepts the Christian community's responsibility to minister this grace even outside itself, then a properly religious ministry through secular institutions would seem appropriate. This would be a ministry of preaching the gospel and reconciling humanity to God in Christ. It would, I believe, be part of the priestly mission of the Christian Church and thus belong to the entire people: clergy, religious and laity.

Dogmatic Constitution on Divine Revelation
Dei Verbum, 18 November, 1965

Donald Senior, C.P.

Reviewing the process that led to the formulation of this conciliar text is equivalent to reviewing the whole agonizing and glorious struggle of the Council itself.[1] The document's formulation took the entire span of the Council, starting with a preparatory schema presented on October 27, 1960 and ending with the endorsement of a decisively different text on November 18, 1965. In between were momentous battles between traditionalists and progressives. Two crisis points were memorable: the famous vote of November 1962 where the traditionalists had managed to alter the usual voting procedure so that now a two-thirds majority was needed to send the original schema back for reformulation. The progressives failed to muster such a vote and the Council would have been stuck with an impossible text had not

---

[1]For a detailed account, see J. Ratzinger, "Origin and Background," in H. Vorgrimler (ed.), *Commentary on the Documents of Vatican II* (London: Burns & Oates; New York: Herder and Herder, 1969). Vol. 3; pp. 155-66.

Pope John XXIII personally intervened to have the schema removed from the agenda and sent to a special commission for revision. During the second session, divisions were so great that some proposed that the attempt to formulate a text be abandoned all together or at least that parts of the text be absorbed into other conciliar documents. But Pope Paul VI in his speech at the end of the second session on December 4, 1963 explicitly mentioned the schema on revelation as an agenda topic for the third session. After continued struggle the finished product was voted on at the eighth public session of November 18, 1965: 2344 positive, 6 negative.

It is not surprising that such turbulence should swirl around the issue of revelation: nothing is more fundamental and nothing so exposes one's theological worldview as this topic. Much of the character of this conciliar text reflects an uneasy compromise between opposing world views: one more traditional, essentialist, heavily supernaturalist and static; the other more historically sensitive, immanentist, dialectical and process oriented. In reading the text and reviewing its history, one can wonder if the battle joined at the Council has not smoldered ever since and threatens now to blaze back into the open.

Commentators on this text emphasize that its real achievements can only be appreciated when it is read in tandem with Vatican I's statement on revelation. Vatican II's *Constitution on Divine Revelation*, particularly in its doctrinal sections, was not meant to be a bold departure from previous formulations but a carefully calibrated advance, in continuity with the old but making vital openings to future developments.

A list of the document's six chapters might be helpful before we proceed to assessment. The first five chapters are devoted to a doctrinal reflections; the last concentrates on the pastoral implications: (1) The nature of revelation; (2) The transmission of revelation (the early church; the relationship of Scripture and tradition; the role of the magisterium); (3) Inspiration and interpretation of Scripture; (4)

The nature of the Old Testament; (5) The nature of the New Testament; (6) Scripture in the life of the church.

The most important doctrinal sections are found in the first three chapters. The chapter on the Old and New Testaments are largely descriptive. The concluding chapter concentrates on the pastoral use of Scripture in the church and has a number of significant exhortations and instructions.

In this instance, as with virtually all of the issues considered by the Council, it is important to remember that subsequent impact on the life of the church was not due solely to conciliar initiatives. The renewal of biblical scholarship in Roman Catholicism had been making progress for almost a century, even if scholars were still harassed and one had to proceed with caution. The landmark document *Divino Afflante Spiritu* (1943) had appeared two decades before the Council and had paved the way for a new generation of Catholic biblical scholarship. Popular movements towards biblical piety were already stirring; translations into the vernacular were underway before the Council had been thought of.

But these movements were uncertain, their validity questioned, their leaders suspect. On the eve of the Council visible Catholic biblical scholars such as Maximilian Zerwick and Stanislaus Lyonnet were purged and attempts were being made to discredit the Pontifical Biblical Institute, the symbolic headquarters of Roman Catholic biblical scholarship. So the role of the Council in validating the biblical movement within Catholicism should not be exaggerated nor should it be overlooked.

The successes and lapses of the text on revelation surely stand out more clearly now than they did in November of 1965. I would like to list some of the positive and negative features of the document that strike me from our present vantage point. Many of these points, I believe, are conditioned by a North American experience.

Positive Achievements

One of the most significant advances of the *Constitution on Divine Revelation* was that it began to speak of revelation no longer solely in metaphysical and static categories but in biblical and personalist categories of dialogue and communication, thereby modeling a style of theology it would recommend to Catholic theologians in the concluding chapter of the text (24). As we will note below, formulations that speak of revelation as God's self-communication to humanity (2), are juxtaposed with more essentialist categories that refer to the disclosure of "doctrine" and "divine truths" and "eternal decrees of his will" (2,6). This is one of the more glaring evidences of the uneasy compromise that made the document possible. But still the achievement is notable and would be further exploited in Catholic theology. Revelation was being conceived of in more fluid personalist and process categories, an advance that would pave the way for the breakthrough of more than one theological impasse.

The document also reaffirmed the Catholic position that authentic revelation takes place on multiple fronts: creation, the history of Israel and the early church, the person and history of Jesus. This is an extremely important aspect of Catholic tradition and, because of it, Catholicism has been spared some of the turmoil caused by biblical fundamentalism. Classical Catholicism does not conceive of Christianity solely as a "religion of the book"; contact with God is possible through human experience and through reflection on created realities (3). Although the Constitution does not exploit it, this affirmation leaves an important opening to other religious traditions and to the authentic human and religious aspirations of all peoples.

The *Constitution on Divine Revelation* also came up with a compromise formulation on the issues of inspiration and inerrancy that at least avoided the worst traps and allowed freedom for theological development. Here again the compromise nature of the text is most apparent. The term "withour error" is used but with sufficient nuance so that it does not apply globally to the Bible, thereby averting the kind of "inerrancy" battles that are plaguing evangelical churches in the United States. Various levels of "truth" appropriate to different literary modes are explicitly acknowledged (12). The original draft, however, had claimed "inerrancy" and absolute truth for the entire Bible without any qualification, even to the point of explicitly affirming that the Scriptures are without error on all levels: scientific, historical, geographical, etc.! If a statement like this had been approved, Catholic scholarship would have been shipwrecked. The present text—"...we must acknowledge that the books of Scripture, firmly, faithfully and without error, teach that truth which God, for the sake of our salvation, wished to see confided to the Sacred Scriptures" (11)—gives sufficient running room even though its precise meaning remains vague.

Likewise, the Council did not end up with impossible formulations on the the hotly debated question of "inspiration." Traditional formulations ("written under the inspiration of the Holy Spirit," "[the biblical books] have God as their author," etc. cf. 11) are used but they are juxtaposed with unprecedented emphasis on the role of the human authors in the writing of the biblical books (11-13). The biblical authors are acknowledged as true authors and, therefore, account must be taken of the time-conditioned circumstances of their writing. The biblical books are as fully human as the Word Incarnate is fully human (13).

This coexistence of two theological emphases, while far from satisfactory as the expression of a coherent theological synthesis, nevertheless allows Catholicism to avoid, at least on the official level, the kind of rigid fundamentalism that seems to be a particular American virus.

Another near miss was the question of the "two sources" of revelation: Scripture and Tradition. This was one of the most hotly debated issues in the formulation of the document and its final version walked the tightrope once more in attempting to satisfy traditionalists and progressives. The final formulation "Sacred Tradition and sacred Scripture make up a single sacred deposit of the Word of God, which is entrusted to the Church", (10) does not adequately deal with Protestant objections that in some instances Tradition seems to go far beyond Scripture or even to be at variance with it, but at least it avoids the mechanistic two-source viewpoint. It should also be noted that the concept of Tradition presented in the text, while sometimes appearing to speak of Tradition in a rather essentialist framework as "truths handed down," in other instances has a much more dynamic and developmental sense of tradition.

One of the most significant achievements of the Council, and one whose impact is just being felt, is its unabashed endorsement of the historical-critical method of biblical research. This endorsement had already been signaled by the church in such documents as Pius XII's *Divino Afflante Spiritu* (1943) and the Biblical Commission's instruction on the historical truth of the Gospels (1964). But the document's implied approbation gave such impulses the solemnity of conciliar approbation.

The endorsement comes in bits and pieces throughout the document: interpreters of Scripture are exhorted to carefully investigate "the meaning which the sacred writers really had in mind" (12). The investigator must be aware, therefore, of "literary forms," of the varieties of "truth" expressed in different literary forms, of the historical and cultural milieu of the biblical writer (12). The stages in the formation of the gospels are subtly noted (19) and it is even allowed that some of the material in the gospels was formulated not from historical recollection but in order to "synthesize" or "explain" traditions "with an eye for the situation of the churches"— a clear reference to redaction criticism (19). In the final chapter biblical scholarship is praised and encouraged (23).

From a later vantage point, one might wonder if the Council knew what it was getting itself into! As we will point out below, there is no explicit suggestion in the text that biblical and other forms of critical scholarship might uncover something that threatened the church's self-consciousness. However, it is surely no accident that for every endorsement of critical scholarship present in the text, there is equal time given to reaffirming the decisive role of church authority in providing official interpretation, and there are repeated words of caution and exhortations to vigilance and fidelity.

Without doubt, the most successful part of the document is its sixth and final chapter—"Sacred Scripture in the Life of the Church"—containing a series of pastoral directives. The theological positions expressed in the first three chapters certainly provide the intellectual running room that made these pastoral injunctions meaningful, but the real success of the Council's directives can be easily ticked off by reading through the final chapter of the constitution.

It declared, first of all, that "access to sacred scripture ought to be open wide to the Christian faithful." (22). To further this, it called for "suitable and correct" translations from the original biblical languages. It also suggests ecumenical collaboration in this area. The explosion of translations, commentaries and other biblical paraphernàlia since the Council is an impressive testimony that the message was heard.

It further encouraged biblical scholarship (23) and called for a revitalization of theology, with Scripture as its "soul" (24). The same biblical emphasis was enjoined for "pastoral preaching, catechetics, and all other forms of Christian instruction, among which the liturgical homily should hold pride of place" (24). When we consider the differences in style between pre- and post-Vatican II christology, catechetics, and at least the aspirations of preaching, there is little doubt that this paragraph may be one of the most revolutionary in all of the Council.

The exhortations close with an appeal to all Christians, but especially bishops, priests and religious (the laity still seem like an endangered species in this text), to read, study and pray over the Scriptures. Again, it is safe to say that even though the Bible remains an untapped mystery for many Catholics, the intrusion of the Scriptures into the devotional life of the church is one of the most successful results of Vatican II and, in the long run, may be its most enduring achievement.

The Unfinished Business of the Declaration

Climbing into the time machine and re-reading this document from a later vantage point also reveals some glaring omissions and some unhappy formulations. It is here, curiously, that reading the text from an American perspective yields the most results.

Many problems in the document stem from its essentially compromise quality. Some of these we have already cited: a) the juxtaposition of a dialectical and mechanistic view of revelation; b) a view of tradition that tries to be both dynamic and static; c) an attempt to safeguard the sacred character of the text by reaffirming traditional formulations of inspiration and inerrancy while at the same time trying to affirm the authentically human character of the biblical literature.

All of these compromises were necessary to some degree if any text at all were to come forth from the Council on the vital topic of revelation. Surely they are a small price to pay for the crucial pastoral freedom they helped protect. But rereading the text now shows how fragile the compromise was, and one can wonder if the opposing world views that rumble beneath this text are once more breaking out into uncompromising factions.

Other issues are more probing and many of them relate to specific American concerns.

THE ABSENCE OF SELF-CRITICISM.

It is amazing to read this text of what was supposed to be a non-triumphalistic Council and see how triumphalistic its statement can be. Within the document itself there is no hint that the biblical movement had erupted out of a hunger for the biblical word, a hunger caused in part by the Church's rationing of the Scriptures in its intellectual and devotional life. The paragraph on translations (22) is a classical instance of how the church can look at history in a self serving way. To support the statement that the church has "always" sought to make the Scriptures available to the faithful, the Council appeals to the church's use of the Septuagint and the Vulgate, thereby overlooking some of the sorry restrictions of access to the Bible for centuries of the church's history.

There is also no hint in the document that one of the main reasons why the biblical movement had an impact on the church was because of the debt owed to the reform churches with their vigorous biblical scholarship and their strong biblical piety.

Such well-known euphemisms ("the church has always taught...") can be soothing or amusing. But they are also symptomatic of an uncritical attitude for which the church ultimately pays a price. Perhaps this lack of self-criticism in its official consciousness explains the lack of preparation in the post-conciliar church for the hard crunch of implementing renewal. There is no reference in the entire document to the critical function of the Scriptures in the life of the church. This was an omission that baffled and even scandalized many Protestant observers at the time the text was formulated; but it seemed to bother few Catholics. The Constitution seems to assume that by endorsing the role of the Scriptures in the life, thought, and piety of the church, those Scriptures would do nothing more than ratify and affirm the church as it is. The text acknowledges that the church is the "servant" of the Word (10) but such service seems to be exercised, according to the text, more in the church's faithfully guarding and disseminating the Word than in its being prophetically challenged or instructed by the Scriptures.

American culture has its own forms of hubris and is not immune to self-deception as recent political history makes abundantly clear. But the complete absence of self-criticism evidenced in the Council's document, I believe, runs counter to the instincts of our own culture and political process where it is expected that public debate and critical reflection should challenge current practice, either by appeal to our founding ideals or to effectiveness or both.

In any case, the post-conciliar church, has certainly not been immune to the prophetic function of the Scriptures.

Since the Council, of course, appeal to the biblical Word has challenged many of the church's most cherished assumptions about its authority, its order, its doctrinal formulations, and its moral priorities. But too often , perhaps because the church's own ideology made no official place for the critical function of the Bible, such challenges have been viewed in many instances as insubordination or as dangerous misinterpretations rather than as the ferment of God's Word in the life of the church.

THE ABSENCE OF PLURALISM AND DIVERSITY

This lapse is allied to the one we have just mentioned; it is also something that the vantage point of American experience highlights. In reviewing the evolution of the New Testament and the early church, the document assumes that one church structure held sway from the very beginning: the monarchical hierarchical structure that characterizes present day Roman Catholicism. This classical viewpoint on the origin of the church covers the following basic scenario: Jesus appointed Twelve Apostles, instructing them with the truths of Gospel and empowering them to teach and guide the church; the Apostles, in turn, appointed bishops and conferred on them their own powers of teaching and order; through an unbroken chain of succession, the gospel continues to be authoritatively preached and interpreted down through the centuries.

There is no suggestion in the document that, in fact, this historical picture is a kind of ecclesiastical shorthand and that the actual historical origin of the church was much more complicated and evolutionary. It might be argued that such issues belong to the documents on the church or on the bishops. But it remains true that in considering the nature of revelation and the place of the Scriptures in the life of the church, one eventually has to face the fact that the Scriptures, especially the New Testament, when critically examined, offer a complicated view of the development of church structures and order. The simple view of apostolic succession put forward in this document simply does not hold up against the biblical evidence, the very evidence the document is recommending that the church include in its theology. It is also true that the New Testament does not offer a homogeneous ecclesiology but a pluralistic one. There are diverse types of church structures and images in the New Testatment but there is no hint of this in the Constitution's review of the origin of the church.

It is noteworthy that since the Council, Roman Catholic biblical scholarship (especially in the United States) has taken up pastoral issues: the Petrine office, the role of Mary, the ordained priesthood, the role of the women, charismatic vs. hierarchical forms of leadership, the dynamics of community, etc.[2] These issues, of course, have also been examined by church historians and systematic theologians. The contribution of the biblical data has been to demonstrate substantial diversity within the very foundational period of Christianity and within its foundational sources. Attention to the scriptural data from a historical-critical vantage point makes anachronistic imposition of later ecclesiological developments back onto our sources less possible, certainly less justifiable. For example, the hierarchical structures of Roman Catholicism have authentic roots in the New Testament, but so may other possible ecclesiologies and attendant structures. Likewise, the controversy over ordination of women has shown that it is impossible to support the church's position exclusively from biblical grounds.

In general, one gets the impression that the Council Fathers were either naive or overly optimistic about the potential, in fact inevitable, critical function of biblical scholarship. And one can ask if, in endorsing the methodology of historical criticism in regard to the Bible, the Council was aware that it was thereby also opening up the Pandora's Box of legitimating historical criticism as it applies to

---

[2]See, for example, R. Brown, K. Donfried, J. Reumann, *Peter in the New Testament* (New York: Paulist, 1973); R. Brown, K. Donfried, J. Fitzmyer, J. Reumann, *Mary in the New Testament* (New York: Paulist, 1978); J. Reumann (with responses by J. Fitzmyer and J. Quinn), *Righteousness in the New Testament* (New York: Paulist, 1982). All three volumes are by-products of the Lutheran-Roman Catholic bilateral dialogues.

dogma and church structures. I think it is safe to predict that Catholicism may be less prepared to deal with a historical-critical analysis of its structures than it is with a critical Appraisal of the Bible.

A LIMITED VIEW OF THE BIBLE AS LITERATURE

Although the *Constitution on Divine Revelation* made important strides by endorsing the analysis of literary forms as part of the legitimate interpretation of the Bible, this endorsement seems limited from the vantage point of present day biblical scholarship. The recognition of the "human nature" of the biblical text still seems somewhat grudging. The impression is given that divine truth is buried underneath its human shell. The literary aspects of the Bible are so much underbrush that the biblical explorer has to cut through before breaking into the clear and being able to imbide the pure message of the text.

Contemporary biblical scholarship, especially in North America, would find this approach too limited. The Bible is viewed much more seriously and positively as literature than it was at the time of the Council. Narrative, metaphor and symbol are not considered simply the by-products of divine condescension (as the text speaks of it in quoting Chrysostom, cf. 13). Rather, narrative, symbol and metaphor are the effective and appropriate media of revelation. The literary forms of the Bible are to be savored as disclosures of the human encounter with the transcendent.

In almost every area of biblical methodology, recognition of the Bible as literature and therefore of the biblical writers as genuine authors has been advanced. Form and redaction criticism, the two basic forms of biblical methodology alluded to in the document, have been joined by further refinements such as composition criticism, structural analysis, sociological analysis, etc.—all of which assume the Bible is the product of human literary skill. Many recent biblical scholars would question the document's focus on the "intention" of the biblical author, which the document sees as leading to an understanding of God's own intention (12).

Many literary critics are diffident about retrieving from a text the historical author's intention and prefer instead to focus on the literary dynamics between the text and the reader. It would be unfair to fault the conciliar text for not expressing all the subtleties of evolving biblical methodology. But the Council's seeming toleration (rather than full endorsement) of the human quality of the Scriptures may be symptomatic of something deeper and as yet unresolved within Roman Catholic tradition: its attitude to creation and to history. In an important but perhaps unexploited intuition, the Council compared the humanness of the Bible to the humanness of the Incarnate Word (13). Catholic christology of recent centuries has had its greatest difficulties in trying to take seriously the *humanity* of Jesus. The same might also be said of the Scriptures: the presence in the document of traditional formulations of inspiration and inerrancy are symptoms of a reluctance to move away from a supernaturalist viewpoint in regard to the Bible. Admission of the full humanness of the Bible might be construed somehow as a denial of its "sacredness." This reluctance had analogies in the church's conception of itself. In his commentary on the Constitution in the Vorgrimler series, Joseph Ratzinger points out that many of the attributes which Vatican I applied to the *church* were subtly transferred to *Christ* in the formulations of Vatican II, a quiet recognition of inflated theological language.[3] The same process may have to take place in regard to the biblical text. Although the *Constitution on Divine Revelation* acknowledged the "humanness" of the Scriptures, there is little follow-through. There is still a need to clearly recognize the "limits" of Scripture and its time-bounded perspective on some moral and doctrinal issues.

[3]Cf. J. Ratzinger, "Revelation Itself," in H. Vorgrimler (ed.), *Commentary on the Documents of Vatican II*, vol. 3, p. 176.

A LACK OF ECUMENISM

Issues of "ecumenism" such as relations with Judaism and other non-Christian religions were, of course, taken up in separate documents of Vatican II. The document on revelation cannot be faulted for lacking a full-scale treatment of these issues, but there are aspects of its views on revelation and Scripture where an ecumenical perspective should have had an impact and did not. Here, too, the American experience of religious pluralism makes such omissions less tolerable.

There are three specific areas under the general heading of ecumenism on which I would like to comment. First of all, in its discussion of revelation, the document makes no mention at all of the question of non-Christian religions, other than Judaism, as a potential source or locus of authentic revelation. It reaffirms the Catholic position that humans can come to know God through experience and through reflection on creation (3,6), but when it comes to speak of history and of religious traditions, the only arena acknowledged as revelatory is that of Israel, Jesus and the apostolic church. No mention, positive or negative, is made of other religious traditions, much less of their sacred writings.

This is a lacuna that Christianity can no longer afford. The reality of long-term religious traditions such as Buddhism, Hinduism and Islam cannot be considered as a passing aberration but as a datum to be reflected on theologically, particularly in the context of the church's doctrine on revelation.

Secondly, the document as it stands fails to exploit sufficiently the opening to other Christian denominations which a consideration of Scripture affords. Mention is made of having common biblical translations with separated brethren (22) but this is the sole reference and it is too little. There is no candid acknowledgement of the debt owed to Protestantism for the stimulus of its biblical scholarship or for the testimony and prophetic challenge of its biblical piety: realities which had a deep impact on contemporary Catholicism.

Post-conciliar experience, especially in the United States, shows that intellectual collaboration among the various Christian denominations has moved more quickly and further on the level of biblical exegesis than in any other field. This is due, in part, to the nature of exegesis where doctrinal, ecclesial and moral conclusions can be deferred and thus deep divisions left unexposed. Certainly the tasks of moral and dogmatic theology will always be more of an ecumenical challenge. Nevertheless some biblical enterprises have been consciously ecumenical, even on highly charged issues, such as the joint studies on Peter, Mary, and the meaning of justification mentioned above.[4] Success in these ventures has been due to widespread and substantial consensus on key points of methodology. Here is a genuine ecumenical breakthrough which if the Council text were to be revised could be highlighted to show how exploration of a common source text coupled with a willingness to suspend denominational anxiety can lead to deeper levels of unity. It may be chauvanisitc to assert it, but I think greater strides have been made in this regard in North America than anywhere else, precisely because of the pluralistic context of American culture.

A third lapse in the area of ecumenism is the weakness of the document's treatment of the Old Testament, and by extension, of Judaism itself. The chapter on the Old Testament (chapter 4) is the document's briefest and surely its most anemic. Some positive value is attributed to the Hebrew Scriptures in their own right (they "give expression to a lively sense of God, . . . are a storehouse of sublime teachings on God, and of sound wisdom on human life, as well as a wonderful treasury of prayers. . ." 15), but this is only after a reminder that they contain some things which are "incomplete and temporary." In general the document's view of the Old Testament is dominated by a "fulfillment" mentality which views the Hebrew Scriptures almost exclu-

[4]Cf. above, n.l.

sively from the vantage point of the New Testament. The principal purpose of the Old Testament is stated to be preparation for Christ and the messianic Kingdom (15). It declares that God has so authored the Bible that the "New (Testament) should be hidden in the Old and that the Old should be manifest in the New" and that the full meaning of the Old Testament is only made manifest in the New (16). Such an evaluation of the Hebrew Scriptures is woefully inadequate. It presumes that Judaism as a religious tradition ceased with the arrival of Jesus and the early church or that its religious message was wholly ancillary to the Christian experience and is now a discarded hulk. It fails to recognize what Paul himself realized: Juadism continues as a living religious tradition that has its own role to play in the salvation of humanity. To overlook this, as the document does, is not only an offense to Jews; something more sinister lurks beneath this attitude. It is a viewpoint that has fed anti-semitism for some two thousand years. By implication it suggests that Judaism is a non-entity, or even worse, an alien being, to which Christianity is superior in every way. It smacks of theological blindness by allowing the church to make assertions about its own traditions without being accountable to historical realities. It is just as important to Christianity as it is to Judaism that we acknowledge that Judaism is alive and breathing. Our assertions about the messianic ministry of Jesus and about the unfolding of history must take into account the "incompleteness" of the Christian experience and the unfinished work of redemption. Otherwise Christian assertions about Jesus become abstract or a form of whistling in the dark.

There are few places in the world where the Christian-Jewish dialogue has gone on with such intensity as in the United States, due in no small part to the size and relative security of the Jewish community in the United States and because of the vital link between the state of Israel and America. It is unlikely that the document's appraisal of the Old Testament would be so framed by anyone who has participated in this Christian-Jewish dialogue. Here, too, is a fact of American experience that was probably foreign to many of the framers of the document on revelation. This issue reminds us again that diversity and pluralism prove to be the most fruitful atmosphere for realistic theologizing.

INCOMPLETE PASTORAL ANALYSIS.

Hindsight shows that the pastoral reflections and recommendations of the document, as excellent as they are, need development. The concluding chapter does mention the need for a revitalization of preaching that is nourished by the Scriptures (23,24,25), but little guidance is given on the art of biblical interpretation. The document recommends that preachers and catechists have "contact" with the sacred Word of God and assures them that the Scriptures will "nourish" and "yield fruits of holiness" in their ministry of the word. But nothing is said about the difference between exegesis and interpretation or about the evocative power of narrative and metaphor and the corresponding need for the interpreter to have literary and personal sensitivity in order to bring the text and experience into creative interplay. This has been an area where North American theology has developed in the past few years. Good preaching or other forms of interpretation are not assured by mere "contact" with the biblical text; it is even possible that the last state of that preacher will be worst than the first through such contact. More needs to be said about the kind of skills a post-Vatican II preacher should have if, indeed, the task of preaching is now seen as a creative interpretation of the biblical word. Here, as in the case of liturgical reform, the Council may not have anticipated how much its emphasis upon the use of metaphorical language and ritual expression in the Church's proclamation would demand personal development in the interpreter.

Conclusion

For all of its flaws, the *Dogmatic Constitution on Divine Revelation* represents an incredible achievement; it is a genuine watershed in the history of Roman Catholicism.

One has only to remember how some things were before the Council: the style of manual theology, the virtual absence of the Bible from Catholic devotional life, the rationalistic approach of our catechisms, the muffling of the Word within our liturgical life, the ridicule directed towards Protestants because of their clinging to the Bible, the pale diet of historical minutiae and archeological questions considered the only legitimate interest of Catholic biblical studies. Such memories help us realize the extraordinary change in consciousness that has come over Roman Catholicism since the time of Council.

Is the turbulence that has accompanied the biblical renewal only a brief spasm soon to subside? Or is it, in fact, an apocalyptic birth pang signalling a new age? I tend to think that it is the latter. The biblical movement in Catholicism does not seem to have leveled off or slowed down. It still has the full endorsement of the official church. The end result is that steadily increasing numbers of Catholic Christians are coming into immediate contact with one of the fundamental sources of their religious tradition: biblical stories, metaphors, symbols, values. This infusion of biblical data can cause some indigestion: strange forms of piety, some flacid religious education materials, a diminution of common sense and vigorous thinking in favor of romanticism and ecstatic fanaticism.

But in the balance the Catholic biblical revolution has been a profound blessing, gradually empowering many adult Catholics with a proper sense of their own religious authority. Now they, too, have access, without layers of mediation, to the sources of our religious tradition. They, too, can grasp images and symbols and values, blessed with biblical authority, which may challenge or offer alternatives to some of the images and symbols and values which dominate in the church. It is no accident that there is such interplay between biblical exploration and the key pastoral issues of our day such as community, ordination, violence, authority, the nature of creation and the human body, etc.

As we mentioned before, many of these issues and movements were in play long before the Council was convoked and some of them have causes that go far beyond the biblical renewal. But Vatican II's document on revelation confirmed and validated the biblical renewal and managed to avoid placing any insurmountable roadblocks in its way. Such may be the very best a Council, or any church authority, can do.

Decree on the Apostolate of Lay People
Apostolicam Actuositatem,
18 November, 1965

Alan F. Blakley

Vatican II and the Laity

Vatican II was the first Council of the Church to address, in a specific way, the question of the laity in the Church. The *Decree on the Apostolate of the Laity,* therefore, became the first Council document in the history of the Church devoted to the role of the laity. The Preparatory Commission for the Apostolate of the Laity held its first plenary session in November of 1960. It was constituted by the Central Papal Commission to develop the following topics selected from the numerous *vota* requested of various instances: 1) the Apostolate of the Laity, its extent, its goals, its relation to the hierarchy, its nature interpreted in the light of present-day needs; 2) Catholic Action....; 3) societies....[1]

[1]Ferdinand Klostermann, "Decree on the Apostolate of the Laity" in Herbert Vorgrimler, ed., *Commentary on the Documents of Vatican II*, Volume III (New York: Herder and Herder; 1969) p. 273.

The Preparatory Commission's work went through many stages and revisions. During this process, Pope Paul VI, on September 15, 1963, made an unprecedented announcement. Paul had invited representatives of the laity as observers to the Council. Vatican II then became the first Council "to invite representatives of the laity to be official observers of the proceedings. They were also the first to be addressed during a regular working congregation by members of the laity. Although the Second Vatican Council was in most aspects a 'bishops' council', it nonetheless paved the way to making, perhaps, the third or fourth Vatican Council a 'layman's council.' "[2]

The vote on the final draft "was held during the 157th general congregation on 10 November 1965; the results of this were 2201 affirmative, 2 negative, and 5 invalid votes."[3] The vote on the *Decree on the Apostolate of the Laity,* therefore, passed the Council with the fewest dissenting votes of any document. It was promulgated on November 18, 1965.

From the beginning of the first session of the Council. October 11, 1962, through the beginning of the third session, September 14, 1964, there was a certain amount of confusion concerning the relationship of this document to other documents. The confusion centered on the question of what belonged to the *Decree on the Apostolate of the Laity,* what belonged to the chapter on the Laity in the Schema on the Church, what belonged to Schema XIII (later to become the *Church in the Modern World*), and what belonged to the Commission for the Reform of Canon Law.[4]

A consensus developed among those working on the *Decree on the Apostolate of the Laity* "that a final position could be adopted toward the draft only when it was known

---

[2]Vincent A. Yzermans, *American Participation in the Second Vatican Council* (New York: Sheed and Ward; 1967) p. 449. While it is not within the scope of this paper to predict Vatican III or Jerusalem I, nor do I necessarily agree with Msgr. Yzermans' statement, it is interesting that he would make this prediction in 1967.

[3]Klostermann, p. 301

[4]To get a feel for the confusion, see Klostermann, pp. 280-285.

what was contained in the chapter on the laity in the draft of the *Constitution on the Church,* as well as in what was then known as 'Schema XIII' on the *Church in the Modern World.*"[5]

The *Decree on the Apostolate of the Laity* became an expansion of sections from *The Church* and *The Church in the Modern World.* One overall theme of the document pulls these other documents together. Chapter III begins: "The lay apostolate, in all its many aspects, is exercised both in the Church and in the world"[6] Thus begins the heart of the document. The Fathers, in this chapter, discuss the various fields of the apostolate. This constitutes the specifics of the Christian call to action in holiness. The previous chapters of the document reiterate items from *The Church* and *The Church in the Modern World.* This chapter specifies those items.

The specific areas of the apostolate are: evangelization and sanctification of the temporal order; renewal of the temporal order; apostolate within church communities; apostolate to the family; and, apostolate of like-towards-like. The laity are called, through their baptism, to sanctify the world. This general challenge becomes specific in their roles in church communities, their families and their everyday activities.

The laity are to be leaven in the world. The witness of their lives is to be such that others may see God through them. Living a Christian life is the foremost task of the laity. In doing this, they sanctify the world. Their task of living and speaking for Christian principles renews the temporal order. The Fathers detailed three specific areas in which this apostolate is to be exercised.

The laity are responsible for becoming active members of their church communities. "Their action within the Church communities is so necessary that without it the apostolate of the pastors will frequently be unable to obtain its full

[5]Klostermann, p. 288.

[6]Austin P. Flannery, ed., *The Documents of Vatican II* (Grand Rapids, MI: Wm. B. Eerdmans Pub. Co; 1975) p. 776.

effect"[7] This statement has little to do with the oft lamented shortage of clergy. Rather the Fathers saw that for parishes to be true faith communities, laity and clergy alike need to work together. The parish needs close cooperation and contact of laity and clergy in the common tasks of sanctification if it is to be viable.

> "Two tasks affected by such cooperation are then named: the laity are to make known to the Church, represented by the parish, the problems which men face in the present world as well as questions about salvation, which may then be considered and resolved in common by laity and clergy; likewise, they are to support the apostolic and missionary initiative of the parish."[8]

The laity are necessary to the effectiveness of the parish. Without contact and cooperation, the clergy knows nothing of the cares and problems of the Church. "In fact, this knowledge is the necessary basis for effective preaching and pastoral care; this alone would be a rich enough fruit of this contact and dialogue between laity and pastors, even on the parish level."[9] The laity are not being asked to take over the roles and duties and responsibilities of the clergy. The laity are being asked to enable the clergy to do their jobs by cooperating with them and contacting them concerning the proper content of their pastoral action.

The proper content of pastoral action for the laity lies within their daily lives. They have an apostolate to the family. The apostolate of the married laity is "to give clear proof in their own lives of the indissolubility and holiness of the marriage bond; to assert with vigor the right and duty of parents and guardians to give their children a Christian upbringing; to defend the dignity and legitimate automony of the family."[10] The Fathers declare that this is the "most

[7]Flannery, p. 777.

[8]Klosterman, p. 336.

[9]Klosterman, p. 337.

[10]Flannery, pp. 778-779

important aspect of their apostolate."[11] The Christian laity who remain dedicated to the Christian life within the family bear witness to their faith to the rest of the world. Through their families, they sanctify and renew the world. They give example to their neighbors as well as raising their children in faith. Both of these activities renew and sanctify.

The other pastoral action proper to the laity is the apostolate of like-towards-like. "It is a fact that many men cannot hear the Gospel and come to acknowledge Christ except through the laymen they associate with."[12] The laity are the Word of God, living and active in the world. Through baptism, their responsibility is to be the living Gospel.

The Fathers are very strong in their exhortation to this apostolate.

> The apostolate in one's social environment endeavors to infuse the Christian spirit into the mentality and behavior, laws and structures of the community in which one lives. To such a degree is it the special work and responsibility of lay people, that no one else can ever properly supply for them... It is amid the surroundings of their work that they are best qualified to be of help to their brothers, in the surroundings of their profession, of their study, residence, leisure or local group.[13]

No one can do this but the laity. The clergy no matter how hard they try cannot provide the day-to-day sanctification of the neighborhood, school, business community, playground. It is the role of the laity and the laity alone. If the laity does not do it, it simply will not be done.

Activity of the Laity Since Vatican II

The evolution of the activity of the laity since Vatican II

[11]Flannery, p. 779.
[12]Flannery, pp. 781-782
[13]Flannery, p. 781

has been very positive.[14] The Church has witnessed a great expansion in the participation of the laity in communities. Programs of spiritual and educational renewal have developed around the country. New and increased opportunities for lay involvement in the Church have been seen for both the 'professional' and nonprofessional laity.

The parish without a parish council and board of education is now the exception. These councils are composed primarily of laity. Their charge is that described in the *Decree on the Apostolate of the Laity* with respect to church communities. Through these organizations, they make known to the Church the problems facing the people of the parish and they work with the clergy to address the issues. This, of course, does not happen with all parish councils or boards of education. It is the ideal, the goal. Yet it does take place in a remarkable number of places. This cooperation occurs much more frequently now than ever before. Diocesan pastoral councils and boards of education have grown in lay participation. Their duty, at the diocesan level, is similar to the parish council and board of education at the parish level.

The past twenty years have brought an increase in lay involvement in liturgies, especially the Eucharistic liturgy. The great majority of parishes throughout this country now have lay men and women as extraordinary ministers of communion. Laity are involved regularly as lectors and commentators at Mass. Worship commissions now seek the input of the laity. They seek to know what the issues and problems are in the lives of the people, so that those may be addressed. Once again, this is not always done well either by the clergy or the laity, but it is the goal in most parishes to make it happen better.

Another interesting phenomenon has occured since the Council. Something called 'lay ministry' has developed. 'Lay ministry' seems to refer to practically anything that is done in the name of the Church by the laity. Depending, of

[14]For an annotated listing of some major events and some post-concilliar documents, see Appendix II.

course, upon who uses the term, it may mean anything from taking communion to shut-ins to volunteering to work in the school cafeteria. Programs designed to encourage, support and train lay ministers have been developed in different places around the country. The Archdiocese of Cincinnati, for example, has a Lay Pastoral Ministry Program. This program is designed to train laity for pastoral positions in parishes. Courses are taught in the evenings, at the diocesan seminary. The program normally leads to a master's degree.

The laity have responded to the events of Vatican II by seeking programs of spiritual and educational renewal within their parishes. Many parishes are attempting to design adult education courses. Bible study groups have been born around the country at the parish or neighborhood level. These are not always the best, but they do illustrate the efforts of the laity to train themselves if the clergy is unable or unwilling to assume that responsibility. There are many programs that have been designed that are available now for parishes to use in adult education. The *Journey* program of biblical study is one such example.[15] It is designed in such a way that it can be used with a bare minimum of clergy involvement.

Spiritual renewal has grown tremendously since the Council. Such programs as *Genesis II, Romans VIII, Christ Renews His Parish* and *Renew* have been used in a large number of parishes throughout the country. Many times these programs have been very successful in building unity and identity within the parish. They attempt to encourage the laity to take a greater role in their communities.

These spiritual and educational programs are not always successful. Nor, do they always have immediate and obvious results in increasing the sanctity of the Christian. Yet the programs do lead to evangelization. Building the faith and understanding of the Christian faithful helps them to live their lives in a more Christian way. They become the leaven in the world. An increased understanding of the

[15]The *Journey* Program's copyrighted by The Divine Word International Centre of Religious Education, London, Ontario.

responsibilities of the Christian life and a deepened spirituality leads, however circuitously, to an increase of the apostolate of like-towards-like.

Beyond the opportunities of the past years for parish-based adult education and in lay ministry training programs, the laity have found new avenues opened for them. Seminary courses and religious and theological education that used to be difficult to find, at best, are now open to the laity. There has been an increase in the numbers of lay theologians—both men and women. These 'professional' laity now find more opportunities at all levels. The laity are finding many more openings for them as pastoral ministers in parishes, directors of religious education, parochial school administrators, in diocesan offices and in Catholic universities. Laity, now more than ever before, are able to find jobs in the Church.

ONE SERIOUS QUESTION

There are problems distinctive to the laity amid all of this good. Some of these are new problems, the results of events since Vatican II. Some are old problems still present. The question may be asked: "Have the laity seen 'what priests do' as the apostolate and, therefore, sought to make their own apostolate center on sacramental activities?" A corollary is; "Is the proliferation of 'lay ministry' another form of clericalism?"

For such a long time, the only people in the Church seen as ministers were priests. Asked what priests do, most people give answers based upon the administration of the sacraments with the additions of visiting hospitals, nursing homes, shut-ins. If one considers the location of the greatest increases in lay involvement since Vatican II, one notices that these surround the administration of the sacraments— lay ministers at Mass, etc.—visiting hospitals, nursing homes, shut-ins and taking on the roles of parish pastoral ministers. All of these were traditional clergy roles.

The taking over of traditional clergy roles by the laity has been a great boon to pastoral ministry on a parish level.

Many more people have been ministered to than ever would have been. Many lay people do better jobs of ministering in certain situations than clergy could do. The growing involvement of the laity has been essential and beneficial for the growth of the American Church in the years since Vatican II.

One does wonder, however, if the attitude has developed that unless one is exercising one's apostolate by performing a formerly clerical role then one is not exercising one's apostolate. If this attitude has developed, then the *Decree on the Apostolate of the Laity* has failed. The apostolate within church communities is one small portion of the apostolate of the laity. The greatest challenges and the portions of the apostolate that can be exercised by no one *other than* the laity are those that are in the world—the apostolate to the family, to neighbors, to co-workers, that is, "the apostolate of like-towards-like."

How often has the following statement been uttered by clergy and laity alike: "he's not much of a Catholic; he never does anything for the church; he only goes to Mass on Sundays!" Perhaps this mythical person is exercising his apostolate in a much stronger way in his family and in his workplace than the president of the parish council who is also a lay minister of the Eucharist and a tireless CCD teacher. Yet the mythical person is not given encouragement and support for the exercise of the apostolate to the family and the apostolate of like-toward-like.

Neither clergy nor laity actively and consistently encourage other forms of 'lay ministry.' Laity are encouraged to work within the church community, sometimes to the detriment of the other forms of the apostolate. It is not too unusual to find examples of parish involvement actually stifling the development of the family through an abundance of programs for the laity. Consider a family of four people actively involved in their parish's programs. If each one of the members is involved in only one parish activity, the week becomes punctuated with absences. The father may be involved with *Christ Renews His Parish.* He is absent one evening each week. The mother may be involved with adult education. She is absent a different evening each week. One child may be involved in parish sponsored sports, thus being absent from the family several times each week. The other child may be a member of the youth group —another evening during the week. Everything must occur at different times so that everyone can do everything. Is the parish really strengthening the family in this way?

One other example may help to illustrate the inclination of clergy and laity alike to discourage the apostolate to the family and of like-towards-like for the apostolate within the parish community. A public school teacher, a young woman in her late twenties, comes to see a priest. She tells him that she wants to be more involved in her religion. What does the priest suggest? He probably asks her if she would like to be a lector or distributor at Mass, or a CCD teacher, because of her teaching experience. He may become even more creative and ask her to work on a particular project that the parish is sponsoring. Or, perhaps, he will ask her to serve on a committee. This is not to be overly critical of the clergy; the majority of the laity would suggest the same activities.

All of the suggested activities are good things and the school teacher might well enjoy doing one or all of them. However, in answering her request for guidance in this way, the apostolate of the laity is not being properly represented. The response encourages a division between religion and world. It also precludes her seeing her secular teaching as apostolic.

What should the priest have said? To be true to the *Decree on the Apostolate of the Laity,* he should have discussed with the teacher the meaning of the apostolate to the family. He could have gone on to show her how her teaching in a secular school could be a genuine and fulfilling exercise of the apostolate. He might have suggested that she might want to do something in the parish as well — good CCD teachers being hard to find!

It is certainly much more difficult to guide and encourage someone to exercise the apostolate in the family or the apostolate of like-towards-like. Neither clergy nor laity have been trained to see this. Perhaps it is the most important aspect of the Council's document, though, because it concerns an apostolate that cannot be exercised by anyone other than the laity. The clergy simply cannot do it. And, a clericalized laity does not have the time, encouragement or support to do it.

Conclusion

The distinctive apostolate of the laity is the apostolate of one business executive to another within the work place. It is an apostolate not of preaching but of example. The distinctive apostolate of a mother and a father to a child is an apostolate of guidance. Until clergy and laity alike can realize the value of this apostolate, the Church will remain mired in an institutionalized format that has lost meaning for so many. Once the laity are encourage to exercise this apostolate, the Church will become more and more a personalized community of faith that is once again viable.

APPENDIX I

An Outline of the Decree

I. Introduction

II. The Vocation of Lay People to the Apostolate
  A. Participation of Laity in the Church's Mission
  B. Foundations of the Lay Apostolate — Baptism and Confirmation
  C. The Spirituality of Lay People

III. Objectives — Evangelization/Sanctification/Renewal of Temporal Order
  A. The Apostolate of Evangelization and Sanctification

B. The Renewal of the Temporal Order
C. Charitable Works and Social Aid

IV. The Various Fields of the Apostolate
   A. Church Communities
   B. The Family
   C. Young People
   D. The Apostolate of Like-Towards-Like
   E. National and International Levels

V. The Different Forms of the Apostolate
   A. Individual Apostolate
   B. Group Apostolate
   C. Catholic Action

VI. The Order to be Observed
   A. Relations with the Hierarchy
   B. Relations with Clergy and with Religious
   C. Special Councils
   D. Cooperation with Other Christians and Non-Christians

VII. Training for the Apostolate
   A. The Need for Training
   B. Principles of Training
   C. Those who Train Others for the Apostolate
   D. Fields Calling for Specialized Training
   E. Aids to Training

VIII. Exhortation

Promulgated on November 18, 1965

APPENDIX II

The following is a list of some events and Church documents concerning the laity since November 18, 1965. The references, in parenthesis following the entry are to specific years and pages in Felician A. Foy, O.F.M., editor, *The National Catholic Almanac* (Paterson, New Jersey: St. Anthony's

Guild). This list does not claim to be complete. There are probably some events of much greater importance than some that are included.

November 18, 1965 — An ecumenical Council for the first time in history voted to promulgate a decree dealing exclusively with the nature, character and duties of laymen and their active role in the Church's mission. (1966, p. 120).

May 20-23, 1966 — Archbishop Paul J. Hallinan calls the First Congress of the Laity of the Archdiocese of Atlanta. (1967, p. 69).

April 2, 1967 — 1500 people attended the First Meeting of the Chicago Conference of Laymen. They requested greater lay participation in the Archdiocese of Chicago. (1968, p. 64).

April 14-20, 1967 — Council of Laity held its first plenary meeting in Rome. (1968, p. 64).

October 11-18, 1967 — Over 2000 delegates, observers and experts attended the Third World Congress of the Lay Apostolate in Rome. The theme of the Congress was "God's People on Man's Journey." 30 delegates and 20 experts were from the United States. (1968, p. 107).

December 27, 1967 — 6000 people attended Pope Paul VI's general audience in St. Peter's Basilica. The Pope said "every Catholic layman can and must be active within the Church." (1969, p. 51).

January 3, 1968 — Pope Paul VI, at a general audience, said, the Church has "demonstrated that she puts her confidence precisely in the apostolate of the lay faithful for the renewal of the awareness and of the efficiency of her mission in our time." (1969, p. 51).

January 11, 1968 — "The Church in our Day" is released as a collective pastoral letter of the bishops of the United States. Section I of Chapter II concerns the laity. (1969, p. 132).

July 29, 1968 — Pope Paul VI releases the encyclical *Humanae Vitae*. (1969, p. 97).

November 15, 1968 — The bishops of the United States release "Human Life in Our Day." (1969, p. 112).

April 30, 1970 — Document on Mixed Marriages released. (1971, p. 278).

July, 1970 — Msgr. Marcel Uylenbroeck, head of the Vatican Council of the Laity, said that laity who expect clergy to speak out on every world problem are not proud or aware enough of their own role in the Church. (1971, p. 87).

August, 1970 — National Office of Black Catholics Established. (1971, p. 89).

October 14, 1970 — Plan approved to form a Natinal Council of Catholic Laity which would merge the National Council of Catholic Women and the National Council of Catholic Men. (1971, p. 127).

December, 1972 — The National Conference of Catholic Bishops issues "Theological Reflections on the Ordination of Women." (1974, p. 117).

January 29, 1973 — *Immensae Caritatis* ("Instruction on Facilitationg Sacramental Communion in Particular Circumstances") approved by Pope Paul VI. It set norms for allowing extraordinary ministers for the distribution of communion. (1974, p. 133).

March 11, 1973 — Terence Cardinal Cooke instituted 213 lay persons as extraordinary ministers of communion at St. Patrick's Cathedral, New York. (1974, p. 74).

April, 1974 — National Coalition of American Nuns issued a study paper disagreeing with the NCCB's conclusions in "Theological Reflections on the Ordination of Women." (1974, p. 118).

May 3, 1973 — Pope Paul VI established a temporary commission to study the role of women in the Church and in society. (1974, p. 117).

July, 1973 — Joint Committee of Organizations Concerned with the Status of Women in the Church issued a paper saying that the NCCB conclusions in "Theological Reflections on the Ordination of Women" were invalid. (1974, p. 118).

November 12-16, 1973 — The bishops of the United States at a national NCCB meeting in Washington agreed by a large majority to seek Vatican permission to establish two new lay ministries open to both men and women — ministry of religious education and ministry of music. (1975, p. 504).

July 4, 1974 — NCCB issued "A Review of the Principle Trends in the Life of the Catholic Church in the United States." The major theme was the tension between secularism/humanism and Christianity. (1975, p. 114).

September 25, 1974 — Department of Social Development, USCC issued "Development-Dependency: The Role of Multinational Corporations." (1975, p. 147).

October 21-23, 1976 — The Call to Action Conference met in Detroit. It was designed to lay out lines for a five year pastoral and social action program for the Church in the United States. (1978, p. 118).

November 8-11, 1976 — NCCB national meeting, Washington. Archbishop Jean Jadot said that in the face of the priest shortage greater responsibilities should be given to lay persons.

— The bishops approved "To Live in Christ Jesus," a pastoral letter reaffirming the Church's traditional moral values on family and sexuality; nation; and, community of nations. (1978, p. 516).

January 27, 1977 — Congregation for the Doctrine of the Faith released "Declaration on the Question of the Admission of Women to the Ministerial Priesthood."(1978, p. 139).

March 17, 1977 — Pope Paul VI, in an address to French

bishops at the Vatican, declared that lay ministries are no substitutes for priestly ministries. (1978, p. 69).

May 3-5, 1977 — NCCB national meeting, Chicago. The bishops voted to ask the Holy See to rescind the penalty of automatic excommunication with respect to divorced and remarried Catholics. (1978, p. 517).

May 19, 1977 — NCCB responded to Call to Action Conference by setting up a committee to develop the five year plan of action in consultation with other NCCB and USCC committees. (1978, p. 118).

September 7-9, 1977 — A meeting of lay ministry coordinators was held in Philadelphia. They agreed upon the need to raise awareness of lay persons about their distinctive ministry. (1978, p. 130).

November 4, 1977 — Archbishop Jean Jadot announced that Pope Paul VI had lifted the automatic excommunication for divorced and remarried Catholics. (1979, p. 95).

November 14-17, 1977 — NCCB national meeting, Washington. The bishops received a report from the Ad Hoc Committee on the Role of Women in Society and the Church which said that women are becoming more involved in decision-making positions in the Church. (1979, p. 516).

December 12, 1977 — A group of 47 Catholics of the Chicago area issued "On Devaluing the Laity." They saw too much emphasis on ministry within the Church and not enough on ministry to the world. (1979, p. 84).

December 9, 1978 — The theme of the 1980 Synod of Bishops was announced as "The Duties of the Christian Family in the Contemporary World." (1980, p. 103).

March 4, 1979 — Pope John Paul II released his first encyclical, *Redemptor Hominis.* (1980, p. 75).

May 1-3, 1979 — NCCB national meeting, Chicago. It was announced that a petition signed by 13,000 people challenging the "Declaration on the Question of the Admission of Women to the Ministerial Priesthood" had been received and was being forwarded to the Vatican without endorsement. (1980, p. 526).

October 1, 1979 — Homily of Pope John Paul II in Limerick said that the specific role of the laity is to express the Gospel in their lives and thereby to insert the Gospel as a leaven into the reality of the world in which they live. (1980, p. 67).

May 7, 1980 — Pope John Paul II, at a Mass in Nairobi, said that the laity are called by God to be involved in the world in order to transform it according to the Gospel. (1981, p. 48).

November 13, 1980 — NCCB approved "Called and Gifted: The American Catholic Laity." (1982, p. 59).

The De-Clericalization of
The U.S. Church

Jon Nilson

In 1889, Archbishop John Ireland addressed these ring-
ing words to the delegates of a National Lay Catholic Congress in Baltimore:

> Go back and say to your fellow Catholics that there is a
> departure among the Catholics of the United States. Tell
> them that heretofore, so to speak, you have done but
> little, but that henceforth you are going to do great
> things. Tell them that there is a mission open to laymen
> ...As one of your Bishops I am ashamed of myself that I
> was not conscious before this of the power existing in the
> midst of the laity and that I have not done anything to
> bring it out... With God's help... I shall do all I can to
> bring out this power.

As plans were being made for another Congress in 1893,
however, James Cardinal Gibbons wrote to Ireland as
follows:

With regard to the Congress, we must act with caution. Any overt attempt on your or my part to suppress it would raise a hue and cry, and the worst motives would be ascribed to us. The best plan is to enjoin on Onahan and our friends a passive attitude that little or nothing should be done to advance the Congress till our meeting in October, and then we would try to kill it, or failing that, to determine that this should be the last Congress.[1]

Anecdotes like this help to demolish two impressions that might easily be gained by reading Vatican II's *Decree on the Apostolate of the Laity.* The first is that the clergy will always welcome the laity's seeking and taking a more active role in the Church. The second is that Vatican II discovered the dignity and importance of the laity.

It seems that a vital, committed laity would be heartening to bishops and priests. Such a laity would be living proof that the pastors had carried out their commission faithfully and well. The *Decree on the Pastoral Office of Bishops* says that the bishop "should ensure that the faithful are duly involved in Church affairs; he should recognize their right and duty to play their part in building up the Mystical Body of Christ" (16). The *Decree on the Ministry and Life of Priests* states that "Priests should also be confident in giving lay people charge of duties in the service of the Church, giving them freedom and opportunity for activity and even inviting them, when opportunity occurs, to take the initiative in undertaking projects of their own" (9). The theological grounds for these exhortations can be found in chapters 2, 4, and 5 of the Constitution on the Church; in the whole of the *Decree on the Apostolate of the Laity;* and in the *Constitution on the Church in the Modern World.*

These statements can and should be understood as a call for an end to any clerical monopolies on the Church's mission and functions. They summon lay people to meet their responsibilities as baptized Catholics. They challenge

[1]See James Hennesey, *American Catholics.* New York: Oxford, 1983. Pp. 190-191.

the clergy to exchange control for mutuality, predominance for community. Given the strongly hierarchical self-understanding and practice of the pre-Vatican II Church, it is surprising that such strong affirmations and legitimations of the lay role in the Church have engendered relatively little tension and conflict. To be sure, there are horror stories aplenty about Fr. Clyde Arrogant's obsession for control and Mr. Jack Charisma's notion that his election to the parish council conferred upon him an infallibility only a little less than the Pope's. Nonetheless, schism (the time-honored way for Christians to deal with irreconcilable differences) is just a word in the history books so far.

The reason is simple. Vatican II created expectations that might have led to schism if it had not also created "valves" that prevented pressures from building up. Among these, the most effective were the recognitions that the Church of Christ was far more extensive than the Roman Catholic Church and that God's saving love is at work outside the formal boundaries of Catholicism.[2] In effect, says Vatican II, the institutional Church is not the absolutely indispensable medium of an intimate relationship with God. Explicit membership in it is not a necessary condition for salvation. "Extra ecclesiam, nulla salus (Outside the Church, there is no salvation)" was put into theological cold storage. This meant that the stakes and consequences of disagreements within the Church were no longer ultimate. The necessity of staying in the Church at all costs evaporated. Now one could "hang loose" or even "opt out" of the Church without fear of losing God's love and imperilling one's eternal salvation. In short, the Council relativized the Church so that the rending conflicts one might have expected between clergy and laity never materialized.

Vatican II neither created nor discovered an active, committed laity for the Church in the United States. The history of Catholicism in this country includes the names and accomplishments of many great lay people. Yet, in contrast

---

[2] Dogmatic Constitution on the Church, 8, 15-16; Pastoral Constitution on the Church in the Modern World, 16 et al.

to the entire number of lay Catholics, these were few and extraordinary. For example, the moving spirits behind the Baltimore Congress of 1889 were hardly typical of the average lay person of their time. Henry F. Brownson was the son of Orestes A. Brownson, one of the most influential Catholics of the nineteenth century. Another, William J. Onahan, was an immigrant who, nonetheless, became extraordinarily prominent socially and politically as well as religiously. The typical lay Catholic was an immigrant or the child of immigrants who had fled the famines in Ireland or the revolutionary upheavals in Europe. From 1870 to 1900, the Catholic population of the United States jumped from 4.5 to 12 million. Without skills or education, the Catholic immigrants were admitted as source of cheap labor for the farmlands and burgeoning factories of the post-Civil War era. Few of these Catholics had the background or free time necessary to take a very active role in Church affairs.

Soon, however, Catholics were moving up the social ladder. Its rungs were the "local mediating institutions: the family, the union, the school, the corporation, the local bank or credit union, the community organization, the parish."[3] The victories of organized labor during the New Deal years moved a large number of Catholics into the middle class.[4] By 1952, well over two million Catholic veterans of World War II had taken advantage of educational opportunities afforded by the "GI Bill of Rights."[5] The election of John F. Kennedy to the presidency in 1960 seemed to many the final, decisive proof that Catholics were no longer second class citizens. They had arrived.

So Vatican II's affirmations of the dignity and role of the laity did not come as a revelation to Catholics in the United States. Rather, it confirmed the validity of their experience of themselves. By 1960, many of them had already invested years in organizations like the Christian Family Movement,

[3]William M. Droel, "Northern Liberation Theology," *America*. Jan. 26, 1985. p. 59.

[4]Hennesey, *op. cit.*, 283.

[5]This is based on statistics given in Hennesey, pp. 278 and 283.

the Catholic Interracial Council, Young Christian Students, Young Christian Workers, the Catholic Youth Organization, Friendship House, and the Catholic Worker Movement. By 1960, many Catholics had educations which made them the intellectual peers of their clergy. By 1960, Catholics were beginning to think of their role in the Church in terms of ideals like fundamental equality among people and inalienable human rights which they had absorbed from their experience as citizens of the United States. Vatican II provided the theological validation for what they had already learned from their own experience about their roles, rights, and responsibilities in and for the Church.

And not a moment too soon. The Council's charter and justification for lay involvement in the Church came precisely when the numbers of ordained ministers and religious began to decline precipitously. To claim that the Council, its theology, and its impact caused the hemorrhage of men from the priesthood and women from the religious life would surely be simplistic. Yet it would also be unrealistic to pretend that Vatican II was not a major factor. In the ten years following its close, an estimated 10,000 priests left the ministry. There were 49,000 seminarians in 1965; by 1978, there were a little over 11, 000. Religious orders of women lost almost 30% of their members from 1966 to 1979.

The future is not much brighter. According to Richard Schoenherr's major study on the priesthood in the United States, the highest possible number of diocesan priests in the year 2000 will be 22,000. The lowest projection is 12,000. We can most realistically expect between 16,000 and 18,000 priests which is about 50% less than the number of diocesan priests in 1970. If the Roman Catholic population remains stable, this would allow one priest for every 3,000 people. Today, there is one for every 880. Schoenherr's remark verges on understatement, "This represents an organizational crisis of huge proportions."[6]

These statistics might yet be cited in the book-length

[6]Lecture by Richard Schoenherr to the Institute of Pastoral Studies, Loyola University of Chicago, July 16, 1984.

obituaries that will be written at the death of the Church in the United States. But it is still quite vigorous because many of the tasks heretofore done by priests and sisters have been taken over by the laity. The first published findings of the Notre Dame Study of Catholic Parish Life show that, with the exception of the pastor, 83% of the leadership in parishes is now lay. Well over half the parish staff with responsibilities for important programs are lay people. Lay people comprise 94% of the unpaid leadership of the parishes. In over one-third of U.S. parishes, pastor and laity share the leadership. A major conclusion of the Notre Dame Study is: "The decline of Church vocations and the limited supply of priests and sisters have certainly contributed to the changing patterns of responsibility for parish ministries. Into that vocation gap the laity have apparently stepped."[1]

Besides parish-based lay ministerial activity, there is also the post-Council phenomenon of organizations similar in conception to the Peace Corps and VISTA. The Jesuit Volunteer Corps is an example. With about 500 members, it is the largest organization of its kind in the U.S. Church. Most of the volunteers are in their 20's and recent college graduates. They are assigned to jobs for which they express a preference and they live in small communities with four or five other volunteers. Most of their $280 monthly salary is put into a common fund to pay rent, buy food, etc. They have $75 per month to spend as they wish. Most of their work is educational or community-organizing in nature.

While the numbers of laity now actively involved in the Church's mission are encouraging for the short term, there are reasons to be concerned about the long range impact of "de-clericalization." Most of the laity now active in ministry are volunteers, so they work for the Church on a part-time basis. They invest the greater part of their time and energy in their family lives and jobs. At best, ministry is third on the list of priorities. Lay people who do ministry full-time are

[1]David C. Leege and Joseph Gremillion, "The U.S. Parish Twenty Years After Vatican II: an Introduction to the Study," Report #1. University of Notre Dame. Privately printed and circulated. p. 9.

usually paid just enough to maintain themselves alone in spartan conditions. They certainly cannot support a family on their salary. So the full-time lay ministers tend to be young, single people between the end of their formal education and the beginning of marriage and parenthood. Their commitment to ministry in the Church is necessarily temporary and short-term.

Compared to the preparation of a priest or sister, lay ministerial training is almost negligible. A priest has spent a minimum of four years in theological studies and pastoral training beyond the baccalaureate degree; in addition, many of these have spent a year or two in a novitiate or formation program. The commitment of religious women to their own formation and education is undeniable; fully 65% of them hold master's degrees. Contrast these backgrounds to the ministerial preparation received by a typical lay minister and you get an image of a sincere, well-intentioned, enthusiastic, and committed individual who is, nonetheless, getting "on the job" training and proceeding largely by trial and error.

These are people whose awareness of human need and whose generosity in responding to it are extraordinary. Yet these same people are all too often ignorant of the theological grounds and principles of ministry in the Church and unaware of the traditions and history which help to constitute Christianity as a distinct form of religion and Roman Catholicism as a distinctive form of Christianity. Consequently, these resources which are replete with inspiration and wisdom and nourishment are just not available to the lay ministers. Their words and activities cannot be measured, shaped, and deepened in distinctively Catholic ways simply because they have not been sufficiently tutored or become sufficiently experienced in these Catholic ways.

To the extent that ministry in the believing community is lay under the present circumstances, the community becomes like a sailing ship without ballast. It may move quickly and respond instantly to each change in the wind but it is very difficult to keep it on course.

The current situation also leaves the Church in the hands

of ordained ministers who, as a group, are getting older and more and more conservative.[8] Granted, all the baptized are the Church. But Roman Catholicism has a distinctive, well defined structure. Like any institution, those who give the most time to it can have the most influence upon it. A part-time volunteer or a full-time but temporary minister may have a dramatic impact around the edges but the center can be changed only by those who have the patience, time, and commitment to reach it. Key decisions, such as the use of physical resources, allocation of personnel, and budget priorities, will continue to be made by the celibate clergy, whose number is shrinking and whose average age is rising. Ministry widely defined may continue to flourish as more and more laity take it up. Yet it will be a face-to-face, one-on-one type of ministry. Administration and control of the institution will remain clerical. It is not surprising that the Notre Dame Study contains good news and bad news on this point. The good news is that 75% of U.S. parishes have parish councils. The bad news is that less than 5% of the pastors name the parish council as one of the five main influences on the life of the parish.[9]

Thus, the Roman Catholic Church of the future looks like a tree whose sapwood is alive and vibrant on the outer edges of the trunk but whose heartwood is dry and crumbling. Yet even this image may be too optimistic, since nourishment to the sapwood is slowly being choked off. From the Constitution on the Sacred Liturgy we know that in both theory and practice, "the liturgy is the summit toward which the activity of the Church is directed; it is also the fount from which all her power flows." (10) So the Church of the future may be marked by a high level of lay involvement,[10] but how Catholic will this involvement be without a sufficient number of ordained presiders to make the celebration of the Eucharist readily accessible? Will the future bring a hybrid

[8]Schoenherr, *op. cit.*

[9]Leege and Gremillion, *op. cit.*, p. 9.

[10]"Almost half of the respondents in our Phase II sample are participating in one or more parish activities beyond Mass." Leege and Gremillion, *op. cit.*, p. 10.

form of Catholicism whose focus is, instead, the Bible and the prayer group? Already the distinctive riches and benefits of the Catholic tradition of Christianity are slowly being dissipated. The axiom, "the way you pray is the way you believe" admits no exceptions.

In short, if we assume that all the factors in our current situation remain the same (which, given the Holy Spirit's sense of humor, may be an utterly unfounded assumption) the long range effect of de-clericalization on the U.S. Church promises to be debilitating. Its authentic vitality is being sapped as it is increasingly deprived of the Eucharist. Its depth and distinctiveness evaporate as its theological and spiritual traditions become *terra incognita* to the majority of its ministers.

The Church in the United States needs to make celibacy optional for ordained ministers in order to obtain sufficient numbers to meet the Eucharistic needs of its people. It needs to require intensive theological and pastoral education for candidates for ministry so that it can draw upon the wisdom of its traditions in meeting the challenges and problems of its mission. This is not a call for re-clericalizing the Church. The Eucharistic ministry of married presbyters and the well grounded ministry of lay people are not likely to take over the Church and introduce a new kind of clerical culture. Rather, they will form living links between the Church and all those sectors of human life which need the light of the Gospel so urgently.

Declaration on Religious Liberty
Dignitatis Humanae, 7 December, 1965

John E. Linnan, C.S.V.

Introduction

As John Courtney Murray, *peritus* at the Council, and perhaps the strongest theological proponent of religious freedom in the Church, wrote:

> It can hardly be maintained that the Declaration is a milestone in human history — moral, political, or intellectual. The principle of religious freedom has long been recognized in constitutional law, to the point where even Marxist-Leninist political ideology is obliged to pay lip-service to it. In all honesty, it must be admitted that the Church is late in acknowledging the validity of principle.[1]

The document's significance lies first and foremost in the

[1]Abbott, Walter. M., S.J. (ed.) *The Documents of Vatican II*, Guild Press, N. Y. 1966, p. 673

fact that at long last the Church did solemnly recognize that "the dignity of the human person consists in his responsible use of freedom."[2] Secondly, at another level entirely, the declaration not only raised the issue of doctrinal development, but was in itself an exercise in this development, authenticated by the Council itself. In this sense it has theological impact which goes far beyond the subject matter of the decree. For these two reasons alone, the *Declaration on Religious Liberty* deserves to be reconsidered in the light of the Church's experience since the decree was promulgated on the day before the Council closed, December 7, 1965.

History of the Declaration

This declaration began its life in 1962 as Chapter IX of the schema of the *Constitution on the Church*. The chapter was entitled "On Relations between Church and State, or on Religious Tolerance." Its teaching was that which has been considered "traditional" for a millenium. In principle all must embrace the true faith, and the civil society through its authorities must promote that faith alone, and publicly participate in its cult. However, on the hypothesis that there are those who do not accept the true faith, while they do not enjoy *the right* to profess another religion, the State may, for the sake of the common good and public peace, tolerate their profession of a false religion. This is the "thesis/hypothesis" teaching on the relationship between Church and State. There was such dissatisfaction with this approach that the section was later removed from the Constitution on the Church.

At the same time, the Secretariat for the Promotion of Christian Unity was also preparing a text on the relations between Church and State. The competence of the Secretariat to deal with this matter was first denied. In October,

[2]Ibid., P. 674

1962 Pope John XXIII recognized the Secretariat's competence to submit drafts to the Council. The first draft of the declaration was submitted to the Council as Chapter V of the Decree on Ecumenism in November, 1963. It was discussed briefly, but detailed discussion was left to the second and third sessions. Suggestions and emendations amounted to 280 pages. But the major change was the decision in April, 1963, to propose a separate declaration on religious liberty.

A second draft of the declaration was presented in April, 1964, and a third draft was presented in November of the same year. No vote was taken. The decree was perhaps the most controversial document presented to the Council. The fourth draft was presented in May, 1965 and was discussed by the Council in September of the same year. The arguments surrounding it were heated. The first vote to approve the direction of the declaration was taken on September 20, 1965. The direction was approved by 90% of the Council. A fifth amended text was approved article by article on October 26 and 27. While receiving overall approval, a significant number of fathers continued to vote negatively, and close to a quarter voted positively but with reservations. It was on December 7, 1965 that the final text (a sixth draft) was approved by 2,308 votes. Seventy voted against the declaration.

The opposition to the declaration was strong and vocal, though perhaps not as numerous as opponents suggested. Major objections centered around the following six issues: 1) abandonment of the "traditional" thesis/hypothesis doctrine; 2) the question of development in doctrine; 3) fear that the Church would lose status; 4) the lack of clear evidence that the declaration was supported in Scripture; 5) fear that the declaration promoted religious indifferentism; 6) concern that it would enhance the power of the State *vis-à-vis* the Church.

The Teaching of the Declaration on Religious Liberty

The Declaration is composed of a prefatory article; two chapters: Chapter I, *The General Principle of Religious Freedom* (Arts. 2-8) and Chapter II, *Religious Freedom in the Light of Revelation* (Arts. 9-14); and a final article on religious freedom in the current situation (1965).

In a very real sense the first article of the declaration is a solemn pronouncement which asserts four things:
1) that the right to freedom in religious matters, freedom from psychological and external coercion, and freedom to seek truth, embrace it, adhere to it, and act on it, *inheres in each man and women by reason of his/her dignity as a person* endowed with reason and free will and therefore endowed with conscience and personal responsibility;
2) that all men and women are impelled by nature and morally obligated to seek the truth and adhere to it;
3) that while Catholics believe that in Jesus and his Church God has made known the true religion, this truth, like all others, can impose itself on the human mind only in virtue of its own truthfulness;
4) that the Council in making this declaration intends *to develop* the teaching of the recent popes on the inviolable rights of the human person and on the constitutional order of society.

Theological Argument

Chapter I contains a closely argued presentation of this right to religious freedom, its ground in the nature of the human person, and the obligation of the human person to seek truth and to adhere to it once it is discovered. In this chapter the Council also insists that since the human person is inherently social, this right has a necessary social dimension which must be preserved and protected by the civil authority; and when necessary, regulated by that same authority.

The Council describes persons, as "beings endowed with

reason and free will and therefore bearing personal responsibility." (2) It argues that the right to religious freedom is grounded in the two-fold obligation of all human beings, given their nature as rational and free, to seek the truth and to seek to do that which is in accord with the truth. Human beings are "both impelled by their nature and bound by moral obligation to seek the truth, especially religious truth." (2) But as the Council declares, human beings "cannot satisfy this obligation in a way that is in keeping with their own nature, unless they enjoy both psychological freedom and immunity from external coercion." (2)

Truth, considered from the perspective of "the highest norm of human life," is the divine law "eternal, objective and universal, by which God orders, directs and governs the whole world and the ways of human community. . ."(3) It is by means of conscience that the human being recognizes truth as a norm of human behavior. And just as persons "must adhere to the truth they have discovered" in order to respond faithfully to their nature, so too the human being "is bound to follow his [or her] conscience faithfully in all his [or her] activity so that he [or she] may come to God, who is his [or her] last end." (3) Consequently no one can be forced to act contrary to conscience nor prevented from acting according to conscience. "The reason is because the practice of religion of its very nature consists primarily of those voluntary and free internal acts by which a man directs himself to God."

But the Council is not content merely to protect the internal acts of the individual person. The Council insists that the human person is inherently social. In the very process by which a person seeks the truth the human being is social.

> The search for truth, however, must be carried out in a manner that is appropriate to the dignity of the human person and his social nature, namely, by free enquiry with the help of teaching or instruction, communication and dialogue. It is by these means that men share with each other the truth they have discovered, or think they have

> discovered, in such a way that they help one another in the search for truth. (3)

Likewise, the social nature of the human person demands the free expression of internal commitment.

> But his own social nature requires that man give external expression to these internal acts of religion, that he communicate with others on religious matters, and profess his religion in community. Consequently to deny man the free exercise of religion in society, when the just requirements of public order are observed, is to do an injustice to the human person and to the very order established by God for men. (3)

And because private and public acts of religion are acts by which people direct themselves to God they transcend the temporal order.

> Therefore the civil authority, the purpose of which is the care of the common good in the temporal order, must recognize and look with favor on the religious life of the citizens. But if it presumes to control or restrict religious activity it must be said to have exceeded the limits of its power. (3)

In Articles 4 and 5, the Council next affirms that the subject of the right to religious freedom is not only the individual person, but religious communities and families. In discussing how this right applies to communities and families, it goes into some detail concerning the practical content of this right.

Article 6 of the Declaration is a succinct primer on the obligations of civil authority with respect to human rights. It asserts as a general principle that:

> the common good of society consists in the sum total of those conditions of social life which enable men to achieve a fuller measure of perfection with greater ease. It

consists especially in safeguarding the rights and duties of the human person. (6)

While it is the duty of all individuals, groups, religious communities, and the Church to protect the rights of all, it is especially an obligation of the civil authority. "The protection and promotion of the inviolable rights of man is an essential duty of every civil authority." (6) However, in any human society rights may be in conflict. The Council therefore considers the need to recognize that the exercise of rights is subject to regulation.

> In availing of any freedom men must respect the moral principle of personal and social responsibility: in exercising their rights individual men and social groups are bound by the moral law to have regard for the rights of others, their own duties to others and the common good of all. All men must be treated with justice and humanity. Furthermore, since civil society has the right to protect itself against possible abuses committed in the name of religious freedom the responsibility of providing such protection rests especially with the civil authority.

The Council insists that in regulating the exercise of human rights, the civil authority be guided by the principles of public peace, morality, and good order which are requisites of the common good. However, civil authority should respect "the principle of the integrity of freedom in society" and, consequently, human freedom "should be given the fullest possible recognition and should not be curtailed except when and insofar as is necessary." (7) This is a powerful principle!

The final section in this chapter is an exhortation on the part of the Council urging education for responsible freedom in the name of religious freedom itself. "Religious liberty therefore should have this further purpose and aim in enabling men to act with greater responsibility in fulfilling their own obligations in society." (8)

Revelation

In Chapter II (Articles 9-14), the Council considers this right to religious freedom from the perspective of divine revelation. The Council points out that the right to religious freedom as known from reason (Chapter I) and as known from revelation (Chapter II) does not differ with respect to the object of the right, but only with respect to origin of the knowledge of the right.

Articles 9-11 argue that while revelation does not state in so many words the right of the human person to be free of coercion in religious matters, it does affirm the almost god-like dignity of the human person in grace and the necessity that the human response to God be genuinely free.

> Man, redeemed by Christ the Saviour and called through Jesus Christ to be an adopted son of God, cannot give his adherence to God when he reveals himself unless, drawn by the Father, he submits to God with a faith that is reasonable and free. It is therefore fully in accordance with the nature of faith that in religious matters every form of coercion by men should be excluded. (10)

The Council also cites the example of Jesus, his free response to the Father and the graciousness of the invitation to believe that Christ addresses to the freedom of his disciples. From this example, the Council concludes:

> For he bore witness to the truth but refused to use force to impose it on those who spoke out against it. His kingdom does not make its claims by blows, but is established by bearing witness to and hearing the truth and grows by the love with which Christ, lifted up on the cross, draws men to himself." (11)

Finally, the Council refers to the example of the preaching of the apostles:

From the very beginnings of the Church the disciples of Christ strove to convert men to confess Christ as Lord, not however by applying coercion or with the use of techniques unworthy of the Gospel but, above all, by the power of the word of God. (11)

It is in the twelfth article of the Declaration that the Council solemnly apologizes on behalf of the Church for past failures to be faithful to the revealed truth in the matter of religious freedom:

Although in the life of the people of God in its pilgrimage through the vicissitudes of human history there has at times appeared a form of behavior which was hardly in keeping with the spirit of the Gospel and was even opposed to it, it has always remained the teaching of the Church that no one is to be coerced into believing. (12)

Perhaps to quiet the fears of those who are concerned that full freedom may indeed harm the Church, the Council insists that it is only in a truly free society that the Church can fulfill her divine mission. (13) It also reminds all who are members of the Church, that freedom of religion does not absolve them from the obligation to Christ,

to grow daily in... knowledge of truth... received from him, to be faithful in announcing it, and vigorous in defending it without having recourse to methods which are contrary to the spirit of the Gospel. (14)

In the concluding article (Article 15) of the Declaration, the Council treats of the current situation (1965) and affirms that people want to be able to profess freely their religion in private and public. This desire is a sign of the times. The Council deplores the fact that there are civil societies where freedom of religion is not possible or is unduly hindered. The Council concludes its declaration on this note:

...to establish and strengthen peaceful relations and harmony in the human race, religious freedom must be given effective constitutional protection everywhere and that highest of a human being's rights and duties — to lead a religious life with freedom in society — must be respected. (15)

The Significance of the Declaration

The primary value of the *Declaration* is that it lays down the theoretical foundations for a new charter governing relations between religious and civil authority in general, and specifically, the relations between Church and State. In this brief *Declaration* the Church returns to a healthier, more realistic, and more evangelical vision of its relationship to the civil society; — a vision it once had but lost for awhile in the glamour of its triumph in the West. Furthermore it affirms that the principles which govern Church-State relationships are accessible to human reason but are also to be found in the revelation God makes in Jesus, the Christ. Finally, this charter recognizes that what is prior to both Church and State is the dignity of the human person, which neither institution can infringe on, and which both are called into existence to foster and serve.

More specifically, the *Declaration* represents a number of important advances in the understanding on the part of the Church in the area of rights, religion, and civil authority.

First, the *Declaration* represents a significant development over the official teaching of the Church since the middle ages. Not only is there real doctrinal development here, but there is also frank acknowledgement of that development as such, and an honest confession of error in the past. Such honesty is not frequently encountered when the Church evaluates her teaching, and is all the more salutary for its infrequency.

A second advance is the clear teaching that rights inhere in persons, not in values, and that they are rooted in human dignity, not in the subjective attitudes of persons. Once and for all the Church abandons the notion that truth alone has the right to exist; error, no right at all. The right to freedom in religious matters is not lost by abuse; it is validated not by beliefs and judgments accounted to be correct, but by the very nature of the human person as endowed with reason and free-will and the personal responsibility consequent on these. The thesis/hypothesis approach to religious freedom was finally put to rest.

Thirdly, of great importance is the Council's effort to define the responsibilities of the state: the promotion of the common good and the protection and fostering of human rights, limiting the free exercise of these rights when, and only insofar as necessary to preserve a just public peace, where people live together in good order and true justice.

Fourthly, the serious endeavor of the Council to root its teaching on human freedom in religious matters in Revelation is very important. For the believing Christian it adds the sanction of God's Word to this teaching. No more can one say that natural rights can be superseded by divine revelation, as if the God of nature and the God of Jesus were not one in the same.

Fifthly, implicit in this Declaration is the notion that God may indeed have larger purposes in the divine plan than the prosperity of either Church or State as human beings may conceive of either at any given point in history. Human institutions are relativized in favor of the dignity of human persons.

And last but not least, the ecclesial experience of the Church in the United States, and the theology it derived from that experience were vindicated by the Universal Church in a variety of ways. The Council recognized and called for the constitutional recognition and legal implementation of those fundamental human rights which validate all democratic governments. The Council recognized implicitly the inherent rightness of that Church-State relationship which the American Church had long experienced and vehemently argued for during its almost two centuries of existence in the U.S. The great proponent of this Ameri-

can Catholic theology was John Courtney Murray, S.J., but
his teaching was rooted in the insights of Spalding, Ireland,
Gibbons, Carroll and many others.

What is Needed Now?

The Declaration on Religious Liberty has worn well. It
still speaks clearly of the inviolability of the rights of human
beings in the face of institutions, be they religious or civil.
Today totalitarianism, religious fanaticism, national security, the elitism of left and right, and terrorism, all threaten to
overwhelm the basic message of this *Declaration.* So the
Declaration as it stands bears repeating.

What more might be needed? Six things suggest
themselves.

1) The *Declaration's* understanding of truth seems too
static. There is need for a clearer recognition of the inherently dynamic nature of truth. We are dealing here with a
human category. The phrases, "to seek the truth, embrace it
and adhere to it," suggest a quantitative, once and for all,
character to truth. What is missing here is the awareness of
the dynamism of truth, its historicity, in a word, its elusive-
ness, always just beyond one's comprehension.

2) Advances in biblical scholarship since the Council
would suggest that a much better understanding of human
freedom in the light of revelation could be developed.

3) There is embedded in this declaration a theology of
institutions, specifically civil and ecclesial institutions. This
theology needs to be made more explicit to enunciate more
clearly the role and value of these institutions for the development of human potential. Needed, too, is a political
theology which clearly delineates the limits of institutions
with respect to human dignity, and specifies the relationship
of human freedom to the common good.

4) The vision implicit in this declaration of the world as a
community of nations needs to be developed, specifically
how this community relativizes nation states and religious
institutions.

5) The principles which require freedom from psychological intimidation and external coercion in religious matters need to be applied to life within an ecclesial community. If believing is not just an act but a process of conversion stretching over a life-time, not only must the act initiating this conversion be free, but the freedom of the person throughout this process must be assured. Even ecclesial authority is human authority, which by definition cannot infringe on the freedom of the person to seek truth through free exchange and dialogue, except when the common good of the Church requires it.

6) Finally, a closer look at what this *Declaration* says about the nature of religion, its relationship to civil society, and the obligation of civil society to enable a human freedom that envisages even freedom *from* religion might put an end to the anachronism of diplomatic relations between the Roman Catholic Church and civil governments. They demean religion and the Church, and they hinder the capacity of civil government to fulfill its duties in matters of religious freedom.

Conclusion

This brief and cursory study of the *Declaration on Religious Freedom* has tried to show that the Council made significant developments in the Church's teaching on human freedom and the relations between Church and State. The *Declaration* is rich in insights. It summarizes a healthy but unfortunately long forgotten political theory. It advances ideas that call for continual reflection and development. Its impact on the Church's relationship to the State and to other religions has been largely beneficial. It is sad, however, that the teaching of the *Declaration* has had so little impact within the Church.

Decree on the Church's Missionary Activity
Ad Gentes Divinitus, 7 December, 1965

William R. Burrows

Certainly the most memorable line of the Vatican II Decree on the Missionary Activity of the Church is that which opens its first chapter: "The Church on earth is by its very nature missionary" (2). Having known one of the decree's principal authors, Johannes Schütte, and having spoken with him about the decree, it is clear to me that it is this line which the decree's promoters wanted etched in the minds both of the council fathers and of the church at large. Each Vatican II decree, to be sure, had its interested backers and detractors, but nowhere could there have been more behind-the-scenes concern for the practical effects than in this one. Its backers believed firmly that an expansive, missionary spirit was not just one mark of the church but *the* mark.

The following paper has three parts of unequal length. Part One attempts to address factors leading to the sort of decree the council finally approved. Part Two attempts to lift out key elements in the text itself, placing special emphasis on post-conciliar implementation instructions (which have received relatively little attention in the broader theological community, and which may have special interest for us considering implications of this decree in the North American Catholic world). Part Three represents personal reflections upon matter of "mission" interest which require critical attention today.

Behind the Text

Suso Brechter, in the fourth volume of the *Commentary on the Documents of Vatican II*, [1] makes the important point that the mission decree is intelligible only in the light of the dynamics that led to the *Dogmatic Constitution on the Church* and the *Pastoral Constitution on the Church in the Modern World*. The decree reflects the victory of the promoters of a biblical-and-patristic-inspired mindset over the more legalistic and curia-dominated preparatory commissions. The decrees on the church's nature and on the church in the modern world, for their part, represent the retrieval of ancient organic mystery metaphors for church self-understanding. While institutional and legal metaphors are not abandoned, they recede from the center of attention. One can fairly ask if the mission decree has been fully successful in overcoming some of the problems created by or reflected in the functioning of the curial Congregation for the Propagation of the Faith (now often known as Congregation for the Evangelization of Peoples), but it is clear that the *intention* of the preparatory commission was precisely that of putting a solid biblical foundation under the mission work of the church.

Finally, however, a background factor in the drafting of the conciliar decree bedevils the attempt to (1) be fully biblical or (2) give us a decree which truly responds to the

[1] Herder & Herder 1969, pp. 87-181.

needs of a church which is by its very nature missionary. This backgound factor is the centrality of the concerns of the missionary congregations and orders for a mission decree which would be of service to them in carrying on the work of traditional "overseas missions". I will build my case methodically in the second and third parts of this paper. Here it is important to stress a series of events that stand behind our present text. [2] The complicating factor is this: as the mission schema evolved beyond the pre-conciliar preparatory commission's somewhat legalistic framework (and became more biblical), it also came to be influenced much more heavily by the religious orders which have carried on so much of the foreign missionary work of the church since the nineteenth century.

When the council opened on the 11th of October, 1962, the work of the preparatory commissions ceased. The Preparatory Commission for the Missions had been dominated by Roman curial personnel and academics, both of which groups tended to have ties to the Congregation for the Propagation of the Faith. The president both of the Preparatory Commission and of the Conciliar Missionary Commission was Cardinal Agagianian, but the Conciliar Commission was wider in complexion than the Preconciliar Commission had been. Its twenty-four members were almost exclusively missionary bishops belonging for the most part to the native hierarchy, and another larger representation of Latin Americans. [3] In the first session, it will be recalled, the burning issues were those concerning the liturgy. Here the "new" theology won the central battles and, paradoxically sought to retrieve freeing ancient traditions.

The Missionary Commission did not even meet once during the first session. But mission issues were not thereby absent from the council proper, for among those who were

[2]If there is interest in going more deeply into this question, the best source is the multi-volume *Acta Synodalia sacrosancti Concilii Vaticani II* (Vatican City: Vatican Polyglot Press, 1970-80). There one can trace the history of the council fathers and gain a broader and deeper appreciation of the dynamics behind the text.

[3]Brechter, p. 91

most active in criticizing the rigidity of the curia-dominated preparatory commissions (as also of the curia-dominated church as a whole) were the mission bishops who made up approximately one-third of the council fathers. Criticism of the Congregation for the Propagation of the Faith was trenchant, and crystallized round the demand that its powers of jurisdiction over mission territories be ended. Thus the ground was dug out from under the seven chapters of the Congregation-prepared pre-conciliar commission document even as other skirmishes in the biblical-patristic-liturgical areas were preparing the foundations for the mission decree adoption of the basic ecclesiology of the Church Constitution and the *Constitution on the Church in the Modern World.* Suffice it to say here that the mission decree must be read in the light of those two documents. Indeed, it became, in effect, the document which dots the i's and crosses the t's which spell out the meaning of Vatican II's ecclesiological revolution for the entities which the decree calls "missions".

In the ambiguity which surrounds the word "mission" lies the second part of the "behind the text" tale of this document. In 1963, between the council's official sessions, the Congregation's Cardinal Agagianian met with the Missionary Commission to thoroughly revise the preconciliar schema. The meetings, though, were thought to be unhelpful, since the Cardinal found it hard to preside over meetings that had as their goal the dismembering of his own Congregation. In 1964 the mission schema was still a conciliar Cinderella, but in the third session of the council Archbishop Felici announced that the schema would be voted upon and discussed. The problem was that it was an open secret that the majority of the missionary bishops flatly rejected the schema. [4] In the end it was rejected. Between the third and fourth sessions of the council it would have to be redrafted to meet the needs and objections of the missionary bishops, or the council would close without a mission statement.

[4]Brechter, p. 97

In January of 1965, meeting as guests of Johannes Schu³tte, Superior General of the Divine Word Missionaries and one of the Commission's experts, the process of re-drafting began in earnest. When the test was finished and ready to be presented in the fourth session, it was the product of two groups' concerns: (1) the mission bishops and (2) the "missionary" orders. The title of the decree was changed to the *Decree on the Church's Missionary Activity.* The ecclesiology was that of the two documents on the church. The missiology, however, was dominated by the mindset of the two ecclesiastical groups which produced the document. On the one hand, therefore, the "mission" tended to become "missions" (thus giving the document a traditional orientation which I would argue is not the only missiology derivable from the two major church constitutions. [5] While the bishops and "sending" religious orders do not have identical interests and outlooks, in fact, they are so closely related in seeking financial personnel and other assistance in North America and Europe that when they composed the mission decree they were interested in the same thing. Namely, they wanted it stated clearly and solemnly that northern hemisphere "sending" churches had an obligation to support the "receiving" mission churches generously with both personnel and financial assistance.

The point to which my argument draws us is this: *the Decree on the Church's Missionary Activity* is a magnificent step forward for the church insofar as it says clearly that the concerns we today tend to call "evangelical" and discuss under the rubric of "out-reach", express the inmost nature of the church as a whole. They are not merely the activities of specialists who go to far off places. Rather each church *is* church to the extent that it is "missionary" (for which term read "active in the evangelization process"). That point is somewhat obscured in the decree however, because the people behind the decree had traditional concern for "over-

[5]"Mission tends to speak of a total evangelization or evangelism process. "Missions" tends to connote that sort of activity under a special aspect: the activities of "missionary" orders in the Third World.

seas missions" in mind. They saw the emerging crisis in First World evangelism but wanted to preserve the word "mission" for Third World church-planting. This has, I believe, impeded the church from facing the evangelization crisis and its ramifications for ecclesial structures in the First World.

The Text and Its Important Points

The Preface of the decree explicitly relates the decree to the theology of the *Constitution on the Church,* seeing the church as "a kind of sacrament or sign of intimate union of humankind with God...(and) an instrument for the achievement of such union and unity" (1). Where the mission decree becomes more precise and specific is in its insistence that the "Church on earth is by its very nature missionary..." (2), and includes the obligation to make visible throughout the world the universal human call to participate in divine life symbolized by the incarnation of God's son (3).

Chapter One of the decree seeks to link the activity, nature and mission of the ecclesial mission to the activity, nature and mission of God. The language attempts to bring the Pauline *mysterion* (cf. Ephesians 1:3-22: Colossians 1:11-28) motif to the modern understanding of mission. The mystery/sacramental language of the Church Constitution Chapter One and Chapter Two ("The Mystery of the Church" and "The People of God" respectively, (1-17) has a completely different flavor from that of Chapter III ("The Hierarchical Structure of the Church, With Special Reference to the Episcopate" (18-29). Already within Chapter One of the mission decree the need to bring pilgrim, mystery, sacramental language into conjunction with institutional language and concerns is seen. In art. 6 we read:

> This task which must be carried out by the order of bishops, under the leadership of Peter's successor and with the prayers and cooperation of the whole Church, is

one and the same everywhere and in all situations, although because of circumstances, it may not always be exercised in the same way. (6)

The decree notes that the mission is carried on by peoples or individuals in various ways, according to the circumstances of their lives. In that context (*mission* being the church's universal vocation of carrying on the evangelical mandate of proclamation and service), there are special activities called *missions*, defined as

> The special undertakings in which preachers of the Gospel, sent by the Church, and going into the whole world, carry out the work of preaching the Gospel and implanting the Church among people who do not yet believe in Christ, are generally called "missions." Such undertakings are accomplished by missionary activity and are, for the most part, carried out in defined territories recognized by the Holy See. The special end of this missionary activity is the evangelization and the implanting of the Church among peoples or groups in which it has not yet taken root. (6)

The same article states that this activity "among the nations differs from pastoral activity among the faithful." In art. 7 it is stated clearly that Jesus Christ is the sole mediator of human salvation and that, therefore, "all must be converted to Him as He is made known by the Church's preaching. All must be incorporated into Him by baptism and into the Church which is His body." The decree does not treat the other side of this doctrine, that is to say, the question of whether those who do not come explicitly to faith are saved or how their putative salvation is related to Christ. One gets the impression that this thorny problem was considered too unsettled and fluid for inclusion in the mission schema. Nevertheless, it should be noted that the *Constitution on the Church in the Modern World* was being debated at this same time, and that it was generally accepted that predestination was positive (i.e., toward salvation). Negative predestination has, of course, had its proponents, but Catholic theology tends to try to find ways to express its conviction that sufficient grace is given to all humans.

In any case the theology of the *Decree on the Church's Missionary Activity* is positive, not negative. Missionary activity itself has a *manifestative* goal, leading to the praise and glory of God, the acknowledgement by creatures of their creator (8-9). Listen for example to art. 8:

> Missionary activity is intimately bound up with human nature and its aspirations. In manifesting Christ, the Church reveals to men their true situation and calling, since Christ is the head and exemplar of that renewed humanity, imbued with that brotherly love, sincerity and spirit of peace, to which all men aspire. (8)

In the context of the critique of missions that was (and remains a hallmark of the post-colonial world), the decree seeks to say that missions have aimed at enhancing humanity's global life:

> ...the Gospel has acted as a leaven in the interests of liberty and progress, and it always offers itself as a leaven with regard to brotherhood, unity and peace. So it is not without reason the Christ is hailed by the faithful as "the hope of the nations and their saviour." (8)

Chapter Two enters into a discussion of the nature of mission work, and does so in terms that are consistent with its premises in Chapter One. Mission, missions and church are in close relationship; witness and preaching aim at conversion; conversion leads to membership in the church.

The new churches, however, look remarkably similar to the churches which sent the missionaries. Chapter Three is one in which the presupposition that the "young" churches or "mission" churches are to be very similar to the "sending" churches of Euro-America is most apparent.[6] In addition to

---

[6]Chapter Three (art. 19-22) is entitled "particular Churches." *Ecclesia particularis* in Vatican II documents has a certain ambiguity to it, as an inspection of even a few of the places in which the term is used will show (v. gr., L.G., 13, 23; C.D., 11; O.E., 2; A.G., 22).

the question of whether and to what extent a local congregation is a particular church, and how such congregations
relate to a particular church, and how such congregations
relate to dioceses and the universal church, the decree on
missions creates a special question when it speaks of non-
self-sustaining churches which depend upon other churches
in art. 19. Whether, when it says "congregation," the decree
means this in its usual sense (a parish under the leadership of
a pastoral priest), or a diocese or group of dioceses is not
immediately clear. What is clear, however, is that the decree
finds itself forced to take cognizance of the fact that many
churches founded in the modern mission era depend heavily
upon outside help. While they have some indigenous personnel, they still require people whom we often call missionaries to serve as pastors of flocks which in many cases have
existed for several hundred years (think of Latin America).
Inexplicably, the decree terms such churches "new." Though
that is, of course, true of many such churches (for example,
in parts of Oceania and Africa), it is not true of many others,
notably in South America.

What the council fathers are intent upon stressing is that
"mission action should furnish help to those churches,
founded long since, which are in a certain state of regression
or weakness" (19). A point I will return to in Part Three of
this paper should be raised here. The *Decree on the Missions* is forced by the realities of a large segment of the
church to violate its own definition of missions as work
carried out "among peoples who do not yet believe in
Christ" (6). The fact is that the bulk of the work carried out
under the rubric of "missions" is in reality not primary
evangelization but on-going pastoral work performed by
foreigners among Catholics who do not yet have pastors of
their own people.

It is my judgment that factors inherent in the Roman
Catholic understanding of what is necessary for ordination
to the pastoral ministry go to keep churches which ought
long ago have become self-ministering dependent upon
Euro-American churches. While the decree on the missions
defines missions in terms which would please conservative

evangelical Protestants, the reality is that the exigencies of taking care of baptized but non-self-ministering Christians brings the church to the state where the majority of our "missionaries" are in fact foreign pastors. This is the nub of several crucial problems.

Chapter Four is an excellent, balanced and far-sighted chapter designed to help prepare future missionaries. It is a distillation of the principles enunciated in the great mission encyclicals of the twentieth century, and embodies the wisdom of the modern mission era. It is interesting to note that this chapter presumes that disciplines such as linguistics, anthropology, history of religions and psychology will help men and women enter into the task of primary evangelization. De facto, however, most of the people whom missionary institutes send from First World countries will be going to do the *pastoral* work spoken of above, not the primary evangelization and church-planting work which the decree defines as missionary in its own specific sense. Still, Chapter Four is a visionary section. Its insights would be equally useful for training a new sort of missionary for our own "neopagan" North America.[7]

Chapter Five, "Planning Missionary Activity" is the mission bishops' attempt to reorganize the Congregation for Propagation of the Faith to change it into The Congregation for the Evangelization of Peoples, the name by which it is increasingly known. Rather than run the affairs of the missions, the Congregation is to become a resource for coordinating out-reach and evangelization efforts, and to serve as a clearing house for vital information and help rationally plan the allocation of resources. *Ecclesiae Sanctae* (1966) devotes 24 paragraphs of instructions to the implementation of the decree on the missions. *Regimini Ecclesiae Universae* (1967) devotes one of its largest sections to spelling out how the Propaganda Congregation is to be restructured, largely in the light of the mission decree, but

[7]See Alfred Krass, *Evangelizing Neopagan North America* (Scottdale, Pa: Herald, 1982) for an excellent Protestant analysis of the evangelization needs of North America.

also in the light of other decrees which lay out the council's understanding of mission. Evangelization will be the activity it coordinates. And to do this the Congregation will carry on numerous related tasks, but primarily those of *aiding* the heralds of the gospel, not *commanding* them.

Missionary cooperation is the subject of the sixth chapter of the mission decree. The chapter has some of the same bifurcation spoken of in other places in this paper, but also useful clarity at a practical level. No church is truly church, nor any Christian truly Christian without awareness of responsibility for spreading the Gospel (35-36). The primary witness is that of personal life, but in the same way that the gospel is directed to all peoples, so each church has to have the world mission in mind (27), especially by retaining contact with and interest in the work of missionaries.

Bishops especially are reminded — although the decree here unfortunately divides the Christian world into sending and receiving churches — that they are ordained for the whole world, not just a single diocese. On bishops especially devolves the responsibility to promote mission concern, raise financial help for the missions, and to stimulate vocations for the missions. One reason for this was the sensitivity of the religious orders, who had such a hand in the drafting of the decree, to the fact that missions had come to be thought of as the preserve of a few congregations who specialized in this exotic work. To counteract that impression, Chapter Six goes to great lengths to drive home the point that the missions are a work of the whole church. A 1969 Instruction of the Evangelization Congregation on the "Cooperation of Bishops with Pontifical Mission Aid Societies"[8] spells out the vital importance of bishops especially to see to it that good people are appointed to the various Pontifical mission societies. Such societies are to be considered "the means of imbuing Catholics from their infancy with a truly universal and missionary outlook." Where societies such as that for Propagation of the Faith were once thought of as primarily fund-raising activities,

[8] Acta Apostolicae Sedis 61 (1969): pp. 276-87

under the new guidelines, they ought to become organizations which aim at galvanizing the faithful for a multifaceted concern for the missions (without, one senses, forgetting to raise money besides!).

Summarizing the argument to this point, the following ideas are central:

1. The *Decree on the Missions* places missions (in the technical sense) within the context of the divine mission to save and enhance human life.
2. Missions, as ecclesiastical undertakings, aim at the preaching of the gospel, the conversion of non-Christians, and the founding of new churches.
3. The Decree makes clear the *universal* Christian vocation to mission; it concretizes this and spells out implications of this for "sending" or "mature" churches in order that they — and especially their bishops — may see that missions are not the stepchild of such mature churches but an integral part of that activity; the mature churches are called upon to aid the overseas missions with personnel and financial assistance.
4. The Congregation for the Propagation of the Faith is to become the Congregation for the Evangelization of Peoples whose primary service is to coordinate efforts to carry on missions and general evangelization.
5. The post-conciliar implementation decree, *Ecclesiae Sanctae*, in its third chapter (17-18) envisages cooperation between missionary institutes and home dioceses, and (9-12) the establishment of missionary councils by bishops and missionary institutes to promote dissemination of information and mutual assistance between churches.

Critical Reflections

Were one to write the *Decree on the Church's Missionary Activity* today, what would have to be redone?

First, to say a word about the basic "sending/receiving" or center/periphery" imagery of the decree. It is hard to see how it could today be allowed to dominate a discussion of either mission or missions. With the deterioration of the institutional strength of Catholicism in much of Europe —traditional homeland of most of our missionaries — specially in the growing crisis in finding pastoral ministers to tend the flock, the church in large parts of Europe is hardly much healthier than the church of Latin America or the Philippines. France was called a "mission territory" by the worker-priests of the immediate post-World War II era. It is hardly less so today. In the '60s it was possible to ignore this situation. Today it is not. In North America the situation is not as critical, but the Schoenherr study[9] makes it clear that patterns are not materially different here from those that have led to the weakening of the European church.

In this context, then, a critical question must be asked: If re-evangelization of the fallen-away and evangelization of the neopagan is *the* most important task of a church such as that in North America, whence will come the personnel resources to accomplish it? It has been observed by various people in various ways that we have moved from an ecclesiology wherein the laity was considered passive and the clergy active to one in which *all* are required to be both committed and active. Nevertheless, the process of helping galvanize such an activist church requires a class of evangelizing ministers of some sort or another.

The *Decree on the Church's Missionary Activity* rather easily defines missions in terms which suggest that there are strong and mature sending churches on the one hand, and receiving churches on the other; that the sending churches have a pastoral clergy which will be able to keep the home fires burning; and that it would be sufficient for us to spell out clearly the obligation of such sending churches to the missions. I would like to suggest that those presuppostitions are dubious today.

In the *Decree on the Church's Missionary Activity* the mission of the church is primarily that of herald, announc-

[9]Madison, Wisconsin, 1981: *Decline and Change in the U.S. Catholic Church.*

ing the Gospel *(evangelion)*, participating in the process of making God's good favor to humankind visible. Missions are enterprises carried on to create new churches in areas where churches have not existed before, so that they may participate in God's mission of reconciling humanity. What the analysis to this point reveals is that as time has marched on the old sending churches have come to a state where they may be little stronger than the receiving churches.

A council today treating the missionary activity of the church would, I believe, find it harder to ignore such realities. It would be clearer that a new *Dogmatic Constitution on the Church* process would have to examine various presuppositions about the institutional shape of Catholicism. In that context then, a new degree on the missions would realize that today there is no center and periphery in mission. The question for the traditional missions would resemble the following: how can we reduce dependence upon northern hemisphere churches and create a Brazilian, Ghanaian or Papua New Guinean fellowship which will carry on the evangelization process under their unique conditions? The question would not be significantly different for Germany, the U.S. or France.

The strength of the *Decree on the Church's Missionary Activity* lies in its praticality. Missionary orders and bishops hammered out a document that concretized a vision of what needed to be done to make missions function better. That is also the weakness of the document. It does not come to grips with the deepest question that faces these missions: cutting the knots that keep them in dependence upon other churches, churches which today are in better shape only in the area of wealth, not a particularly evangelical criterion of strength!

Mission today is an activity with no center and periphery because it is everywhere. Missions would be better defined as the attempt of *each* Christian community to reach out to neighbors to announce by deed and word the Gospel that even Tridents, Smith & Wesson .38s and burglar bars can be melted into plowshares, surgical instruments and playground equipment — people would repent, and let God's Spirit make them into a new creation.

That said, Chapter Four of the *Decree on the Church's Missionary Act* (23-27) could serve as a far-sighted core to a revised *ratio fundamentalis* for training the sort of missionaries needed in places as diverse as Chicago, San Diego and Clinton, Iowa. Finding ways to reach out to people today alienated from the church will certainly require missionary evangelists as resourceful as Ricci and de Nobili, for the cultures which traditional churches look out upon today are as different — *within a country such as the U.S.* — as China's or India's were from these sixteenth and seventeenth century Jesuits.

At the risk of introducing an element which preoccupies my own thoughts and may be idiosyncratic, may I dwell for a moment upon a line from article 6? The decree states clearly that, "... missionary activity among the nations differs from pastoral activity among the faithful." One of the primary difficulties of Catholic mission activities among the nations since the sixteenth century has been in bringing missions to a close and fully self-ministering and sustaining local churches to birth. Missionaries have included religious brothers and sisters especially since the nineteenth century. In more recent times lay volunteers have become more prominent. But in the main, missions have been clerical enterprises directed by ordained priests and bishops, guided by the decisions of the Propaganda. Thus, willingly or not, priestly and clerical concerns have dominated missions since the people with authority thought of themselves as priests.

The recent work of Vincent Donovan, C.S.SP. has influenced me greatly in what follows.[10] Donovan went among the Masai of East Africa as a missioner, not as a priest. He spent a good deal of time learning from them what *their* own most inmost values were, and dialogued with them to learn *their* religious beliefs. He preached Christ sensitively and creatively; he allowed the form of church that would grow

[10]See *Christianity Rediscovered* (Maryknoll: Orbis, 1982).

up to take shape according to *their* experience of Christ, not be shaped by Roman Catholic presuppositions. The tragedy of Donovan was that finally his initiatives hit the reefs of Roman presuppostitions, especially regarding ordained ministry and ecclesial structure. What may there be to learn from Donovan? Just this: that a new ministry is required — *that of evangelist.* It would correspond roughly to that of Paul's wandering apostleship, but not allow itself to be caught in questions of pastoral nurture and ministry. Paul boasted that he was not so involved (1 Cor. 1:14-17). Men and women we tend to call "Missionaries" have become, in effect, "foreign pastors," because churches founded since the 16th century have generally not been able to find sufficient personnel to take over pastoral ministry. Why? Has it been because the early missionaries could envision no other form of mature Christian fellowship but that of Europe and North America? Would things have been different if the missionaries had been set apart ("ordained") not as priest-pastors but as missionary-evangelists? Should part of their instructions have read that they were to preach and invite people to convert, but also to leave it up to the converts to decide upon the form of fellowship that their churches would assume?

In the North American context today, when looking at the men and women who have fallen away from traditional Catholicism and have joined no other church, might we not get further by sending evangelists with similar instructions, rather than inviting them back to a form of fellowhship with which many of them have serious problems? Would similar methods perhaps not work better with those who have never been members of our own or any other church?

I am not so naive as to be unaware of the cans of worms such questions uncover. The nature of the problem is one that befuddles any simplistic approach, whether traditional or revisionist. Much of what I have seen written and heard said about evangelization since the Synod of 1974 and *Evangelii Nuntiandi* runs aground on the same reef that eventually forced Fr. Donovan to leave Africa. It remains the presupposition of the *Decree on the Church's Mission ary Activity:* that our present form of Church is the only valid one for Catholics. The great questions facing us today in terms of mission can only be posed when we are able to have horizons broader and more expansive than those of the Decree on The Church's Missionary Activity. The too facile way in which the decree's articles 2-5 narrows to article 6's ecclesiastical outlook and then, in a seemingly untroubled way, expands again to articles 7-9's scriptural, organic and mystery-language horizon amazes me.

Lonergan warns that the pernicious thing about blind-spots is how they function to keep us from looking precisely at the more basic and mistaken presuppositions upon which we base our lives. An examination of problems that prematurely turns to discussing practical issues — which is what the *Decree on Missionary Activity* ultimately does — ignores Lonergan's truth: that a long and sustained investigation, involving many knowledgeable people, is required to unearth the radical sort of solutions which our culture's and church's crisis demands. The need to get a document on the floor for the fourth session, the practical outlook of the mission bishops and the superiors of missionary congregations, and general Roman Catholic commonsense conspired to keep the Decree on Missionary Activity from being a prophetic document. One wonders if we are today much more ready to face the full panoply of questions which mission and missions involve.

Decree on the Ministry
and Life of Priests
Presbyterorum Ordinis, 7 December, 1965

Timothy E. O'Connell

The *Decree on the Ministry and Life of Priests* is yet another of those conciliar decrees that exist by the express will of the Council Fathers. It was not originally envisioned as one of the fruits of the Second Vatican Council. Instead, according to Bishop Guilford C. Young, it emerged when the Fathers found inadequate the discussion of the priesthood in The Constitution on the Church. This relationship to the Constitution on the Church is theologically significant and will be discussed later. Suffice it to say now that the *Decree on Priestly Ministry and Life* is a self-conscious reflection of the mind of the Council Fathers as their thought matured during the various sessions.

Summary of the Decree

After a brief preface, the decree presents itself in three chapters. The first chapter relates the decree to the *Constitu-*

tion on the Church by a theological exposition of the relationship of the ordained priesthood to the life of the church. The exposition is significant for a number of reasons. First, there is the way in which the Council fathers relativize the notion of priesthood, and make it dependent on the reality of church. Indeed, the first paragraph is devoted to a proclamation of the priesthood of the church.

> "The Lord Jesus...makes his whole Mystical Body sharer in the anointing of the Spirit." (2)

The distinctiveness of ordained priesthood is, of course, defended, but it is located in the substance and shape of the ministry which priests exercise in and for the church. A second significance of this chapter is the fact that it appears to identify the ordained priesthood with the reality of ministry. The text is a bit ambiguous but there certainly is no affirmation of the notion of ministry broader than priesthood. Thirdly, a "cosmic" sense of the mission of the church and of the priesthood is presented. "Through the ministry of priests the spiritual sacrifice of the faithful is completed in union with the sacrifice of Christ the only mediator" (2). Its aim is that " 'the whole redeemed city...be offered as a universal sacrifice of God.'" (2 — quoting St. Augustine) The purpose, therefore, which priests pursue by their ministry in life is the glory of God the Father as it is to be achieved in Christ."

The second and third chapters of the decree are far longer. They discuss the ministry and the life of priests, respectively, with these two terms functioning as useful umbrellas for the various observations the fathers wished to make. In all candor, there is a certain arbitrariness to the way in which the topics are organized. But the division that the fathers chose is probably as good as any.

In discussing the ministry of priests, the decree addresses, first, priestly function, second, the relationship of priests to various other individuals and groups, and third, the distribution of priests and the issue of priestly vocations. It has been widely noted that the fathers made a significant contribution to the tradition when they isolated as the primary duty of priests "the proclamation of the gospel of God to all." Cultic and liturgical services were clearly subordinated to evangelical and kerygmatic work. The second ministerial duty of priests is sanctification, occurring in and through the liturgy and the other sacraments. And in the third place, priests lead the church by convening and promoting community as well as by serving the individual members of that community with love.

As priests exercise their ministry to preach, sanctify and lead, they do not act in isolation. So the second part of this chapter discusses various relationships. First, priests relate to the bishop and the college of bishops. This relationship involves mutual rights and responsibilities, so "a group or senate of priests should be set up" (7). But it is fundamentally rooted in the fact that the presbyteral priesthood is a participation in the fullness of orders possessed by the episcopacy. In light of this common participation, priests, secondly, relate to one another; they are a presbytery. This should call forth a fraternal spirit among all priests, particularly between old and young.

In the third place, priests relate to the laity. This relationship puts the priest in the role of "father and teacher," of course. But more fundamentally, it shows them to be "members of the same Body of Christ which all are commanded to build up" (9). I do not think it is an exaggeration to note a schizophrenia in this part of the text. On the one hand, priests "in common with all who have been reborn in the font of baptism, are brothers among brothers" (9). They are to be sincere in their appreciation and promotion of lay people's dignity and of the special role the laity have to play in the Church's mission (9). On the other hand, there is a note of caution and the sense that authority abides in the priest and is delegated to the lay person. Indeed, there is almost a sort of condescension: "Priests should also be confident in giving lay people charge of duties in the service of the Church, giving them freedom and opportunity for activity and even inviting them, when opportunity occurs, to take the initiative in undertaking projects of their own" (9).

The third part of this chapter proclaims the relationship of the priesthood to the church universal. It reminds the reader that priests are called to the service of the whole church. They should therefore be concerned to distribute themselves in terms of actual need. It also encourages (with less than total success, as it turns out) the willing acceptance of priestly vocation. And towards that end, it encourages a variety of vocational projects.

Thus far the ministerial service of priests. How are they to live as they pursue these activities? The third chapter of the decree discusses issues pertaining to the life of priests. It begins with a general discussion of the vocation to Christian perfection. In the second place, it talks about the special spiritual issues of priestly life, and in particular, obedience, celibacy, and the use of wealth. In the third place, it talks about various aids to the spiritual growth of priests, aids both spiritual and economic.

All Christians are called to be perfect as the heavenly father is perfect. But because of their identification with Christ the priest, priests experience a particular challenge to growth in holiness. In the first part of this chapter, the fathers describe that call to perfection. The assertion that priests have a particular challenge to growth is not noteworthy. The relationship of that spiritual life to ministry, however, is. For the most part, this section of the decree simply returns to the three ministries mentioned earlier —word, sacrament and leadership — and describes the ways in which these services are themselves the arena and the occasion for growth in holiness. Thus ministry is not just the fruit of holiness. Even less is it the occupation that fills whatever hours are not devoted to spiritual exercises. On the contrary, ministry is itself the act of spiritual purification and growth.

> By adopting the role of the good shepherd they will find in the practice of pastoral charity itself the bond of

priestly perfection that will reduce to unity their life and activity. (14)

In a second part, the decree deals with the specific issues of a priestly spirituality: obedience, celibacy and the relationship to wealth. In each case, the discussion is marked by challenge and yet balance. Obedience, for example, is viewed primarily not as adhesion to the will of the superior, but as commitment to the will of God. In the case of human superiors, what is required is "hierarchical communion," which may come to the same thing but has, it seems to me, a different nuance. There is no doubt that the Fathers expect the priests to do what they are told. But at the same time, they also call for initiative in service, in frankness, in contributing judgement. Similarly, in the case of celibacy the decree recommends the traditional discipline of the church while not pretending that it is intrinsically related to priesthood. It acknowledges and approves the discipline of the eastern church while at the same time defending and recommending the practices of the West. I think it is worth noticing also that in general, celibacy is equated with continence and not with virginity. That is, it does not celebrate as particularly meritorious the mere fact of sexual inexperience. Rather it recommends the ethical and spiritual integration of sexuality into a lifestyle of dedicated unmarried service.

The decree also addresses the question of the use by priests of material goods. Here again, there is the balance that calls for detachment and liberty without any dualistic suggestion that material things are evil. Some comments about the use of ecclesiastical goods and the value of relatively equal pay for those in various ministries are included here. Finally, the charismatic acceptance of an even more radical poverty is applauded.

The third part of this chapter outlines recommended aids to the spiritual growth of priests. It is a list that is reminiscent of many traditional items of spiritual reading. Meditation on Scripture and participation in the Eucharist are recommended. Frequent reception of the sacraments and particularly of the sacrament of Penance is mentioned. Attention to the model of the Virgin Mary, visits to the Blessed Sacrament and mental prayer are suggested. Nor is the list limited to pious practices. Priests are urged to continue their theological study, and to enrich themselves with knowledge of the social sciences and ministerial techniques. The bishops are urged to provide opportunities for continuing education for the clergy. Finally, the document acknowledges the ways in which physical needs can affect spiritual growth. It urges a just wage for priests, a wage that is decent, relatively equal to all, distributed on the basis of need, and supplemented with appropriate arrangements for old age.

A concluding exhortation brings the decree to a close.

Reflections on the Decree

"The priesthood is not a job, not just a role, not a mere function. No, the priesthood is a way of life, a commitment of the total person. The priesthood is a vocation."

Comments like these are often heard. They are the stuff of formational conferences in seminaries, first-Mass homilies and retreats for priests. And it seems that there is a sense in which they are altogether true. There is a spirituality of priesthood, a religious core to this activity that requires that it not be viewed as a "job," but rather as a "vocation."

Still, one wonders if the juxtaposition of these sets of terms does not somehow distort the reality. Do the terms, with the connotations that arise from their being contrasted with each other, represent the only actual choices? Perhaps not. There is no doubt that the polarized language of the quotation is in tune with the *Decree on Priestly Ministry and Life.* But is the vision espoused by the Decree the only possible theological vision of priesthood? Again, perhaps not.

In the life of the contemporary Church, and particularly in the American experience of Catholic Christianity since Vatican II, there has emerged an alternative vision. And it deserves to be seriously considered. First will be an attempt to characterize and consider the vision that seems to undergird the Decree. Next will be the presentation of this alternative vision that seems to be forming in the American Catholic experience. Thirdly, some of the implications of this latter vision for the "ministry" and "life" of priests will be noted.

First, then, let us try to describe the vision of priesthood that seems to undergird the Decree. For the sake of clarity we can characterize this vision as *ontological*. By this I mean that it understands priests to be some *thing* different than other human persons. Ordination to the priesthood is seen to effect some sort of radical and essential modification of the person. The result is that one becomes intrinsically or ontologically different. This change may be conceptualized in the categories of the "character" theology of the scholastics, or perhaps there is some other way of thematizing it. But in any case it suggests that the priest is essentially different than other persons. Indeed, the vision seems to presume that from the viewpoint of someone or other (perhaps only the inhabitants of heaven) the priest is *observably* different.

What else can be said about this vision? There are several other characteristics which are noteworthy. The first is that it implies and encourages a descending view of ministry. If priests are understood to be ontologically different, then the obvious question is: how do they become that way? The inevitable answer is: ordination. But to discuss ordination is to raise the question of succession. This highlights the participation of priesthood (and diaconate) in the episcopacy. The hierarchical ordering of those three ministries is thus emphasized. The current church practice of preceding ordination by the installation of the candidate into the ministries of reader and acolyte encourages a sense of slowly accumulating power. The imagery chiseled in the steps of one seminary chapel, where minor orders are literally steps on the way to priesthood, is not coincidental. One ascends toward the priesthood. Or to put it the other way, one is the recipient of descending power.

This vision almost inevitably leads to an understanding of

all ministry as derivative. Just as the diaconate and priest-hood are participations in the fullness of the priesthood in the episcopal order, so also the various other ministries in the church are participations in the ordained priesthood. That is, if not logically necessary, at least psychologically inevitable. The entire vision of church is therefore shaped by this descending metaphor. Episcopacy generates priest-hood. (In many psychological and sociological ways, priest-hood generates diaconate.) And ordained ministry generates non-ordained ministry. All are valuable, of course; but the lower are derived from the higher. Thus the Decree can say:

> Priests should confidently entrust to the laity duties in the service of the church, allowing them freedom and room for action. In fact, on suitable occasions, they should invite them to undertake works on their own initiative (9).

It follows, as another characteristic of this overall vision, that for purposes of understanding ministry, the central sacrament is Holy Orders. Holy Orders is the sacrament of service to the Church. Even though "priests, in common with all who have been reborn in the font of baptism, are brothers among brothers" (9), it is not baptism that author-izes service. It is Holy Orders. All forms of service come from that sacrament or lead to it.

Finally, it seems that this vision results in a style of church life that is condescending. We would like to think, indeed the Council would like to think, that it is possible to have a descending theology of ministry that does not lead to a condescending style of ministry. The American experience suggests that this is not possible. Somehow the invitation to a self-righteous conception of priesthood is overwhelmingly seductive. All but the very strongest priests end up, in little ways and at various times, being condescending. The inspir-ing statements of the Council Fathers notwithstanding, the laity are encouraged to be dependent, to sit and wait, and to accept "Father's words."

This condescending style is not true in every case, of

course. Indeed, its exact statistical frequency is not the point. Rather, the observation is that priests and laity alike avoid the style only when they, at least implicitly, reject the ontological theory with its descending metaphor. There seems to be no other way. But if that is true, one must ask: Is there an alternative to this theory and its metaphor? It seems that there is.

An Alternative

In recent decades, theologians have utilized increasingly the tools of biblical study in their pursuit of dogmatic study. They have discovered that careful exegesis in combination with a thoughtful hermeneutic can shed important light on the documents of the historical church as well as on the books of scripture. And in particular, they have often discovered that doctrinal statements do not always have dogmatic force. That is, they have found that to a large degree, doctrinal statements are shaped by the cultural milieu and philosophical presumptions of the age in which they were formulated. Thus, to distill the actual dogmatic commitment of the church, it is necessary either to prescind from those other factors or to translate them into the comparable qualities of one's own age.

It is possible that the use of these biblical tools would make a major difference in our theology of ministry and of priesthood. For the ontological theory of ministry, or at least of orders, may tell us more about medieval philosophy than it does about Christian faith. In scholastic philosophy, for instance, accidents always reside in substance, *fieri* is always dependent on *esse,* becoming is always a function of being. But is that the only way things may be understood? Evidently not. There is a different philosophy today, a philosophy that recognized the centrality of history, the significance of process, and the meaning of experience. This philosophy, however, would view ministry quite differently. Let us, then, sketch this different view so that we may consider viability and usefulness.

We can call this an *existential* understanding of ministry, for it starts with the question of existence, of actual function. What are the roles that exist? And what needs do they meet? Obviously, to answer these questions one needs to look at the context for the activities. And the context is church. What is the purpose of church? The answer is simple: church exists to mediate the presence of Christ to the world. Church is *ekklesia*, the community of "the called." Church is the gathering of explicit and self-concious believers seeking to live their faith and to share it with the world. Apostolic service to the world, then, is a function of membership in the church. Or to put this another way, the mandate to serve and love the world arises from the sacraments of initiation, Baptism and Confirmation (which are completed in the celebration of Eucharist).

This service of the world is both sacrificial and salvific. That is, since the church itself is a sacrament of salvation, Christian service makes present the Savior it proclaims. The result is that in some mysterious way, love of the world saves the world. But in saving the world, it offers it to God. And if, as the Baltimore Catechism said, "God made us to know him, love him and serve him in this world, and to be happy with him in the next," then this service of the world and call of faith to the world is itself an act of praise of God. "The glory of God is man fully alive," said Irenaeus. Therefore, care of the world is praise of God. All of this means that the very human act of saving service is in its own way a sacrifice of praise. It is the offering of the victim as radically reunderstood in the Christian perspective. It is Jesus Christ in his mystical body offered in love to the Father.

But the offering of sacrifice is a priestly act. It follows, then, that service to the world is an exercise of priesthood. Yet, as we have said, service to the world finds its justification in the sacraments of initiation. If this is true, then membership in the church makes one a priest. And, of course, to say this is simply to mimic the words of I Peter 2:9, that we are a priestly people. We are a people who, by means of membership in the church, become the agents of sacramental service, a service which is, by being sacramental, both salvific and sacrificial.

This love is, of course, not limited to those outside the church. If we want to avoid the elitism that cares only for fellow Christians, we do not want to go to the opposite extreme of neglecting the brethren. As various commentators have pointed out, love always has the twin aspect of *diakonia* and *koinonia* (service and community). So this service to which Christians are called by their sacramental membership in the church is a service also to their brothers and sisters in the church. Why is this service necessary? It is necessary precisely that the church may live. And the church is necessary that the world may be saved. Thus there arises something a bit different than Christian service simply taken. There arises that service within the church whose purpose is to nourish the church for the sake of the world. There arises, in other words, ministry. Indeed, in the vision of Ephesians 4, there arise many ministries, all existing for the building of this world-saving community.

Ministry, then, is not identical with Christian service. Ministry is that form of service which is, in a way, inward-oriented, but which exists in order to nourish the church for the sake of the world. Nonetheless, for all of its attention to the church, ministry is still an exercise of love and, as such, finds its justification in Baptism and Confirmation. It is an exercise of one's Christian identity.

Place of Holy Orders

There is, however, an obvious need: all this activity must be organized, orchestrated and ordered. It is inevitable, then, that a ministry of overseeing should emerge, a ministry of ordering. It is not the starting point; it is the last and least of the services. It presupposes the existence of those independent and self-authenticating ministries, which themselves presuppose an independent and self-authenticating vocation of saving service to the world. But it is, for all that, absolutely necessary. Moreover, since the whole church is a holy priesthood, sent to make the world holy, it is not inappropriate to speak of this critical ministry as an exercise of Holy Ordering. Indeed, it is a sacramental act, for it makes present the mystery of Jesus for the sake of the world. And thus this humble rank may rightly be termed a Holy Order of service.

In one sense, then, this alternative conceptualization seems no different than the more traditional one. It ends up saying the same thing. But the way in which ministry is first understood, the way in which one approaches the phenomenon of Holy Orders, does seem to make a difference.

In the first place, this alternative presents a conception which is rooted in a lateral metaphor. And this metaphor makes clear that what is more fundamental is not ordination but ministry and, indeed, not ministry but service to the world. It follows that this lateral metaphor leads us to recognize the autonomy and the self-justification of lay ministry. The laity do not need to wait upon the permission of the ordained in order to serve either the world or their brothers and sisters in the church. Their right to exercise that service, indeed the expectation that they should exercise that service, is theirs. They are, of course, expected to serve in a cooperative way; to do otherwise would be to contradict the very premise of their service, which is love. And therefore an openness to the orchestrating ministry of those ordained to Holy Orders is to be expected. But at the same time, it is an openness to the ordering by another of one's autonomous and rightful exercise of ministry.

It follows that since the reality of ministry is grounded in membership in the church, the sacraments which are pivotal for the understanding of ministry are Baptism and Confirmation, not Holy Orders. Holy Orders is, in a way, a subdivision of the sacraments of initiation, whereby one assumes a specific role within the chruch. But for purposes of a theology of ministry, it is the sacraments of Baptism and Confirmation which require our attention.

In this regard, it is worth noting that the growing appreciation for this understanding of ministry is in large part due to recent attention to the sacraments of initiation. And that, in turn, is due to the widespread study of the Rite of Christian Initiation of Adults (RCIA) in the United States. If we take seriously the notion of initiation into the church, that notion will lead us to a new theology of ministry, a lateral metaphor, and an existential perspective.

Notice, too, that the philosophical roots of this theology are not "transcendental," but rather "experiential." Given the Catholic doctrine that grace builds on nature, that God is found in the whispers of our experience, it seems to follow that there are no realities, whether of daily life or of faith, that are not somehow experienced. And if this is true, then there seems to be serious question about the ontological understanding of sacramental character, and particularly of the character of ordination.

The root idea of character is, of course, part of the full richness of Catholic tradition, found even in patristic writings. But the particular articulation that understands it as involving ontological change is of medieval vintage. And it seems to owe more to the exigencies of the philosophy of the day than to the necessities of the faith. What the faith seems to affirm is that in becoming Christian, and in accepting the task of Holy Ordering, one is to become truly different. It is not just a job, not a set of tasks with which one may successively be engaged and disengaged. Becoming a parent is not something that can be undone; one is forever different because of the event. Becoming a member of a profession such as medicine or law should analogously make one different; for since one cannot unlearn what one knows, one also cannot eschew the responsibility which that knowledge brings. So also does the entrance into Holy Orders challenge one to be different. Indeed, one *is* different because of the learning, the commitment, the responsibility. And the difference should be not transitory but abiding.

The difference, then, is existential, not ontological. The priest is not ontologically different. He is a member of the church exercising service for the world. He focuses on that service through ministry to the church. And he exercises a very important form of ministry by ordering and orchestrating the ministries of others. His ordering is holy because the church is holy.

Implications for Priestly Ministry

Thus far an alternative vision of priesthood. If the first chapter of the Decree had been more fully based on this view, what would have been different in the other two chapters? Let us pursue that question, looking first at ministry.

In one sense, the most obvious implication for the ministry of priests has already been pointed out: namely, the fact that it is subsequent and collaborative. Priests, it has often been said, are relational beings. They exist not for their own sake but for the sake of the people they serve. So also they serve those people preeminently by encouraging and expediting their service.

Moreover, this ministry of ordering is done in the three ways highlighted by the Decree at the beginning of this second chapter: by preaching, liturgical leadership and community service. For the proclamation of the kerygma challenges the people of God to their own ministry, liturgical worship empowers them for that ministry, and priestly service coordinates and expedites that ministry. So, to speak of these three elements of priestly ministry, far from preempting the ministry of others specifies the ways in which priests are in service to the many ministries of the people.

But there is one other implication of this existential view for the lived ministry of priests. We can pursue that implication by asking a simple question: Is the ministry of ordering a full-time occupation?

The correct answer seems to be: sometimes yes and sometimes no. There are some cases where the three tasks mentioned above are sufficiently time-consuming as to be a full-time job. One thinks in particular of some bishops and the pastors of some large parishes. But often it seems that this is not the case.

If one is to argue that priesthood is commonly a full-time occupation, one will have to show which of the tasks occupies the time. Is it proclamation of the word? Perhaps adequate preaching should require major attention in the course of a priest's week. But it is not likely that it claims a major portion of the professional life of most American priests.

Is it liturgical leadership? Many priests argue that this is the activity which claims much of their life. And in truth, with the shrinking numbers of clergy, that is often the case. But the tragic consequences of this development are becoming obvious. Karl Rahner once pointed out that the assertion that "if one Mass is good, two are better" denies the reality of human nature. Grace touches the human person only to the extent of human readiness. And readiness is affected by, among other things, fatigue. Consequently, random multiplication of liturgical experiences, far from increasing devotion, undermines it. The same thing is being experienced by many American priests. They find in the demanded multiplication of liturgical activities a burden and a threat to Christian faith. So there is a limit to how much liturgical leadership an individual priest can exercise in a healthy manner; and that limit, set by human nature, prevents this task from occupying a major portion of a full-time professional life.

But what of the third task: minsterial coordination? It would seem that this is what truly fills a priest's day. But does it? Observation of priestly activity leads one to deny this. Priests' days are full not because they coordinate the ministries of others, but because they do the ministries they seek to be coordinating. That is, their days are full with teaching in a school or visiting a hospital, with counseling the troubled or preparing people for marriage, with financial administration or the leading of prayer. And none of these is a properly priestly role.

They are worthy projects, of course. Indeed, they are ministries essential to the life of the community. That is the reason priests are inclined to pursue them. But for all that, they are not priestly ministries; they are ministries authorized by Baptism and Confirmation. Indeed, on the American scene they are ministries increasingly exercised by many who are not ordained. But if this is so, how is it that priests can be doing these things? The answer is clear: in most settings priesthood, as such, is a part-time occupation. This implication of the existential vision has, in turn, several implications of its own. And since these implications have often been cited in discussions of ministry in America since Vatican II, they will be mentioned here only briefly. First, if these activities are "ministry," then priests should be subject to the same tests of competence as anyone else. The priest-chaplain or the priest-catechist should be no less skilled than the nonordained person exercising these roles. Secondly, if priesthood, as such, is often a part-time role, then priests are under no obligation to defend their other activities on grounds of being "priestly." The activities are not priestly. Rather, the tasks must be justified on grounds, simply, of being helpful.

Thirdly, it is said that ordinary members of the church can involve themselves both in ministry (as defined here) and in apostolic service to the world (what some call "market place ministry"). Indeed, they are urged to give priority to the latter, since ministry exists only for its sake. But if priesthood is often a part-time occupation, is there an intrinsic reason why the rest of a priest's time must be spent in "ministry?" Might he not also appropriately give himself to this apostolic service; that is, to some honorable but "worldly" contribution to the humanization of the world? Indeed, is this not now the case? At the present time the institutional church seems inclined to support certain activities of priests, for example teaching of subjects other than theology, adminstration of charitable activities, journalism and publishing, and to discourage others, for example political office, artistic endeavors, medicine. But the distinction between the activities supported and those discouraged seems fluid. All these activities have potential for facilitating the salvation of the world. And none of them is plausibly priestly.

In conclusion, then, the implication of an existential view of priesthood for the ministry of priests is this: priests are liberated to exercise whatever forms of ministry, or apostolic service, their gifts and opportunities allow. But at the same time, they are confronted with the burden of proving their competence in the same way and to the same extent as anyone else.

Implications for Priestly Life

What of the third chapter of the Decree? What of the "life" of priests? Let us mention and develop one often-cited point in this regard, and be content with that single set of reflections on the American scene.

If priesthood is an essential function within and for the community, then the absence of a number of priests sufficient for the exercise of that function is intolerable. There ought to be ordained a number of people sufficient to provide the needed services for the community. Those able and willing to provide the needed services ought to be ordained. And one might even argue that those able and willing to provide those services, and actually providing them in some manner or other, ought to be acknowledged to be priests by virtue of that very fact.

But if human nature sets limits on how much liturgical leadership an individual priest can provide, then a reduction in the number of priests must necessarily result in the unavailability of that portion of priestly service. And that, of course, is the current situation. Sociological studies have made clear that the number of priests in the United States in the year 2000 will be approximately one-half the number in 1980. These studies make equally clear that the reason for the reduction is not the ministry of priests, but rather their lifestyle. Primarily this involves the obligation of clerical celibacy, imposed upon all who wish to exercise priestly ministry. To a lesser but still significant extent, it involves the necessity for most priests to live in the work-place and with their work-colleagues, an arrangement which is not typical in many other countries and which many priests find burdensome. Finally, it is being increasingly asserted that the reduction in the number of priests is due to the refusal to ordain women, whether married or celibate.

For American Catholics, then, the question arises: do we

have a crisis of vocations or a crisis of vision? Is the difficulty an absence of candidates or our inability to see the candidates who are there? Is the problem that men (and women) are unwilling to accept the burdens of a prophetic lifestyle, or that the details of this lifestyle have revealed themselves as antithetical to, or at least irrelevant to, the tasks of priestly ministry?

Several things are clear. Obligatory celibacy (as obligatory) is fundamentally a discipline of the church, not something connected always and everywhere with priesthood. Obligatory celibacy has flourished most easily in eras marked by a negative and unchristian vision of sexuality. The affirmation of a positive and healthy theology of sexuality makes the obligation of celibacy (as distinguished from the freely accepted prophetic charism of celibacy) increasingly difficult to defend. Devout American Catholics, both clergy and lay, are increasingly undisturbed by the prospect of married clergy or of women priests; at least, they find both these developments far preferable to life without Eucharistic assembly and the sacraments.

But there is another angle on this issue that ought to be mentioned. The currently intense interest in lay ministry, especially career ministry in the Church, is largely due to the reduced number of priests. Perhaps this should not be so, but it is. In noncatholic traditions which welcome married and female clergy, there is no analogous group of professional lay ministers. Ironically, then, a change in ecclesiastical policy regarding the ordination of women or the married might have the effect of reversing the tide of lay involvement in the internal affairs of the church.

Conclusion

These reflections have, of course, raised more questions than they have provided answers. That is to be expected, given the period of time that has elapsed since the *Decree on Priestly Ministry and Life* was promulgated. But hopefully the reflections have at least focussed the questions and, in that way, advanced the conversation.

The Decree discusses priestly ministry and life, but it does so on the basis of a theology of priesthod, an ontological view. That view is questionable from several points of view, and is being questioned by many in the rank and file of the American Catholic church. At the same time, an alternative view, an existential view, presents itself as worth consideration, and is being increasingly considered. But if one affirms this latter view, there are several implications for the ministry and life of priests; and serious concerns about the criteria for eligibility for priestly office are raised. Indeed, in the years since Vatican II, those on the American church scene have noted these implications and raised just these concerns.

That, it seems, is the state of the question at this moment. The resolution of these matters will be a major theme in the next decade. And given its large and active, well-educated laity, given the strong impetus toward an equal and initiating role for women, given the egalitarian tradition of the land, with its support for dialogue and discussion, one can expect that the church in the United States will play an important role in that resolution.

Pastoral Constitution on the
Church in the Modern World
Gaudium et Spes, 7 December, 1965

Joseph Gremillion

The *Pastoral Constitution on the Church in the Modern World* is by far the longest document issued by Vatican II. It also has a breadth of interest and perspective which is unequalled. Because of its length and complexity, as well as its originality in conciliar history, this essay can do no more than offer some preliminary reflections. Nonetheless, some of the tradition-shattering significance of the document can be noted.

Content of the Constitution

The Pastoral Constitution (even the name is unprecedented) is divided into two main parts. The first presents the theological and pastoral principles of the Church's involvement in the world. The second attends to five areas of special urgency for our time.

> The joy and hope, the grief and anguish of the men of our time, especially of those who are poor or afflicted in any way, are the joy and hope, the grief and anguish of the followers of Christ as well. Nothing that is genuinely human fails to find an echo in their hearts (1).

These famous opening words of the Pastoral Constitution encapsulate not only the content of the document, but also its motive. This work was prepared by the Fathers of the Council because of a profound concern for the people of the world and out of a genuine commitment to their welfare.

Still, the concern is not unnuanced. The Church brings a particular perspective to the concerns of the world, a perspective colored by the Church's theological convictions about the meaning of human life. The document offers an introduction that details this theological phenomenology, describing the situation of our time. For "the Church carries the responsibility of reading the signs of the time and of interpreting them in the light of the Gospel." (4) Essentially, what the Church finds is a world suffused with change, burdened with inequities, but also challenged by sharpened perceptions of how things ought to be. And the Council Fathers proclaim "that Christ, who died and was raised for the sake of all, can show man the way and strengthen him through the Spirit in order to be worthy of his destiny" (10).

What is the way that Christ shows? What is the vision of life which the Church offers to the world? These are the questions answered in the first major part of the Pastoral Constitution. Through four chapters the fathers articulate a theological anthropology and an ecclesiology that responds to the needs of the human community in our time. And along the way they also comment on some of the specific concerns that confront us.

Chapter One describes "the dignity of the human person," observing that we are created in God's image but also caught in the web of sin. The noble realities of human freedom and intelligence, the beauty of moral sensibility, are set over against the mystery of death. The tension between these two aspects is viewed as a source for a peculiarly modern issue:

atheism. This phenomenon is examined in some detail. And a characteristically pastoral conclusion is offered:

> Atheism must be countered both by presenting true teaching in a fitting manner and by the full and complete life of the Church and of her members... What does most to show God's presence clearly is the brotherly love of the faithful who, being all of one mind and spirit, work together for the faith of the Gospel and present themselves as a sign of unity (21).

All of this is then recapitulated in a vibrantly proclaimed Christology.

Chapter Two develops the notion of the human person as communitarian. In so doing, it establishes itself as in continuity with one of the richest and most constant themes of the Catholic Christian tradition. Far from a naively individualistic vision of the human, the Church proclaims a socially sensitive perspective.

> God desired that all men should form one family and deal with each other in a spirit of brotherhood... Furthermore, the Lord Jesus when praying to the Father "that they may all be one... even as we are one" implies a certain parallel between the union existing among the divine persons and the union of the sons of God in truth and love (24).

This proclamation leads to a description of the societal nature of the person and, therefore, of the importance of the "common good." Related themes are developed: the irreducible worth of the individual person, the challenge to a concern for enemies, the fundamental equality of all, the challenge of human solidarity.

Chapter Three extends this vision into the arena of human activity, affirming the human person's *right* to act and to affect the environment, at the same time noting the difficulties faced by this desire for human autonomy and self-expression. Life is so complex; there is so much interconnectedness; there is the burden of sin. Still, the valid call to autonomous and mature human action remains. Indeed, it is forcefully asserted by a Christian vision. For

> of all the Spirit makes free men, who are ready to put aside love or self and integrate earthly resources into human life, in order to reach out to that future day when mankind itself will become an offering accepted by God (38).

This eschatology which nonetheless keeps a vital place for human activity and for "worldly" concerns sets the stage for the Council's "pastoral" understanding of the Church. Chapter Four expresses this ecclesiology. It begins with the simple but far-reaching statement that the Church and the world are mutually interrelated. It is not simply a matter of the Church giving to the world; rather, it is a matter of "mutual exchange" (40).

> In pursuing its own salvific purpose not only does the Church communicate divine life to men but in a certain sense it casts the reflected light of that divine life over all the earth, notably in the way it heals and elevates the dignity of the human person, in the way it consolidates society, and endows the daily activity of men with a deeper sense and meaning (40).

We must note that this quotation refers to the three aspects which were the subject of the first three chapters. In so doing it also indicates the focus of the rest of the fourth chapter. For the fathers express in some detail what the Church offers to the world of human person, human society and human activity.

> There is no human law so powerful to safeguard the personal dignity and freedom of man as the Gospel which Christ entrusted to the Church (41).

> Christ did not bequeath to the Church a mission in the

political, economic, or social order: the purpose he
assigned to it was a religious one. But this religious
mission can be the source of commitment, direction, and
vigor to establish and consolidate the community of men
(42).

Let Christians follow the example of Christ who
worked as a craftsman; let them be proud of the opportunity to carry out their earthly activity in such a way as
to integrate human, domestic, professional, scientific and
technical enterprises with religious values, under whose
supreme direction all things are ordered to the glory of
God (43).

At the same time the Church is the recipient of the world's
ministrations.

The Church learned early in its history to express the
Christian message in the concepts and language of different peoples... Indeed, this kind of adaptation and
preaching of the revealed Word must ever be the law of all
evangelization...
The Church has a visible social structure, which is a
sign of its unity in Christ: as such it can be enriched, and it
is being enriched, by the evolution of social life-
... Whoever contributes to the development of the community of mankind on the level of family, culture,
economic and social life, and national and international
politics according to the plan of God, is also contributing
in no small way to the community of the Church insofar
as it depends on things outside itself (44).

And all of this is so because of the cosmic centrality of
Christ, "the alpha and the omega" (45).

Part Two

The second part of the *Pastoral Constitution on the
Church in the Modern World* is devoted to a discussion of

five of the most pressing human issues of our day.

Chapter One focuses on "the dignity of marriage and the family." It notes that the health of the family has to be seen in the context of the health of society. Hence, as a component of their concern about society, the fathers "present certain key points of the Church's teaching in a clearer light," (47) on the one hand, reiterating traditional doctrine and, on the other hand, providing a new emphasis.

This new emphasis is manifest in the first words, which provide a definition of Christian marriage.

> The intimate partnership of life and love which constitutes the married state has been established by the creator and endowed by him with its own proper laws. (48)

Procreation is then viewed as a goal and consequence of this.

> By its very nature the institution of marriage and married love is ordered to the procreation and education of the offspring and it is in them that it finds its crowning glory. (48)

The reproclamation of traditional doctrine is exemplified in the discussion of sexuality, marital fidelity, respect for life, including prenatal life, and the meaning of human fertility. And on the question of artificial contraception, a delicate balance is maintained.

> In questions of birth regulation the sons of the Church ...are forbidden to use methods disapproved of by the teaching authority of the Church in its interpretation of the divine law (51).

A footnote at this point adds this comment:

> By order of the Holy Father, certain questions requiring further and more careful investigation have been given

over to a commission for the study of population, the
family, and births, in order that the Holy Father may pass
judgment when its task is completed. With the teaching of
the magisterium standing as it is, the Council has no
intention of proposing concrete solutions at this moment.

Finally, this chapter recognizes the deeper role which the
family plays in transmitting the values of a society and the
Church. All have a responsibility to support the institution
of the family; and organizations and associations within the
Church are encouraged to build up the well-being of family
life.

Chapter Two considers the "proper development of culture." The Council understands this term quite broadly.

The word "culture" in the general sense refers to all those
things which go to the refining and developing of man's
diverse mental and physical endowments... Hence it follows that culture necessarily has historical and social
overtones;... in this sense one can speak about a plural-
ity of cultures (53).

Still, the Council has a relatively concrete view of its contemporary content. In what seems a sort of recapitulation of
the phenomenology that appeared earlier in the document,
contemporary culture is described. It is "a new age in human
history" involving

... the tremendous expansion of the natural and human
sciences, the increase of technology, and the advances in
developing and organizing media of communication (54).

These developments cause difficulties, but they are also
occasions of grace. They can work to human good so long as
one realizes that "culture must be subordinated to the integral development of the human person, to the good of the
community and of the whole of mankind" (59).

This observation provides the fathers with a criterion,

allowing them to make some rather specific comments. All human persons have a right to access to the goods of culture. Special attention should be given to the provision of education to all. And respect should be developed for the specific forms of communication characteristic of the culture, in particular to literature and the arts.

The focus for Chapter Three is "economic and social life." This section begins by once again stressing the dignity and vocation of the human person. It calls for a reform of the world's economic system so that all may benefit. For the true success of the economy is not merely in producing more, but that all may live better (64). There is thus a need to remove huge economic differences, and to be sure that the most powerful nations do not dominate and control the world's riches.

Human labor has a value beyond the means of production or raw materials. Human beings have a right and a duty to work. For

> human work, whether exercised independently or in subordination to another, proceeds from the human person, who, as it were, impresses his seal on the things of nature and reduces them to his will (67).

This section of the Pastoral Constitution also encourages participation in the running of an enterprise by the workers and affirms the right to form labor unions. Indeed, it views this right as "among the fundamental rights of the individual" (68).

There is a common purpose to created things, which are for the good of the entire human race. Therefore the human community is obliged to come to the relief of the poor, and not just from superfluous goods. At the same time,

> property and other forms of private ownership of external goods contribute to the expression of personality and provide man with the opportunity of exercising his role in society and in the economy (71).

So concern for the needs of the poor does not lead to the collectivist solution.

In the end, these tensions must be resolved as Christians put socio-economic life into the context of Christ and work to build his kingdom, "accomplishing the task of justice under the inspiration of charity" (72).

Since human persons are social creatures, they incarnate their yearnings in political structures. This the Council Fathers celebrate in Chapter Four.

> Men are repudiating political systems...which hinder civil and religious liberty or victimize their citizens through avarice and political crimes, or distort the use of authority from being at the service of the common good to benefiting the convenience of political parties or of the governing classes (73).

That is not how it should be. Rather the political order "must be exercised within the limits of the moral order and directed toward the common good according to the juridicial order legitimately established or due to be established." (74)

All have a right to participate in this public life, and all should do so with "a generous and loyal spirit of patriotism, but without narrow-mindedness, so that they will always keep in mind the welfare of the whole human family" (75). Finally, precisely so that this may take place, the Church must not be confused with the political community, nor be bound to any political system. Rather the Church must insist on her right always and everywhere

> to preach the faith, to proclaim its teaching about society, to carry out its task among men without hindrance, and to pass moral judgment even in matters relating to politics, whenever the fundamental rights of man or the salvation of souls requires it (76).

Finally, in Chapter Five, the Council fathers move to the fostering of peace and the establishment of a community of nations. "In our generation . . . the whole human race faces a moment of supreme crisis" (77). For there cannot develop a more human world without a renewed determination to bring about the reality of peace. Therefore, in this very extensive chapter the Council calls for a peace based on justice, and urges the establishment of agencies of peace.

"Peace is more than the absence of war" (78). But it is that. So the first half of this chapter deals with the issue of war. The document condemns terrorism and war without limitations, the methodical extermination of peoples, and the subjugation of other nations. In a series of strongly worded statements, the Council fathers declare that "the development of armaments by modern science has immeasurably magnified the horror and wickedness of war, and that every act of war directed to the indiscriminate destruction of whole cities or vast areas is a crime against God and man" (80). Still, the Council also recognizes a country's right to legitimate self-defense. It asks nations to honor conventions and agreements about the waging of war and, in particular, notes that the arms race is no way to preserve peace.

> Rather than eliminate the causes of war, the arms race serves only to aggravate the position. As long as extravagant sums of money are poured into the development of new weapons, it is impossible to devote adequate aid in tackling the misery which prevails at the present day in the world (81).

So, they express words of support for efforts, especially international efforts, to curb war and to work for peace.

But if peace is to be built into the structures of the international community, then it is necessary to eradicate the causes of dissension and to continue efforts to create agencies of peace. And so, in the second half of this chapter the Pastoral Constitution emphasizes the need to establish stuctures that will facilitate the development of an international community. Specifically, there is need for agencies that are attentive to the poorer regions of the world, regions that still lack sufficient food, health care, education and employment. There is also need for structures that will control the excesses of profit-taking, nationalism and militarism. Finally, there is need to promote international cooperation in the matter of population.

All of this is not something which Christians should simply observe and commend. Rather there should be an active role.

> Indeed it is the duty of the whole people of God, under the teaching and example of the bishops, to alleviate the hardships of our times within the limit of its means, giving generously, as was the ancient custom of the Church (88).

Indeed, the Fathers suggest that the institutional Church should have an active role. In a prophetic comment

> the Council suggests that it would be most opportune to create some organization of the universal Church whose task it would be to arouse the Catholic community to promote the progress of areas which are in want and foster social justice between nations (90).

Just this happened when the Pontifical Commission for Justice and Peace of which one of the present authors was the first director, was established by the Holy See in 1967.

Conclusion

And so this long and intricate document nears its conclusion.

> Drawn from the treasures of the teaching of the Church, the proposals of this Council are intended for all men, whether they believe in God or whether they do not explicitly acknowledge him (91).

The fathers of the Council commit themselves to this fraternal vision. They acknowledge that

> such a mission requires us first of all to create in the Church itself mutual esteem, reverence and harmony, and acknowledge all legitimate diversity (92).

And they commit themselves to respectful collaboration with all men and women of good will. "For our part, our eagerness for such dialogue...excludes nobody." (92) The authors of the Pastoral Constitution do this, after all, because of a profoundly theological and deeply humanistic conviction:

> Christians can yearn for nothing more ardently than to serve the men of this age with an ever growing generosity and success...It is the Father's will that we should recognize Christ our brother in the persons of all men, and love them with an effective love, in words and in deed, thus bearing witness to the truth; and it is his will that we should share with others the mystery of his heavenly love (93).

Significance of the Document

In assessing the continuing significance of the Pastoral Constitution, it seems that there are two pivotal ideas that should be highlighted. The first is the dignity of the human person. The second is the work of the Church.

Out of the experience of war and slaughter, science and technology, the document affirms the dignity and destiny of the human person. It is a bold and heroic affirmation, standing in contradiction to the litany of atrocities, economic theories, scientific and technological advances proposed as the reality of the modern world. This human dignity is affirmed especially in the context of community. Human rights are a logical consequence of that dignity and living in community.

The second critical idea is a redefinition of the work of the Church. Along with the work of conversion and sanctification, the Church is to be a voice and a moral force to bring about an environment in which humanity can reach its dignity in imaging the Creator. To be about such work demands an engagement with the entire human community. It means that the Church has to confront the world. Indeed, the salvation of the Church can only be worked out in the context of the world.

But this redefinition of the Church and work implies a redefinition of membership in the Church. Before the Council, to be a Catholic might have invoked a definition which had to do with one's place in the Church structure, the reception of the sacraments, adhering to a code of personal morality, participating in devotions, and earning one's salvation. To be a Catholic in the context of Vatican II and the Pastoral Constitution refocuses those demands. It calls for an acute awareness of married life, culture, socio-economic life, politics, peace and war.

It calls for a struggle against social sins generated in these areas and hindering men and women from coming to God. With the *Constitution on the Sacred Liturgy,* it demands an engaged liturgy and spirituality to work out salvation in the context of the community. With so many of the Council documents, it speaks of evangelization as a natural function of Church membership, sharing the good news in the world and not in opposition to the world. These consistent themes revolving around social concern, evangelization, and spirituality begin to articulate this qualitive redefinition of what it is to be Church in the modern world. The question becomes not whether outside the Church there is salvation; rather it is whether outside of justice, evangelization, and spirituality there is Church or salvation.

The leaders of the Church who gathered for Vatican II, and the experts they brought to advise them were formed by the experience of two great wars. They were painfully aware of the holocaust, the ravages of modern weapons, the potential for nuclear destruction. They were bishops who for the first time brought to a Church Council the variety of world culture. They brought, too, the personal experience of a Church confronting political and economic systems. They were engaged culturally, economically, and politically. Along with these experiences the bishops were exposed to perhaps the greatest revolution of our time: the development of science and technology. Almost all of them had access to instant communication, and not a few were comfortable with world travel. This essay cannot fully document the profound effect which historical, cultural, and societal influences had in shaping this document. But it is sufficient to say that these influences did not allow the bishops to rest content with an internal definition of Church.

Influence of the Document

Did the Pastoral Constitution have a continuing influence on Church life? Did the leaders of the Church accept this redefinition and attempt to live it out? The answer is yes. Perhaps we can exemplify this by noting some of the writings and some of the structures which seem to emerge from this initiative. We begin with the papacy itself.

The teaching of both Paul VI and John Paul II clearly reflect the developing influence of the document. Paul ended the Vatican exile with papal visits to a global flock. John Paul II has been even more vigorous in bringing the papal message to nations and cultures around the world. Both popes have visited and addressed the United Nations. Paul VI, in addition to writing *Progressio Populorum* which explored in depth some of the themes of the Pastoral Constitution, also convoked the Synods on Justice and on Evangelization, and established the World Day of Peace each year. John Paul II's encyclical *Redemptor Hominis* addresses the dignity of the human person. His series of talks on marriage might even be viewed as a development of the section on Marriage and Family Life in the document. *On Human Work* finds its roots in the context of the section on Socio-Economic Life. The Section on Peace and War finds a strong affirmation in the papal address at Hiroshima.

The same could be said for its influence in the various Bishops' Conferences on national and regional levels. The work of the Latin American Bishops' Conference at Medellin and Puebla would be an obvious example. So also are a number of American initiatives. But we will return to those in a moment.

Finally, the Pastoral Constitution has literally changed the face of the institutional Church. The Roman Curia is no longer Roman or even Italian. New offices such as Justice and Peace and the Council of the Laity have been created. A new perception of the role of the laity in sanctifying the world, calling for a more informed and articulate laity commissioned not only to do the work of the Church, but also to be the Church in the modern world, has been increasingly structured into Church life.

The involvement of the pope and the bishops, as well as the local Church, in social and political issues speaks of this newly developing social critique. The final configuration of these shifts is far from certain, but it is obvious that the Pastoral Constitution has profoundly influenced their shaping during these past twenty years.

The Impact of the Pastoral Constitution on the North American Church

Many historians would say that the years since World War II have witnessed the coming of age of the Church in the United States. The American Catholic is now typically middle class, comfortable, and upwardly mobile. Catholics, except for a growing Hispanic presence, are post-immigrant people. They are well educated.

At the same time the United States itself has faced an astonishing number of challenges in this period. The tradition of isolationism has broken down, to be replaced by the cold war and the arms race. The war in Korea was frustrating and the conflict in Viet Nam divisive. Both actions taught us to paint our moral battles in more shades than black and white. These same times also brought our nation unprecendented affluence and an astonishing growth in science and technology. The frontier of space has just begun to open. Yet even with these successes there has still been an uncomfortable dissatisfaction. The solution to social problems of racism, poverty, and so many others remain unsolved.

It is no simple task to measure the influence of a document such as this in such a context. Certainly the influence has not been a one way street. As Americans our culture and times have affected and colored our reading of this document. The questions of special urgency considered in the second part of the document have an unique application to a nation and a local Church struggling with the litany of these challenges. So the impact of the document might best be measured in the light of these areas which the decree outlined.

The first area to be addressed by the Constitution is the Dignity of Marriage and the Family, and it is perhaps the area in which it is most difficult to assess the significance of the document. It is clear that the American Church pays far greater attention to preparation for marriage and to the cultivation of quality married life. Numerous programs have been established to this end. At the same time, the debate about contraception, and about other sexual matters, continues to trouble the Church.

Given the multiple issues present here, both theological and sociological, a balanced assessment is simply beyond the scope of this review. Still, let it be said that the continued discussion of these issues, the clarification of the current situation, and its evaluation in light of the themes of the Pastoral Constitution is a most important project. All we can do is commend that project, and urge that it be actively advanced.

The second problem of special urgency is the Proper Development of Culture. To deal with the impact of culture is always an elusive quest. It becomes more complicated when it is brought to the American scene, where we are a nation too often unsure of our own cultural identity. The process of coming to terms with our diverse cultural roots is still very much a part of the American agenda. The United States is a country blessed and plagued with affluence which often degenerates into conspicuous consumption. Technology, communications, and television threaten to homogenize our culture even more. The American Church is only beginning to address some of these major issues.

Two areas which have been deeply affected by this section of the Constitution have been American Catholic missionary efforts and regional pastoral concerns.

Since the first part of this century the United States has supplied an enormous number of missionaries to countries around the world. The affirmations of the document, especially in the development of culture, have been an occasion for North Americans to reexamine our approach as a local Church to other cultures. Certainly it has made us more respectful and sensitive to the heritage of other people. With the added impetus of the *Decree on the Church's Missionary Activity* the missions in the last twenty years have become quite different. We have come to realize their reciprocal nature. And we have begun to define more sharply the difference between preaching the gospel of Christ and exporting the gospel of the American culture and politics.

In the United States, the appreciation of the local culture has also been apparent in the publication of regional pastoral letters by local bishops seeking to name the gifts and values of their people. The bishops of Appalachia wrote "This Land Is Home To Me." It seeks to affirm their people and to explore the problems which prevent them from overcoming poverty, ignorance, and the lack of human dignity. The bishops of the Heartland have published a statement, "Strangers and Guests," which deals with the unique cultural expression of a Church seeking to preserve the values of the rural community and the family farm. In both cases it is the Church respecting and owning the culture while dealing with the questions which affect people's lives.

The two 1984 pastorals on the Hispanic and the Black communities address at last their own ethnic contexts, cultural values and dramatic histories, after years of neglect. Notably, there are now ten Black Catholic bishops and a dozen Hispanics in our nation, as compared with two or three before Vatican II.

This section of the Pastoral Constitution is very subtle and speaks of a complicated interaction with the experience of society. It is a guide to dealing with diversity and tradition, an ongoing question in ethnic American Catholicism. It is also a guide to dealing with the emerging influence of cultural patterns worldwide.

The Socio-Economic section of the document deals primarily with the issues of labor, goods, and capital. With the Church in the United States becoming more middle class and upwardly mobile, some real challenges are presented to the American dream. How do we live with affluence and consumerism? What is our responsibility to the poor here in our own country and around the world? Where do labor unions fit into a Church which is moving beyond its working class roots?

This section fits very comfortably into the social tradition of the last ninety years both in the Church universal and especially in the Church of the United States. It found a strong reflection in the words of John Paul II, when he spoke of sharing not just from our abundance, but from our substance. It has also influenced the statements and writings of the United States bishops. A pastoral letter on Marxism was published in 1981, and now a pastoral on the Economy is being developed. In addition, a number of statements by the National Council of Catholic Bishops and the United States Catholic Conference reflect the strong influence of the socio-economic principles laid out in the conciliar statement. In development, in economics, and in labor issues the principles of the document are evident. (Some examples: the Statement on the World Food Crisis: A Pastoral Plan, NCCB, 1974; Development-Dependency: The Role of the Multinational Corporations, USCC, 1974; The Economy:

Human Dimensions, USCC, 1975; Farm Labor, NCCB, 1968; Resolution on Farah Manufacturing — Amalgamated Clothing Workers Dispute, USCC, 1973)

The stirring struggle of the Farm Workers, largely led by Mexican-Americans, under the banner of Our Lady of Guadalupe, was greatly strengthened by Vatican II teaching and the ecclesial support this generated.

Finally, it is interesting to note the use of union boycotts in this country and the support they receive from the Church. Most all of the successful or ongoing boycotts, whether they were lettuce or grapes, of Campbell, Farah, or Nestle, have all sought the blessing of the Church by appealing to the principles articulated in the Pastoral Constitution. In this issue of boycotts, as with so many other areas of socio-economic concern, the agenda of this decree continues to influence the directions of the American Church

Perhaps one of the most significant shifts in the American Church may have been precipitated by the section on the Political Life of the Community. During the first part of this century, one of the tasks of the Church seemed to be to establish the position that Catholics "belonged." Now, with the patriotism and loyalty of Catholics established, the challenge of the Constitution has brought the Church to a position beyond uncritical Americanism. Individual Catholics are part of government at all levels. But more significantly, the Church has developed a political agenda as it faces the American government. The major issues it lists as priorities includes: Abortion, Arms Control, Capital Punishment, The Economy, Education, Family Life, Food and Agriculture Policy, Health Care, Housing, Human Rights, Mass Media, and Regional Conflicts in the World.

In many ways, the Church has remained a sleeping giant. in its political influence. But signs of its awakening are certainly present. Along with the traditional concerns of abortion and education, the intervention of the Church in American policy in El Salvador and Latin America has had a significant impact. The recent pastoral on topics of war and peace marked a break with the government stand of opposition to Russia and communism at any price. Over sixty official statements have been issued by the NCCB and the USCC dealing with the Church and the political life of our country. Still the effectiveness of the Church as a voice in the political arena is still uncertain. The next few years could be a critical time in assessing the response of the American Church to the challenges of this section on political life.

The final problem of special urgency addressed in the Pastoral Constitution is the issue of Peace and the Promotion of the Community of Nations. In the United States the build up of the arms race and the conflict in Viet Nam have caused the Church to issue a number of statements on war and the military. As was mentioned above, the most significant influence in this area is the bishops' pastoral on war and peace, as it examines the morality of modern conflict and the role of the Christian. The potential impact on the Church and the possibilities for lessening the threat of the weapons of ultimate destruction are just beginning to be felt.

Along with the official statements of the NCCB and the USCC, there have also been a significant number of individual bishops who have spoken out on the nuclear question. Local pastoral letters have expressed concern and opposition to various aspects of the nuclear threat. Catholics, and especially bishops, have had an important influence in the peace movement in this country. Yet it is not certain that the impact of the teaching of this section of the Pastoral Constitution has filtered down into the lives of the ordinary Catholic, or that the witness of Church people on this question will translate into the lives of ordinary Catholics.

Through Catholic Relief Services-USCC the American Church extends emergency and development assistance to millions of the poorest in fifty countries of the Third World, and helps to resettle refugees. This outpouring of compassion to the needy beyond our shores began after World War II and was intensified by Vatican II. Undocumented refugees within our own country are now helped by the Santuary Ministry, with grave risk often to these new apostles.

Conclusion

It would not be fair to end this essay without mentioning one other aspect of the American Church where the Constitution has had a significant influence. Like the Church in Rome, so also the structures of the American Church have been affected.

Religious Institutes, especially those of women, have been at the forefront for implementing *Gaudium et Spes* in all the areas outlined above, and at all levels. They provide much of the personnel, research and animation for Justice and Peace centers in all their variety. Laity have begun also to find their role, through Pax Christi, for instance, and by introducing social concern into family and professional circles, and through educational and retreat programs.

In 1967 the bishops of the United States significantly revamped their national body to form the National Conference of Catholic Bishops, and the United States Catholic Conference to serve as their societal arm. Much of the work of both bodies reflects the agenda of the Pastoral Constitution. Again, in 1971 the bishops established the Campaign for Human Development to combat the causes of poverty in our society. Again, its charter could have been an addendum to the Council document. Similarly, on a diocesan level over one hundred offices of justice and peace have been established throughout the United States. A look at a local or national Catholic Directory today, in comparison to one in the mid-sixties, would show even more significant structural changes wrought by the Council and especially by the impact of this particular document.

Perhaps it would be best to conclude by imitating the conclusion of the document itself. Though it is general, the conciliar plan has impacted the lives of individuals, the structures of dioceses, and the shape of the national conference in the United States. It has provided a relevant agenda as the Church faces the modern world. Yet the most important contribution of all may be that it presents us with the challenge to promote the spirit of love and to recognize the spirit of hope in the world today.

Vatican II: Setting, Themes, Future Agenda

Timothy E. O'Connell*

In the movie *Family Affair*, Bea Arthur portrays a Catholic woman beset with many of life's troubles. Her husband was grumpy. One of her sons was getting a divorce. Her daughter said she might not "wait until marriage." And in the wider world there was war, inflation and perpetual smog. How to explain all these catastrophes? She has an answer. "Ya know what it is Harry? It's that ee-ku-menical council. That's what. It's all their fault!"

While Ms. Arthur may be stretching things a bit, there is

*The group of scholars and pastors who developed the various papers which constitute the chapters of this book also shared in concluding discussions. Those discussions, with exciting insights contributed by all the participants, form the basis for this final essay. The author frankly acknowledges his dependence on the contributions of all. At the same time, he accepts all responsibility for the formulation appearing here, and particularly for any deficiencies which may become apparent.

no doubt that the Second Vatican Council was a significant event. The previous essays have detailed the content and impact of the various documents issuing from the Council. They also offered insights into the significance of those documents. Still it may be helpful to attempt some reflections on the overall project that was Vatican II.

What follows will consider three points. First, an attempt to highlight some elements of the Council's setting, some items of historical context that help to explain its approach. Secondly, an enumeration of several of the more powerful themes that emerged within the Council. Thirdly, an indication of the continuing agenda for the Church, agenda including both items not considered by the Council and items generated by the Council.

Setting

From the point of view of the secular world, it is clear that Vatican II was the first council convened in the Global Village. It was not a happy village, of course. But it was real, and its reality could not be ignored. Something new was afoot in the world.

In Europe there was the debris of two world wars in thirty years: Economic dislocation and instability of governments. In the Third World there was the emergence of self-consciousness, the end of colonialism and the affirmation of diverse identities. The United States and the Soviet Union were firmly established in their cold war relationship, and other nation states were increasingly drawn into this polarized world map. Throughout all of the northern hemisphere the age of the industrial revolution, with its basis in the transportation of materials and people, was giving way to the cybernetic age, rooted in instantaneous communication.

The dawn of a new day was at hand. No one could guess what the weather would be, much less what the events of the day would bring. But the day could not be avoided. Perhaps the Second Vatican Council is neither more nor less than the honest admission of this new day, and the sincere attempt to respond to it from the perspective of Christian faith.

This interpretation is even more convincing when we take into account the context of religious history. The Council of Trent had established the Church in an adversary relationship with other Christians. And the affiliation of various Christian leaders with national governments had the effect of replicating these polarities in the secular sphere. This set of coalitions and antinomies was deeply shaken by the revolutions of 1776 and 1789, and by the rise of the secular nation state. Inasmuch as the Church was identified with the old order, it was a simple matter to redefine the scene as an opposition between Church and the secular world.

There were efforts to think more positively of the world in general and of secularity in particular. In the field of theology, the early nineteenth century finds considerable effort in this regard. Perhaps the center of this open theology was the University of Tubingen in Germany. But its initiatives were not always received with enthusiasm. From Rome there issued a long series of documents opposing these integrative and open-minded approaches. The *Syllabus of Errors* (1864) and several other writings of Pius IX. Various documents from Vatican I (1870) and the encyclical *Aeterni Patris* in which Leo XIII called for a return to the perennial philosophy of Thomas Aquinas (1879). The condemnations of Modernism in *Lamentabili* and Pius X's *Pascendi* (1907).

Needless to say these various documents dealt with differing specific questions. But there was a common theme. Indeed, for a hundred years the Roman Catholic Church has wrestled with a single fundamental issue: what is the significance of the secular world, of human life lived on its own terms. And in varying ways, each of these documents gave the same suspicious answer. The estimation of the human and the secular was negative. The Church and the world stood in opposition to one another.

This question was not reserved to Roman Catholicism. To a large extent the Protestant tradition had become identified with secular culture. But the Neo-Orthodox movement represents the same suspicious movement emerging in Protestantism. But it was, nonetheless, characteristically

Catholic. And it was a concern that would not end. We will see that Vatican II raised the question of the significance of human life, and that it responded with an affirming and appreciative stance. For now, however, it is important to note that Vatican II was not raising a new question. It was returning to an old question and formulating a new and different answer.

In enumerating the factors which constituted the historical context for the Council, we should also take note of the internationalization of the Church. The very membership of the Council exemplified the Global Village. Karl Rahner has pointed out that unlike Vatican I where the bishops representing the Third World churches tended themselves to be Europeans, the members of Vatican II were the natural sons of the churches they led. ("Toward a fundamental Theological Interpretation of Vatican II," *Theological Studies* 40 [1979], 716-727.) It was an ecumenical council in the fullest sense of the term, and perhaps to an unprecendented extent.

Themes: Experience

In Studying the documents produced by the Second Vatican Council, one discovers a series of pivotal themes. The themes were not themselves the topics for the writing. Indeed, one suspects that the various Council fathers were not equally conscious of their presence and influence. Nonetheless it is clear that they exercised major influence upon the product of their deliberations. In this section I will describe several of these themes.

There is one motif that appears over and over in the course of the Council. Indeed, in many ways, it may be the heuristic key to the entire enterprise. And that is the legitimate significance of human experience. John XXIII had reversed the policy of antagonism between Church and world when he called for an aggionamento and an opening of the windows. And it was clear that he foresaw not only a stronger proclamation to the world of the Church's message, but also a reception by the Church of a genuine worldly wisdom. In doing so he implicitly affirmed, and the Council ratified, human experience as a true *locus theologicus.*

Over and over again in their Council speeches the fathers would declare, "Our pastoral experience reveals..." They reflected on their experience, and on the experience of other members of the Church, fellow believers, and of men and women of the world. And they attempted to read and learn from the "signs of the time" that this experience revealed.

Having affirmed the significance of experience, the bishops were led to several related conclusions. First, one's experience ought to be genuinely meaningful. People have a right to experience that is genuinely responsive to human needs and inclinations, not only in the secular sphere but also in the ecclesial. Perhaps especially in the ecclesial sphere. Hence the call for a reform of the liturgy which would introduce the vernacular, would clarify and emphasize symbolic language attuned to contemporary humankind, would challenge celebrants to an interpersonal style of liturgical presiding. Hence also the programs for priestly formation and religious life mandated by those documents. Hence also the very existence of the *Decree on Communications,* with its recognition of the human right to know.

Experience ought also to be influential. Men and women have a right to act on their experience, to draw conclusions from it, and to shape their lives in light of it. Hence the *Decree on Religious Liberty* and on *Ecumenism,* with their affirmation of the rights of conscience.

Finally, experience ought to be inspirational. That is, it ought to be the sort of experience able to express the presence of the spirit of God. It ought to be uplifting, respectful, and humanizing. Hence the very existence of the Council's finest moment, *The Pastoral Constitution on the Church in the Modern World,* calling for continuing efforts to humanize the world of our day.

And perhaps all three of these, human experience as meaningful, influential and inspirational, were powerfully expressed in the Council's attitude toward revelation. First, there was the reaffirmation of Scripture as central to the life of the Church. Both in the liturgy and elsewhere the biblical texts were brought close to the people, and by implication the people were invited to render their own interpretation. The importance of technical exegesis was not overlooked, of course. But the reading of Scripture in the vernacular and the increasing emphasis upon preaching encouraged applied interpretations that would be rooted in and responsive to the dynamics of personal experience.

But there is more. The *Constitution on Revelation* may have spoken of Scripture and tradition as a special font of God's presence. Still between the lines of this document and of all its proclamations, the Council affirmed the fact that all the world is somehow revelatory. It proclaimed the sacramentality of creation. Indeed, in some ways it complemented the theology of revelation with the theology of creation. And in so doing it relativized the explicitly religious by grounding it in and making it accountable to the presence of God in human experience.

The *Constitution on the Liturgy* was pivotal in effecting this change. We are well aware of the dislocation caused by the liturgical reform. But those who suggest that this pain was due simply to a clumsiness of implementation miss the point. The *Constitution on the Sacred Liturgy,* and the reform which it mandated and initiated, are the very incarnation of the *geist* of Vatican II. By themselves the other documents could easily have become mere verbiage. The concreteness of the liturgical reform enfleshed the Council's dream. It exemplified the Council's conviction. And it submitted the Council's decisions to the acid test of ordinary life.

Some have said that the difficulties surrounding the liturgical reform were due to the fact that this document was the first to be issued by the Council. And to some small extent that may be true. But it is equally true that with the publication of this document, the die was cast. In some other, very real sense all the other documents are simply glosses on the symbolic text of the new liturgy. The *Constitution on the Church* may, for example, speak eloquently of the Church as the People of God. But for the members of the Church, the real proclamation of that truth occurred the first time a priest looked out at his congregation and said: "Let us exchange with one another the sign of Christ's peace."

...History

The message of human experience was only one of the sources for the proposed liturgical reform. A review of the theological literature in the decades before the Council would make clear that an equally important source was historical study. Indeed a second, related but also complementary motif within the Council's product is "return to the sources." John O'Malley, S.J. points out that Vatican II was the first Council with a consciousness of its own location within history. ("Reform, Historical Consciousness and Vatican II's Aggiornamento," *Theological Studies* 32 (1971), 573-601.) The bishops, and even more their theological periti, came to Rome with an unprecedented knowledge of the Church's past. They might still be tempted to use the courtly formulation: "As the Church has always taught . . . " But they knew that this was rarely the literal truth. The fruits of this historical consciousness were many.

For one thing the concept of tradition underwent a redefinition. It is part of the Catholic genius to provide always a counterforce to the seductive power of one's individual and present experience. It is precisely the role of "tradition" to neutralize our sad potential for solipsism. But often enough, tradition indicated nothing more than what some authority had been taught as a child. Tradition was "ways within memory," and the superior's memory at that. Hence the interaction of tradition and experience often degenerated into thinly disguised authoritarianism.

Under the influence of historical consciousness all this changed. Tradition became "ways beyond memory." It became the counterforce to the experience of *all* the members of the Church. It ceased being something in the immediate possession of anyone, it began to be something to be searched out by everyone. The invocation of tradition was not a command for docility but a call for critical thinking. What's more, in implementing this "return to the sources," in submitting the experience of the whole Church to the test of a long and diverse history, the Council fathers were redefining their own role. They were reconceptualizing the function of scholarship. They were rearranging the elements of magisterial action. And they were establishing on a throne of unprecedented power the true reality of ecclesiastical tradition.

Historical consciousness does not, however, speak only of the past. It is an awareness also of a transitory present and a genuinely new future. With its decision to return to the sources, the Council no doubt was particularly interested in retrieving the full richness of the Church's past. But the correlative insight about the future could not be avoided. In O'Malley's judgement, Vatican II is also noteworthy because it was the first Council to be aware of its own mortality. Unlike previous ecclesial gatherings, Vatican II knew that it was not speaking the last word. It was a creature of history. And like all such, its statements could only be provisional. It, too, must some day become part of the past, part of tradition, a source and dialogue partner with new, perhaps redically different, but equally legitimate human experience. That development of doctrine which had been described by Cardinal Newman might still not be comfortably named, it might not even be consciously affirmed by all the members of the Council. But its reality had been acknowledged in a decisive and irrevocable way.

. . . *Tensions*

Yet another noteworthy characteristic of Vatican II was a tension, a certain inconsistency with its conceptual positions. No doubt some degree of disunity is to be expected in any product of so many diverse individuals functioning in a collegial fashion. Nonetheless, that is not the only source for the Council's lack of integration. Another source seems to be the very specifically transitional character which the Council possessed. At least two examples of this tension can be named. First there is the coexistence of two diverse ecclesiologies. This is worth highlighting, precisely because it is so often overlooked. But the fact is that the vision of Church expressed in the *Dogmatic Constitution on the Church* is quite different from that found in the *Pastoral Constitution on the Church in the Modern World.*

The *Dogmatic Constitution* looks *into* the Church, defining its various parts and analyzing their relationship to one another. It views the Church in essentially hierarchical terms, with power, truth and supernational life itself flowing down from the top. It is true that the *Dogmatic Constitution on the Church* complements the hyperpapalism of Vatican I with the doctrine of episcopal collegiality. It also rejects a self-righteous regalism by insisting that Church leaders maintain a spiritual basis and a genuinely apostolic commitment. But the vision is still hierarchical, and the central sacrament of Church life is Holy Orders.

In many ways the goal of the *Dogmatic Constitution on the Church* was the reformation of the old ecclesiology, and it is arguably the best articulation that ecclesiology ever had. Still, it is the old ecclesiology. Despite the presence of organic metaphors such as People of God and Body of Christ, the ecclesial image remains essentially mechanistic. If the documents of Vatican I and related writings conceived of the Church in pyramidical terms, so does the *Dogmatic Constitution on the Church.* Where the material was once unyielding iron, it may now be warmly stained wood or even some friendly fabric. It is still a pyramid. It is understood not in the categories of botany or biology, of living things, but in the categories of geometry and physics, of things that are dead.

But something happened in the course of Vatican II. Besides this long planned treatise on the Church, even in its much modified revised and improved form, something else was needed. The world was still there. And, as we have seen, the relationship of the Church and world was at the heart of the Council. And so there emerged the *Pastoral Constitution on The Church In the Modern World.*, ungainly, unorganized, unaesthetic, an expression of instinct and intuition, not of the finely tuned insight. Still it presents another vision of the Church, the first clumsy expression of a new ecclesiology.

Here we look outward, viewing the Church in relation to the world. We understand the Church as an actor in the world, justifying itself by the fruits of its labor. The world needs the Church, and therefore the important thing is that it is present and active. The Church is a living organism, the fruit of the dynamic inter-relationship of its members, where the sum is synergistically more than the accumulation of its parts. To discuss the relative importance of the part is an exercise in narcissitic foolishness. The really significant thing is not one's role but one's membership. Indeed, within this Church all members are radically equal. The pivotal sacraments are those dealing with membership (Baptism and Confirmation) not with function, for all functions are interdependent.

Indeed, functions must justify their very existence, being measured against the ultimately pragmatic benchmark of fruitfulness. The Church is a very particular sort of body politic. And just as the parts of the human body, under the principle of totality, justify themselves through their contribution to the whole, and the whole justifies itself by its contribution to the world, so it is with the Church. Ministries there surely must be. But in the vision of the *Pasoral Constitution,* ministries are for the sake of mission and must justify themselves by the contribution that they make. Here, truly, is an organic image, the part ever changing and evolving, as the mystical but living body of Christ seeks ways to make itself more salvifically effective in the world.

There is, then, no doubt that the *Dogmatic Constitution* and the *Pastoral Constitution* present us with diverse ecclesiologies. Indeed, both visions remain with us to this day. (One can learn a great deal about one's conversation partners by asking them to name the most significant document of the Second Vatican Council!) To the extent that the

Council fathers gave expression to both of these visions, there is an evident tension in their teaching. But given the realities of this moment on the Church's history, that may be a blessing. Perhaps it is too soon to choose between them. Indeed, there may even be some way of synthesizing the mechanistic and the organic visions of Church. But at least, for the present, we can be conscious of the character of these visions and of how different they truly are.

There is a second tension. It is a truism of systematic theology that doctrines are at least partially the creatures of the philosophies in which they are expressed. The limitations of a particular philosophy establish the limits in which the faith can be articulated at any given moment. And similarly, changes in philosophic vision inevitably occasion changes in both the articulation and the understanding of the faith. It is therefore worth noting the coexistence at Vatican II of two philosophical visions.

The Council was convened out of the perspective of a renewed scholasticism. Its task was aggiornamento, the modification of the cultural forms of the faith without violence to its central essence. The Council was to give its attention to the "accidents" of faith, while all the time protecting its unchanging "substance."

And yet the Council's growing appreciation for historical consciousness was representative of the emerging insights of a new philosophy of process. What is real is not essence but existence, not being but becoming. Human persons exist not apart from history or above it, but within it. And consequently the distinction between substance and accidents, even if it is meaningful, is not useful in practical affairs. What the Council did changed the Church, changed it in the totality of its living reality. It will never be the same. In the dynamic interraction between the faith community and the living world, all has become somehow different. For example, translate the Roman Mass into Swahili, and one does not have a translation, one has a new experience.

From this perspective, fidelity to the faith is faithful fidelity to the process. In the evolving action of the Church's mission its identity and the active presence of God are progressively revealed. No doubt this appreciation of process was far from the minds of many Council fathers. Still, it is implicit in the decisions that they made, the actions that they took. Their affirmation of experience, their return to the sources, their openness to a new future, point inevitably to the truth affirmed in this new philosophy. And so, again, we must settle for noting the coexistence of these two worlds of thought. The power and the ambiguity of this Council reside precisely in this continuing tension. This leads us to the last motif.

... *Americanism*

As a last theme present in the Second Vatican Council we should point out its peculiarly American character. This is not to say that the Council was consciously American. Far from it. But it is to say that the vision implicit in the Council documents was extraordinarily consonant with the *geist* of American people and that the direction initiated by the Council found a ready audience in the members of the American Catholic Church. Indeed, one might even argue that the Council was least readily accepted by those members of the American Church least attuned to American life and most alienated from its spirit through European connections such as Roman ecclesiastical education.

What is this American spirit? Perhaps it can be potently exemplified in the advertising jargon: "New improved ... " An American approach to life incorporates an extraordinary openness to, even enthusiasm for change. Inasmuch as the entire national identity is understood as "the American experiment," there is an expectation of growth and development, revision and replacement.

America is, of course, a young country. It does not have a long tradition to maintain or defend. There is a sense in which America is short on history. But for all that, there is a peculiar historical consciousness, in the sense of an awareness of one's presence in process. The process is, of course, temporal. Yet in a curious twist, Americans often conceptualize it in spatial, not temporal terms. Theologian Joseph Sittler once pointed out that Europeans are long on history and short on space, whereas the converse is true in America. As a result, says Sittler, Europeans tend to view life in temporal terms; if something is a problem, wait it out. All things will pass, patience is the key. Americans, on the other hand, are characteristically impatient. When confronted by a problem, they move! They do something, going to another place where their short time may more happily be spent. In this regard, it is interesting to note the many meanings of the metaphor "frontier" in the American usage of the English language. We have frontiers of science, art, and of all knowledge. We have the political event of the New Frontier. We see space as the last frontier. The founding American experience is thereby transformed into an ideology of all human life.

The attack upon the frontier is a group experience, of course. But as a limit and testing experience, it is also notably dependent upon individual initiatives. Hence the American spirit accords great worth to the individual. At an extreme, it can degenerate into a self-serving individualism. At its best, however, it includes a profound recognition of the worth of the individual person. In so doing, moreover, it acknowledges the diversity among persons. As individuals came together in order to confront the American frontiers, they had to deal with their diversity. They had to recognize and resign themselves to the reality of pluralism. For a while the ideal of a melting pot was proclaimed. But homogeneity was never achieved. In the end the melting pot was replaced by a mosaic, where differences survive, are cultivated and flourish.

Pluralism, then, is not a price to be paid for survival. It is an asset which enriches life in human society. Americans do not yearn for identity, they struggle for coalition. They seek ways to work together in mutual recognition of diverse needs, interests and approaches.

Finally, inasmuch as the American experiment is a success, the American spirit exhibits unusual optimism. There is the abiding expectation that things will work out. That diverse individuals will find a way to work together. That in cooperation and collaboration they will find new and different and better ways to do things. That they will, through active intervention, construct a future that will be rewarding for all those involved.

This, then, leads to the American Myth. It has never been totally verified in experience, of course. Indeed, ample evidence could be provided to demonstrate that it is hypocritical. Nonetheless it survives as a dream, as an ideal vision of life.

Nor is it an essentially secular vision. The American Myth has been theologized into an American Doctrine whose feast day is Thanksgiving. According to this doctrine God is alive and active in history, working through us and helping us to shape that distinctive future whose frontier we confront. It is no accident that we find ourselves at this time and place in history. We have been placed here by God and are confronted with the promise and the challenge that divine action involves. Again, this doctrine comes in many forms. At its worse it can express the self-righteous narcissism of Manifest Destiny. At its best it can grow into a humble sense of responsibility, that fruit of undeserved giftedness which we call *noblesse oblige*.

Finally, the American Myth and the American Doctrine give rise to an American Strategy: action! The American approach to life is essentially and inevitably pragmatic. What develops loyalty is what works. And whatever works, works because human persons are active, and in their activity are intelligent, using their wits to pursue achievable goals.

Onto this stage, then, walks a council whose preeminent characteristic is a respect for human experience, immediate, powerful, active and diverse. Is there little wonder that Americans should find themselves resonating to the tunes that the Council played? Is it any wonder that American bishops should so easily take to the coalition-building that the Council required? Is it any wonder that sympathetic vibrations should develop not between the American Church and the established Mediterranean Churches, but between America, the pluralistic Churches of Germany and Low Countries and the young Churches of the Third World? And finally (and perhaps debatably), is it any wonder that in the years after the Council the center of innovative Catholic thought and action should cross the Atlantic and establish itself in the central region of the American Church?

Agenda

The Second Vatican Council generated a large number of agenda for life in the Church in the years following. A significant proportion of these agenda were established quite consciously, as the Council sought to implement its decisions. In large measure the years since have been spent dealing with these items of agenda. And at this point it is worth noting what a gargantuan task it has been.

First of all, there was the restructuring of the central ecclesiastical bureaucracy. A whole range of new secretariat were established, for liturgy, ecumenism, peace and justice, non-Christian religions, laity, unbelievers, and so on. There was the creation of structures to monitor (and hopefully encourage) a whole series of mandated changes. One has in mind liturgy, programs of priestly formation, and the renewal of religious life. There was the attempt to give lasting substance to the notion of collegiality, which resulted in the creation of the Synod of Bishops. There was the work around the world to organize bishops into functioning conferences of national hierarchy. And there was an analogous phenomenon at the diocesan level, with the development of presbyteral senates and pastoral councils.

But in the midst of these activities addressing administrative agenda, other agenda were being revealed. These dealt with underlying issues, with radical changes that would ultimately be required by the new vision which the Council spawned. Four of these can be mentioned.

First, there is the question of the relationship of the various bishops to the Bishop of Rome. Some have argued that the two Vatican Councils shared a common concern with the nature of the episcopacy. Vatican I spoke its understanding of the nature and role of the Bishop of Rome, and articulated an unprecedented hyperpapalism. Vatican II attempted to complement this with a clear statement on the meaning and duties of all the bishops. But as of now, these two Councils stand in uneasy proximity. The essential question remains: what is the true role of the Bishop of Rome? The answer of the nineteenth century was "universal jurisdiction." But the return to the sources that has characterized twentieth century Catholicism makes clear that this answer is not the only one to be found in our tradition. Is it the right answer for our time and for the future?

This question involves not only the role of the Pope but also the role of every bishop. One American bishop was recently heard to say: "I am first of all a bishop of the Roman Catholic Church and only secondly bishop of this diocese." We now know that his view is in many ways a characteristically nineteenth century one and that most of Catholic history would have seen matters in just the opposite way. They would have believed that one became a member of the College of Bishops precisely by assuming the mantle of leadership service in a particular local church, and that one best served the Church universal, the Roman Catholic Church, precisely through faithful and creative service to the local Church one led.

Hence in seeking to clarify the relationship of Pope and bishops, one is dealing with evolving definitions of both. The clarification of the individual terms and of their relationship is, moreover, not something that can be resolved through short-term intellectual investigation. Rather, if historical counsciousness teaches us anything, it is clear that this clarification will only emerge at the end of a slow process of interaction between faith and experience, between the full past of Church tradition and the present of lived discipleship.

The second item of the underlying agenda concerns the evolving definition of Church membership. The traditional core of that definition has, of course, been "faith and baptism." But inasmuch as the Church is a human institution, involving incarnation in sociological structure, this core definition has always been supplemented by requirements of discipline. In the European Church of the middle ages, identified with the secular state and incorporating many of its methods, these details could become quite extensive and their enforcement quite rigorous. Now, however, we are presented with the world-wide phenomenon of a disestablished Church. In Europe some semblance of affiliation may remain; but the actual conduct of government, in Italy for example, makes clear that it is more apparent than real. The United States, of course, has a conscious policy separating Church and state. An analogous situation obtains in most of the Third World, where if anything, it is anti-clericalism that is established.

In this relatively new situation it becomes utterly evident that the Catholic Church is a "voluntary society." It may not be completely accurate to say that the hierarchy exercises authority on the consent of the governed, as the phrase was used in classical social contract theory. But there is a certain sense in which that is really true. From a sociological point of view, the Church survives because of the ongoing consent given in faith by its members. In light of this, then, the question of what constitutes Church membership must be raised ever anew. What is it that allows one to count as Catholic? In a world where diversity is inevitable and, indeed, desirable, what are the limits of legitimate pluralism? How do these limits pertain to the orthodoxy of faith? To the orthopraxis of behavior? These questions are part of the abiding agenda bequeathed to us by Vatican II.

The third item concerns the relationship of the Roman Catholic Church to other Christian denominations. The presence of observers at the Council sessions as well as offices established since the Council to promote relations between the traditions made a strong statement about a new posture of interdenominational respect. Beyond this, however, the documents of Vatican II affirmed that other Christian traditions incorporate genuine "signs of the spirit." God acts through them, and they contribute to his saving design for the world.

This is a radical affirmation, but its implications for Church life and practice remain undeveloped. One would think that this conception of the various Christian denominations would suggest a new approach to intercommunion, to the faith-education of the off-spring of mixed marriages, to the regulation of the validity of sacramental marriages celebrated in the presence of a minister other than a Catholic priest. And beyond all this is the issue of reunion itself. Must reunion presuppose absolute uniformity of theological expression, of ritual practice, of spirituality and piety, of bureaucratic structure and of discipline? There seems to be no overwhelming reason why it should. In any case, these questions stand before us in light of the declarations of the Council with regard to the "separated brethren."

Finally, the Council left us with extensive agenda dealing with the relationship of the Church's mission to the life of the world. In traditional language, the Church saw itself as the repository and mediator of salvation. The Church protected the deposit of salvation, made God's presence and grace available to people, allowed people to be the recipients of salvation, and acted as judge of the legitimacy of their conscientious response to that gift. The scriptural text: "whatever you bind on earth is bound in heaven," was widely viewed as giving the Church power and justification for excluding individuals from the process and fruits of salvation. Indeed, while there has been extensive debate and careful nuancing of the dictum: "outside the Church there is no salvation," the notion retains wide currency.

Vatican II has changed all that. The Council's recognition of the significance of human experience has introduced us to a whole new theology of sacramentality. We now recognize that all of creation is sacramental, and, indeed, in some ways salvific. The Church does not monopolize God's action in the world, but rather highlights, explicates and facilitates it. But if this is true, how shall we define the supernatural, as distinguished from the natural? Grace, as distinguished from nature? Ecclesial faith, as distinguished from human good will? Indeed, underlying all this, how shall we understand the role of Jesus as savior (soteriology)? Or the role of the Church as proclaiming his saving deeds (missiology)? What can we say to those communities of men and women dedicated to the missionary project, or the whole Church in its function of evangelizing?

It is not surprising that soteriology and missiology have been neglected branches of theology in recent years. They provide more questions than answers. And that is due, according to this analysis, to the issues raised at the Second Vatican Council.

Conclusion

It has been more than twenty years since the conclusion of Vatican II. In some ways twenty years is a long time, in other ways it is the briefest of moments. From one point of view there has been insufficient time to implement the Council. But from another, there has been the space that allows us to assess it more clearly.

This volume of essays seeks to contribute to that assessment; and this concluding essay, with its observations regarding the Council setting, its principal themes, and its emerging agenda, seeks to highlight some of the more significant points. But the essay, and the volume as a whole, cannot avoid incompleteness. There is much more that could be said about what we now know. And there is much more that we will come to know after further time and attention.

But perhaps an incomplete collection is not inappropriate in this case. For Vatican II was an incomplete Council. The bishops knew they were not speaking the final word on any topic, that they were contributing to an ongoing conversation. There is always more to be learned, more to be shared, more to be appreciated, more to be implemented. In Christ's Church, as in God's world, the process is never complete. Creation and redemption go on.

Let this incomplete project, then, be a gift of respect to those who shaped the Second Vatican Council. We have heard your lesson. And learned.

The Contributors

Alan F. Blakley is chaplain at the College of Mount St. Joseph in Cincinnati, and is an Adolescent Counselor at Juvenile Detention in Cincinnati. He holds an A.B. from Davidson College and a M. Div. from the Atheneum of Ohio. He has served in parishes in the Archdiocese of Cincinnati. He did special study and has written on the theology of work through time spent at the Hastings Center in New York. He has been part of the North American Theology Group since it began in 1979. Recently, he has been named to the steering committee of the Peace Studies Consortium of Ohio Colleges and Universities.

J. Patout Burns is Vice President of Academic Affairs at Georgia State University in Atlanta. He holds a M.Div. from Regis College and a M.Th. from the University of St. Michael's College, both in Toronto. His Ph.D. in Religious Studies was conferred by Yale University in 1974. His books include *The Development of Augustine's Doctrine of Operative Grace* (Etudes Augustiennes, 1980), *Theological Anthropology* (Fortress Press, 1981), and *The Holy Spirit,* with Gerald M. Fagin (*Message of the Fathers of the Church,* Vol. 3, Michael Glazier, 1984). He has published in *Theological Studies, Journal of Theological Studies,* and *Augustinian Studies.* He taught Historical Theology at Jesuit School of Theology in Chicago, Catholic Theological Union, Lutheran School of Theology at Chicago, and Loyola University of Chicago.

William R. Burrows holds a License in Sacred Theology from the Gregorian University in Rome and a Master's Degree from the Divinity School of the University of Chicago. He is currently a candidate for the Ph.D. in theology at the Divinity School, and is finishing work on a dissertation entitled "The Roman Catholic Magisterium on Other Religious Ways: Analysis and Critique from a Postmodern Perspective." Till 1985 a priest-member of the Society of the Divine Word (S.V.D.) and lecturer in systematic theology at Catholic Theological Union in Chicago, Mr. Burrows is author of *New Ministries: The Global Context* (Orbis, 1980) and numerous articles and book reviews on questions of mission, church order and structures of ministry. Mr. Burrows is also working on a book tentatively entitled "Recovering the Evangelical Dimension in Catholicism" for Orbis, and is a member of the Board of Directors of the American Society of Missiology.

Agnes Cunningham, S.S.C.M., is Professor of Patristic Theology and Early Christianity at Saint Mary of the Lake Seminary, Mundelein, Illinois. She holds an M.A. in Theology from Marquette University and an S.T.D. from the Facultes Catholiques, Lyon, France (1968). She has written numerous articles and book reviews which have appeared in *Chicago Studies, Emmanuel, Ecumenical Trends, Journal of Ecumenical Studies, Theological Studies, The American Benedictine Review* and *Soundings.* She has contributed to several volumes on the international level and is author, translator and editor of *The Early Church and the State* (Fortress, 1982), *Prayer: Personal and Liturgical (Message of the Fathers of the Church,* Vol 16; Glazier, 1985) and *The Bishop in the Church: Patristic Texts on the Role of the Episkopos* (Glazier, 1985).

Joseph Gremillion served 1967-74 as the first Secretary of the Vatican's Commission for Justice and Peace, established by Pope Paul VI in follow-up to Vatican Council II; 1960-67 was Director for Social Development, Catholic Relief Services of U.S. Bishops Conference, New York, promoting social ministry and community development, nutrition and health programs in Latin America, Africa, Asia and the Middle East; did pastoral work in his native Diocese of Alexandria-Shreveport, Louisiana, 1943-58, and returned there 1978-83 as Director of Social and Ecumenical Ministry. Author of seven books, including *The Gospel of Peace and Justice* (Orbis 1976), and *Food Energy and the Major Faiths* (Orbis 1978), both written while adjunct professor, University of Notre Dame, 1974-78. Msgr. Gremillion returned to Notre Dame in 1983 as Director of its Institute for Pastoral and Social Ministry. *The Church and Culture Since Vatican II*, edited by Gremillion, will be published in 1985 by the Notre Dame Press; and *The Gospel of Peace and Justice, Vol. II, 1975-85,* by Orbis in 1986.

Robert F. Harvanek, S.J., is Professor of Philosophy at Loyola University of Chicago. He holds a M.A. in Classical Studies (Greek) from Loyola University, and a Ph.D. from Fordham University. He was general editor of the Library of Living Catholic Thought published by the Henry Regnery Co. His articles and reviews in the fields of philosophy, education and spirituality have appeared in *Thought*, the *International Philosophical Quarterly, Studies in the Spirituality of Jesuits*, and the *Jesuit Educational Quarterly.* He taught philosophy in the scholasticates of the Chicago Province of the Society of Jesus, and served as Prefect of Studies and as a Provincial of that Province.

Kevin W. Irwin is Associate Professor of Liturgy and Sacramental Theology at the Catholic University of America, Washington, D.C. He holds an M.A. in Liturgy from Notre Dame and a doctorate in Sacramental Theology from San Anselmo. He is the author of six books on liturgy and sacraments including *Sunday Worship* (Pueblo, 1983) and *Liturgy, Prayer and Spirituality* (Paulist, 1984). His book reviews and articles have appeared in *New Catholic World, Pastoral Music, Worship* and *The Thomist*. He served in parishes in the Archdiocese of New York for six years, was Director of Liturgy at the North American College (Rome) and taught in the Graduate School of Religion and Religious Education at Fordham University.

John Linnan, C.S.V., is President of Catholic Theological Union, Chicago, Illinois. He holds the following degrees from the University of Louvain: S.T.B. (1961), M.A. (1962), S.T.L. (1964) and S.T.D. (1966). He is Associate Professor of Systematic Theology at C.T.U. He has served in provincial administration of the Clerics of St. Viator, and is on the Executive Committee of the N.C.E.A (Seminary Division).

Jon Nilson is Associate Professor and Chairman of the Theology Department at Loyola University of Chicago. He received his doctorate from the University of Notre Dame and has taught at Illinois Benedictine College and the University of Dallas. He is the author of numerous articles and essays. His book on marriage, *From This Day Forward*, was recently published by Abbey Press.

Carolyn Osiek, a Religious of the Sacred Heart for twenty-three years, is Associate Professor of New Testament Studies at Catholic Theological Union, Chicago. She holds a doctorate in New Testament and Christian Origins from Harvard University, and is an associate editor of *Catholic Biblical Quarterly, The Bible Today,* and *Scripture in Church*. She is the author of four books, several tapes, and numerous articles on biblical studies, spirituality and religious life, women in the Church, and the social world of early Christianity. She is also Editorial Director of the *Message of Biblical Spirituality* series published by Michael Glazier, Inc.

Donald Senior's educational background includes a Bachelor of Arts degree in philosophy from the Passionist Seminary College in Chicago (1963); a Licentiate in theology (S.T.L.) from the University of Louvain, Belgium (1970); and a Doctorate in New Testament Studies (S.T.D) from the University of Louvain (1972). He has also pursued further studies at Hebrew Union College, Cincinnati, and Harvard University. Donald Senior, C.P., is Professor of New Testament Studies at Catholic Theological Union, Chicago, where he is also Director of the school's Israel Study Program. He has lectured and conducted retreats and workshops throughout the United States and abroad. He is associate editor of *The Bible Today*, book review editor of *The Catholic Biblical Quarterly*, and co-editor of the twenty-two volume international commentary series *New Testament Message*. He is the author of numerous books and articles including the 4-volume *Passion Series* published by Michael Glazier, Inc.